JULIE TUDOR IS ~~NOT~~ A PSYCHOPATH

About the Author

Jennifer Holdich obtained an MA in Scriptwriting in 2014, won the Cardiff Writers' Circle Short Story competition in 2021 and has had multiple short stories and pieces of flash fiction published.

Julie Tudor Is Not A Psychopath is her debut novel.

JULIE TUDOR IS ~~NOT~~ A PSYCHOPATH

Jennifer Holdich

HODDER &
STOUGHTON

First published in Great Britain in 2025 by Hodder & Stoughton Limited
An Hachette UK company

1

Copyright © Jennifer Holdich 2025

A CIP catalogue record for this title is available from the British Library

Hardback ISBN 978 1 399 73344 1
Trade Paperback ISBN 978 1 399 73345 8
ebook ISBN 978 1 399 73347 2

Typeset in Sabon MT by Hewer Text UK Ltd, Edinburgh
Printed and bound in Great Britain by Clays Ltd, Elcograf S.p.A.

Hodder & Stoughton policy is to use papers that are natural, renewable
and recyclable products and made from wood grown in sustainable
forests. The logging and manufacturing processes are expected to
conform to the environmental regulations of the country of origin.

Hodder & Stoughton Ltd
Carmelite House
50 Victoria Embankment
London EC4Y 0DZ

The authorised representative in the EEA is Hachette Ireland, 8 Castlecourt
Centre, Dublin 15, D15 XTP3, Ireland (email: info@hbgi.ie)

www.hodder.co.uk

For Nanna, Grandma, and uncles Mike, John & Neil,
who aren't here to see this, but I think would be impressed.
And for Harry.

PROLOGUE

Sean's unhappy 'ummph' as he bounced down the last four stairs convinced me the pulley system was not going to work. Even with gravity on our side, getting him down had been a difficult job. Getting him back up was going to be a Herculean feat.

I followed him to the bottom of the stairs and looked up towards the bathroom. The distance seemed vast. Still, Sean wasn't in any state to use the bathroom, and my mind strayed grimly to thoughts of adult nappies.

The dangers of keeping him downstairs were myriad. Picture the scene if a social caller dropped by, expecting tea and a natter, only to find this young man – strong and healthy just yesterday – prostrate on my lounge floor. Imagine the mayhem that would ensue. If I was going to keep him downstairs, I would have to be very careful indeed.

'Ugg, gllg, glllg,' Sean gurgled, and I looked down to find him choking on his own saliva.

I heaved him to a sitting position and kicked his leg into place. Poor Sean would be covered in bruises at this rate! I straightened up, stretching my back, and he began to slide sideways. I caught him by the shoulder and balanced him against the banister.

'Cup of tea?' I asked, and he gurgled. 'Come along then!'

I hitched myself between his ankles, like a horse between the shafts of a cart, and started moving forwards. As Sean's upper body slid to the floor, I realised it wasn't going to be as easy as that. After a few jerky steps, I turned around and started pulling backwards. But that was worse; I turned again and walked forwards.

'We'll get you into the dining room and take tea at the table,' I said, to rally his spirits. Although Sean's days of sitting up at a table were almost certainly behind him. 'Maybe we could have cake? I've got some left over from your wedding. I froze my piece. You're meant to freeze some and keep it for the christening. Did you know that? Did you do that?' At my age, the chances of having a baby to christen were roundabout zero, but I like to stick to traditions. Though traditions were out of the window now. 'No time like the present,' I said. 'I can defrost it.'

Or maybe I wouldn't defrost it. Sean's cake-eating days were also a thing of the past. He would almost certainly choke on the crumbs, coughing his way into the next life, as the tiny morsels tickled their way down his throat.

The kitchen door was open and through it, as I dragged Sean down the hall, I could see the blender sitting on the worktop. It would be seeing a lot of business in the weeks ahead: I may be in the market for a sturdier model. Along with the nappies, this was shaping up to be an expensive enterprise.

Perhaps Sean could eat baby food, although I'd need to buy it in vast quantities. People would think I'd opened an orphanage.

'Aaarggh!' he said. As I rounded the corner into the dining room, something snagged. I looked up from my toils and – goodness me! – what had happened to his arm? Something was pulling it above his head, back towards the hall. On investigation, I found it was still entangled in the pulley, tethering him to the stairs.

I unravelled him, crouching down to untwist his sleeve and giving myself time to catch my breath. I gazed at Sean's woebegone expression, ran my fingers through his hair and sighed.

'Be careful what you wish for, eh, Sean?' I said.

CHAPTER ONE

2009

On the Thursday before *She* came, I took two pieces of fish out of the freezer before remembering: Sean went straight from work to football on Thursdays. I popped one piece back in, then, jacket on, bag over shoulder, I took a quick look round . . . nearly forgot . . .

The picture needed turning. My own invention, a reversible picture. On one side was a scenic landscape, copied from a postcard; on the other a rather racy image I had conjured up of Sean and I in the throes of passion. I don't tend to leave that one on display – just in case of unexpected visitors.

I glanced outside into the garden where the guinea pigs were buried in their hutch, checking they were out of sight, out of mind: away from the prying eyes of nosy neighbours.

Then a final squiz to make sure everything was shipshape, a peaceful and harmonious haven to come back to in the evening.

When all was well, I headed out to the office.

On the train I gazed out of the window at the mountains around our town and thought how lovely it would be to walk up them one weekend. I imagined Sean and I cresting the top and standing hand in hand, slightly breathless, looking down at the track winding along to Cardiff. Not a care, none of the worries of the day-to-day. But if we tried, we would probably find ourselves lost. We are city people, after all.

The office was a ten-minute walk from the train station. On that early autumn day, with the sun high in the sky, birds singing and people out in their summer clothes for perhaps the last time that year, the walk was a pleasure.

I passed the security guard at reception and showed him my ID, even though he saw me every day. He grunted and continued his conversation with the receptionist. I caught the lift and headed up to the seventh floor.

I turned right from the lift. I skipped around the bend, through another door then – breath held – there he was.

The office was open plan, with desks on either side of an aisle. The desks were in groups – 'pods', they called them – and each pod contained four people, who sat, backs to each other, looking out at the rest of the office.

The décor was muted: the walls a purplish grey, the carpet dark grey, medium grey chairs, the desks were some kind of cheap wood, often with snags which caught your clothes, and stainless steel cabinets stood against the walls. The only colour was added by the odd staff member who opted for a bright top, instead of the standard white shirts and blouses.

The atmosphere on the other hand, was upbeat with the hectic sound of people on a mission: heated conversations as we discussed the day's work. From time to time members of our own team nipped across the aisle to confer with their counterparts in the neighbouring department. It really was a busy hive.

Sean was frowning slightly as he peered at his PC monitor. Probably another tricky case.

'Morning, Sean!' I trilled as I approached him.

'Eh?' he was deep in concentration. He looked around for where the voice was coming from and saw me. 'Morning, Julie,' he said.

'Good night, last night?' I asked.

'Yeah, not bad. So-so. You know. Wednesday night.'

'Yeah, yeah, Wednesday night. Football tonight, is it?' I said.

'I'm not going. It's the Pink concert tonight.'

My heart nearly stopped beating in my chest. I'd thought that was next week! I'd only taken out one piece of fish!

'Didn't think that'd be your kind of thing,' said one of The Lads, Dave, giving me time to recover myself.

'Hey-ho, it's give and take, isn't it,' Sean replied. 'My sister's friend dropped out. Pink and Drink, I'm calling it.'

'What will you do for your tea?' I asked, still a little panicky.

'I don't know. Probably get a burger or something, if there's time,' he said. 'Why?'

'I just thought you perhaps wouldn't want to be drinking on an empty stomach.'

'I've survived it before. I wouldn't lose too much sleep over it, if I were you,' he said.

'No, no. I won't be losing any sleep!'

'Catch you later, then,' he said. 'I'm up to my neck in this.'

'Catch you later,' I said.

I went to my desk, turned my computer on and watched as, a minute later, Sean followed another of The Lads, Mike, to the drinks machine. They stood by it, talking and laughing about something, Sean throwing his head back in that carefree way of his.

Sean wasn't good-looking in the Hollywood sense of the word. He wasn't particularly tall, he was slightly chubby, his eyes were a bit close together and now, in his mid-twenties, his hair was already starting to thin.

Yet he had a way of drawing everyone to him, a magnetism that pulled people in and held them there.

'He hangs on your every word when you're talking to him,' Jayne from the post room once said. 'You feel like you're the most important person in the world.'

The day rumbled on. Cheerful, bouncy Ffion, our representative from HR, came down to announce that new health and safety training was being rolled out across the company. She handed out leaflets and advised us to acquaint ourselves with the differences between trips and slips because we would be tested. I hate to fail a test, so I spent what was left of the morning making sure I was in no doubt.

Thursday morning became Thursday afternoon. And, as sure as night follows day, Thursday afternoon became Thursday evening.

Having seen Pink, Sean came into work on Friday looking a bit green. He merely grunted when I said good morning.

By mid-morning, he was talking about going home. Marcus, our manager, said he'd have to take it as a half-day holiday; he couldn't be put down as sick when we all knew he had a hangover. Marcus could be such a killjoy.

I saved the day though, when I said I was going over the road for coffee and offered to get him an espresso. He nodded his gratitude and reached into his pocket for change, but I said it was my treat.

'Thanks, Jools,' he said. 'I owe you one.'

Only he calls me Jools. I would only allow it from him. A few minutes later I stood by his desk – watching as he stirred so much sugar into his drink, Tate & Lyle's share price must've hit an all-time high – anticipating a few shared moments together. And sure enough:

'What's the plan of attack for the weekend then, Jools?' he asked.

I giggled: he had quite the turn of phrase. 'Well,' I said. 'I'm in tonight. Might do some painting in the garden since the light's so vivid at the moment. After that, who knows? The evening's my own. I'm not going anywhere. I have a leg of lamb to roast, with veg and roast potatoes. I have wine in, a really nice Australian red.'

I'd once heard him describing a wine tasting session and how much he had enjoyed an Australian red.

'I won't be opening it before nine,' I said. 'I'll probably have a bath first, light some candles, put a film on. I'll be in all evening. Just a laid-back evening. Just me and . . . whoever.'

He nodded, his eyes slightly unfocused. 'Well, have a good one, then,' he said.

That evening, I followed the routine, exactly as described, but I didn't hear anything from Sean. He probably went home and straight to sleep. I wouldn't blame him. In fact, maybe it was my mention of wine that put him off, in his delicate state.

I started watching Jonathan Ross but it was a bit dull. I picked up my phone: no one had called or sent me a text. I skimmed the news headlines: nothing had happened. I checked my emails: no one had emailed me.

On waking that Saturday, I shook off the disappointment of the previous evening. Sean would have had his reasons. Meanwhile, the world was my oyster, having recently subscribed myself to Sky television.

I had already recorded a few romantic comedies, and I set a few more to tape. In the spirit of harmonious living, I added a few action films for you-know-who. Then, having the house to myself, I sat down to watch *Little Miss Sunshine*.

Halfway through I paused it, fancying a glass of wine.

I don't really know how the film finished. I watched a couple more, but they were unremarkable. When the last of them was over, I turned my attention to cooking.

And that saw me through the rest of the afternoon: chopping, frying, blanching, beating. Pouring, tipping, sipping, swallowing . . . chatting away about this, that and whatever. At six on the dot the meal was on the table; I had evolved into the domestic goddess my late sister, Angela, was always expected to become.

The seating arrangements looked out over my garden.

'The roses really were a success this year,' I remarked, thinking as I said so that, success aside, it really was time I cleared away their dead heads. 'Dessert? I shouldn't really, but we all deserve a treat at the end of the working week.'

I cleared away the plates. I was still slightly peckish, so in the kitchen, out of sight of the dining area, I polished off what was left of Sean's portion, which was pretty much all of it. Except for the mushrooms I'd already pinched from his plate at the table.

I returned with two sundaes I had put together and gobbled mine down. By the time I'd finished, Sean's had pretty much melted, so I tipped it away, just picking out the Flake pieces for myself. I poured the remains of his wine into my own glass: I had my drinking head on by then and felt I could drink until dawn.

The meal over and the washing-up done, it was time to wind down in the lounge, and Sean had assured me that *Pirates of the Caribbean* was very good.

It was alright, the plot was a little hard to follow. Eventually the wine took possession of me, and I drifted off to sleep where I sat. I woke at four in the morning with my mouth hanging open and a crick in my neck – the joys of the weekend – and stumbled off to bed.

CHAPTER TWO

2009

Well, Monday was a new week and as always on a Monday we were insanely busy in the office, catching up with whatever has piled in by phone, email or post. Sean and I hardly had a moment to speak to each other.

By rights, no one should have a moment. We are meant to be a team and that means all hands to the pump on a Monday morning. But that didn't stop several of the others sauntering round the office as if they were on holiday.

Gareth, my sidekick and desk-mate, and I sat together, the other two desks in our pod empty. I wouldn't have known Gareth was in at all that morning were it not for the pile of personal items – phone, keys, wallet, headache tablets – he always poured out of his pockets and onto his desk on arrival each day. I looked around and spotted him talking to someone in our neighbouring department – Gareth always seemed to know everyone – waving his hands in the air and doing what looked like a belly dance, to the hilarity of all. It was not yet nine o'clock, but already, his shirt was creased and his hair looked as if it hadn't seen a hairbrush for weeks.

Gareth, it seemed, had had a particularly racy weekend involving an inflatable flamingo and a male model from Basildon. How the other half live. I'd thought I'd seen some sights on my streaming service, but Gareth made Hollywood sound tame by comparison.

Eventually the room settled down, Gareth found his way back to his own desk and wrestled himself into his seat.

'Does my bum look big in this?' he asked, as the chair seemed to close in around him. He had put on some weight in the time he had worked with us, although he was big by nature. He could probably have been a rugby player, if he'd had any co-ordination, speed, strength, aggression or aptitude for sport whatsoever. A big, dishevelled rugby player, in bright clothes that always tested the limits of the office dress code.

When he was sat down, you could see that his eyes were very pale blue, his nose rather long and his skin always very smooth, hardly troubled by stubble. But the main thing you noticed about Gareth was that he was always smiling. Even in the middle of a last-minute batch of scanning that was going to make him late, he was always smile, smile, smile.

Once settled at his desk, Gareth and I were nose-to-grindstone catching up for the rest of the day. I left the office somewhat dazed at having exchanged not a word with Sean.

Consequently, I wasn't my cheery self when I returned to the house. But it was only Monday, and I resolved to have a pleasant evening. Tomorrow would be another day.

The weather was still fine that evening, more like summer than mid-September, so I took my easel and paints out into the garden for an hour before dusk to make the most of the remaining September sunshine.

I set myself up facing towards the back of my small garden, in close proximity to the hutch which housed the guinea pigs, Bert and Mabel Jackson. They had the same names as my next-door neighbours, but that was just a coincidence.

After some time, I heard a wheezing from behind and when I turned round, Bert – the neighbour, not the guinea pig – was leaning over the fence.

'Evening,' he said.

'Evening.' I turned back to my painting.

'Beautiful weather.'

'It is.'

'More like August than September.'

'It is.'

I paused in my work and stared straight ahead, hoping he'd go away, but he just rubbed a hand over his florid face. Bert once told me he'd had a career in the civil service, but he looked like he'd lived a life in the great outdoors: his hands and face were leathery and weather-worn. He cleared his throat and continued. 'You know, if you don't mind my saying, my niece had some dark times. She could put you in touch with someone who could help.'

I turned around and he was staring at the picture I was painting.

'I'm not having dark times,' I said. 'I'm just not very good at painting shrubbery.'

'Oh,' he said. 'Alright. It's just with the talking and everything . . .'

'Talking?'

'We can hear you. When you're in the house. Alone in the house.'

'Mr Jackson, I have a budgerigar. How will he learn to talk if I never speak to him?'

'Oh,' he said. 'Oh. I didn't realise. He's very quiet, your budgerigar. I hear you, I never hear him.'

'I told you, he's still learning.'

'Doesn't he sing? Birdsong?'

'No, Mr Jackson. Apparently, he does not.' I turned my back and dipped my brush to the paint to signal the conversation was over, and presently I heard him whistling on the other side of his garden. Should budgies sing? I didn't know. I couldn't remember. I'd have a look on the internet later.

I'd lost some of my enthusiasm for painting after Mr Jackson's rather harsh critique, so I went back inside and checked my emails – none; texts – none.

I think it was the heat that made it so hard for everyone to concentrate. Only a couple of weeks before we'd had a real taste of autumn and this last flash of warm weather had made everyone a bit giddy. Each time I glanced up at Sean he was gadding about, chatting to a colleague, not the industrious man I had fallen in love with.

But who can blame us? We all knew we had a long, hard winter coming up. There was no harm, for once, in a relaxing of the protocol.

'You not feeling the heat, Jools?' Sean asked me. It took a moment before I realised he was commenting on my jumper. It may have looked a little odd on a hot day, but you never knew what the air conditioning was going to bring.

'She's acclimatising herself for hell,' Gareth said. Sean seemed to think that was funny and walked away, laughing like a drain. He was called back seconds later though, to look at something on Gareth's phone.

They were fans of the Facebook and it had uploaded a short video of amusing giraffes. I didn't think they were quite as funny as Sean and Gareth found them, but I was in the minority: within minutes most of the department were huddled around Gareth, guffawing with laughter over it.

'Can't believe you're not on Facebook yet, Julie,' Gareth said when the fuss had died down. 'My gran's on it. There's loads of stuff like that and you can see what people you know are up to when you're not with them.'

'How do you mean?' I asked. I'd heard of the Facebook but had thought it was just a collection of animal videos. I had no idea it was also a surveillance tool.

Well, it wasn't quite the in-depth insight I'd imagined when Gareth said I could see what people were up to: I couldn't track them minute by minute, I couldn't see into their homes and some people provided more information than others. But it certainly was an eye-opener. We looked at the profiles of a few of our colleagues and I had to admit, I had had no idea Jayne from the post room was a ballroom dancing champion – she looked so frumpy round the office.

'What do you have to do?' I asked Gareth. 'Do you have to subscribe? Do you have to apply?'

'No,' he said. 'Watch.' And within minutes he'd set me up an account of my own. All I had to do when I got home was fill in the details and request a few friends.

He showed me how to add pictures to my profile. I had experimented with the camera on my phone in the past and had taken a few around the office: Sean at the drinks machine; Sean at the printer; Sean at the coat stand.

Gareth stared at them for a moment. He looked as if he was going to say something, but instead of speaking, he just scrolled between them again.

'You can't use any of them,' he said in the end. 'Julie, you can probably get sued for this.' Finding nothing suitable, he said, 'Smile', and took a picture of me. He added it to my page next to my name and I had my first proper look at it. I recoiled: I thought I'd smiled, but it turned out I'd grimaced and the angle made it look as if I had a double chin. My hairstyle is timeless, early Princess Diana but brunette: the light here made it look flat and shapeless. No one who knew me would recognise me from that!

Luckily, Gareth then explained how to change it.

That evening, I logged onto my laptop and opened up my 'Pictures' file for a better photo. My options were limited. The only real contender was from Sean's late wife, Susannah's, funeral. It didn't seem entirely appropriate, but I wear black most of the time anyway; you'd have to be pretty eagle-eyed to notice that I was wearing a funeral outfit. It was the best photo I had: glass raised, big smile for the camera and a great outfit. I'd bought it especially for the occasion; the last funeral I'd been to was Angela's and I was just a young slip of a girl back then. So up it went. Then I went to the search box, typed in a name: Sean O'Flannery – and there he was!

He's very photogenic, really knows how to pose for a snap. My hand shook a little as it hovered above the 'Add Friend' button, but I took a deep breath, stabbed my finger down and off went my request. I spent a few minutes scrolling through the others in the office, but none of them really interested me.

I returned to my page, looking for any change, but there was nothing from Sean. I read the news headlines, Tony Blair would be at the Labour Party Conference. Nothing from Sean. I was about to switch off my laptop, when there was a ding and a small red circle appeared on the top bar on the Facebook. HE HAD ACCEPTED MY REQUEST! And so quickly! It must have meant as much to him as it did to me.

But when I looked more closely at his page, I found out something else about Sean. Someone had posted on his page the heading 'HAIR OF THE DOG!!!!!!!' above a picture of Sean with four other gentlemen of a similar age and state of inebriation. It had been posted the night after Pink. While I was waiting for him and wondering what he was doing.

CHAPTER THREE

2009

We were all caught completely off guard the day that *She* came. After all, who starts a new job on a *Wednesday*? And not just a Wednesday, but a Wednesday *afternoon*.

Turned out she'd been meant to start on the Monday morning, like any normal person. She blushingly explained that there had been a family emergency – her dad had a problem with his heart. Apparently, he'd been rushed to hospital on Sunday night and this had been the first day she could make it. Not really the level of dedication we expect in an office as busy as ours.

It had been a hectic morning. Gareth and I could barely be seen under the piles of post that had come in – all you could hear all morning was the slit-slit-slit of my letter opener – and it was gone lunchtime before I could start on the spreadsheets. Then *She* walked in.

Xanthe. Xanthe? I looked it up. It means blonde. Which she was. Natural, she claimed. *Natural as nylon.*

The Lads all stared as Marcus took her on a tour of the office. They arrived at our desks. Xanthe.

'Julie, Gareth,' Marcus said, 'this is Xanthe, she's going to be working as a case reviewer.'

Xanthe smiled. 'Hi,' she said. I stared at her silently. 'Nice to meet you,' she mumbled, trying to break eye contact – and my goodness, her eyes were *enormous* – but I continued to stare and she couldn't look away.

Gareth swivelled round in his seat. 'Hi Xanthe, lovely to meet you. I'll tell you now, because Marcus always forgets, that the last Friday of every month is dress down.'

'Lovely to meet you, Gareth, thanks for the heads-up.'

'Over here for all the important info,' he said, 'And the gossip.'

'Xanthe's going to be on my team,' Marcus told us. I visibly juddered. She'd be working with Abi and Lorna and The Lads. That meant she'd be working with Dave and Mike and Sean. She'd be working with *Sean*. I cleared my throat.

'Isn't there the small matter of the exams before anyone joins your team?' I asked him.

'Xanthe already has the qualifications,' Marcus said. 'She's quite experienced.'

She didn't look like someone who would have experience with much, other than applying lipstick, which was something she had certainly done with aplomb. It was so bright you could probably see it from space – if you could drag your attention away from her ridiculous eyes. They took up half of her face, she only had room for a tiny little nose and mouth underneath them. She looked like a cartoon character, especially with her skinny body that made her head look too big.

But I seemed to be in the minority in thinking she looked like some sort of cartoon alien.

'She's very pretty,' Jayne from the post room whispered as she came by.

'She's OK if you like that sort of thing,' I told her. 'Far too much make-up if you ask me.'

'Really?' Jayne said. 'I didn't think she was wearing much make-up, just lipstick.'

'Yeah, it's skilfully applied so it doesn't look like much, I'll give her that, but she'll be taking it off tonight with a chisel.'

'Oh.'

Sean's desk was the next place Marcus took her. He sat her down with Sean; he was to show her the ropes. I watched all afternoon as they sat chatting and giggling, the other blokes gazing over enviously, boys from other departments wandering by to have a look. The carpet was starting to wear thin by the end of the day. As was my patience.

It was around a year and three months since Sean's wife – of one afternoon – passed away, and Sean had been single since then.

In the immediate aftermath I had been somewhat dismayed that Sean kept his distance from me, but I understood that for appearances, he had to observe a mourning period people would consider respectable. Yet, as we passed the one-year mark I began to wonder for how long he was going to carry on the charade. When I had guinea pigs as a child, the average gap between pigs was just a few weeks. When my sister died, we didn't replace her. Judging by the way Sean was looking at Xanthe, he thought a year and a quarter was about right; the grieving process was coming to its conclusion.

I stabbed the letter opener hard into the pile of post and it went some way through. My letter opener is quite the curiosity in this office. It was found some years ago when they replaced the old stationery cupboard with the cheap models we have today. It was buried beneath a pile of ancient documents and caused something of a stir when it was uncovered, due to its remarkable length and sharpness; it was almost in the style of a sword. I was the obvious recipient of this prize, but not before it had been put through a rigorous health and safety assessment to decide if it could legally remain in the building.

Post stabbed, I took my worry dolls out of my bag and headed for the stairwell. Down at the bottom of the stairs, in the cove by the fire escape, I opened the case and looked at the tiny dolls staring up at me. Six of them: I chose Lucy, she had the same blond hair as Xanthe so it seemed appropriate. I took her out and told her my fears. Then I dug my fingers past the others to the pin at the bottom; I took the pin and stabbed it through Lucy's heart.

The worry dolls came with instructions when they were first given to me by my sister. You are supposed to tell each of them your troubles and they will make them dissipate. I have somewhat modified their use, bringing them to a point somewhere between worry and voodoo. The jury is out on whether they work or not, though there have been some startling results.

Returning to the office with the dolls hidden up my sleeve, I was, for a moment, surprised to see Xanthe sitting there next to Sean, still hale and hearty. But it would have looked odd for her to suddenly drop dead. So, I walked nonchalantly past, back to my desk.

I caught up with Sean at the coffee machine. I was doing the run for just Gareth and I on that occasion.

'Hi, Sean,' I said. The drinks area is too public to hold any meaningful kind of conversation, but chit-chat is as much a part of a relationship as any other verbal exchange, so it's important to connect in these circumstances. 'I would have brought your drink over for you if I'd known you wanted one,' I told him.

'Nah, that's cool, Jools,' he said, reaching for his cappuccino. 'I need to stretch my legs as much as I need a coffee. Not good for you to sit still all day.'

I giggled coquettishly. 'I don't think you need to worry about losing your figure,' I reassured him.

Sean had been lifting his drink towards his lips but stopped dead when I spoke. Then he stood up straight, pulled his shoulders back and rubbed his stomach where, if the truth be told, a small paunch was developing.

'I'm more worried about my circulation,' he said. 'You have to keep the blood flowing.' He turned his full attention to the drinks machine.

'Ah,' I said. 'I see.' I looked over to where Xanthe sat. I pressed the buttons for a cup of tea — it takes the machine forever to make tea — to buy myself time. Sean was waiting for a drink for someone else, I didn't like to think who, but it was only a coffee, which pours quickly, so I blurted out:

'Is Xanthe married?'

'No,' he said, still staring at the machine. 'I think she's single.'

'You *think*?' I asked him.

'Yeah, I think.'

I had to take a different tack, a slightly defensive tone had crept into his voice.

'I just ask,' I said, 'because she is looking very . . . flirty, and gossip is flying around already.'

He turned towards me then. 'She only started today, for god's sake,' he said. 'Anyway, I'm not looking to get involved in anything new at the moment.'

And with that, he mooched back to his desk. But he'd made his point: 'not looking to get involved in anything new.' It was a message to let me know he considered himself taken.

It helped me ignore for the rest of the day, the fact that whenever I looked up, he was laughing and joking with Xanthe, as she fluttered her eyelids over those peculiar eyes. It was part of his job to make her feel welcome; it was good for office morale for everyone to get along; it was only a professional interest. To celebrate I handed out nice, easy cases to all.

CHAPTER FOUR

2009

I practically floated into work the next morning, but as I turned the corner, into the main office, what should I see?

Sean was there as usual, but was he hard at work, nose to the monitor? No, he was not! He was leaning back in his chair, turned away from his PC, laughing about something with Xanthe!

'Morning, Sean,' I hmphed as I stormed past.

'Morning, Jools,' he replied.

'Morning, Jools,' Xanthe echoed. I hadn't been talking to her.

But as I glanced over my shoulder, I saw Sean had, briefly, swung his glance and his chair towards me and I calmed. I believe myself to be a competent reader of body language and the fact his eyes and body were turned to me, even while he was ostensibly talking to her, showed where his real feelings lay. Sean is a man of honour, he treats everybody well – it's one of the things I love about him – but his heart belongs to just one woman.

Nevertheless, I kept a weather-eye on them as they sat there.

'My tea has sugar in it, do you want it? Sweeten you up a bit?' Gareth, standing at my shoulder, cast a shadow over my desk, although when I looked up, he was as bright and sunny as ever, big grin and a smiley-face outfit, even though it wasn't dress-down day.

'Beg your pardon?' I said.

'You're looking like you could kill someone,' he told me.

'Am I? Really?' I smiled my sweetest smile. 'Do you think I look like a killer?' He was looking a little doubtful. 'Well, do you?'

He opened his mouth to answer, but then Ffion from HR burst in, loudly reminding everyone to complete the staff survey to be in with a chance of winning a weekend break in the luxury hotel about 50 paces down the road.

I knew I was worrying over nothing, but even so, it was disconcerting to see exactly how much help Sean was giving Xanthe over the course of that day. Surely, she'd been shadowing him for long enough? Shouldn't she be doing some work of her own by now?

And when Sean was down here, she was all he talked about: Xanthe this and Xanthe that. 'She chews ice, did you know?' he asked us. 'When she has a cold drink she likes to have loads of ice in it and she chews all the cubes and drinks down to the slush at the bottom.'

Well, if that was the most interesting thing about her, it wasn't going to take long for the novelty to wear off.

'Most people put flavouring in it and call it an ice pop,' I said.

'Eh?' Sean replied, looking as if I'd just introduced quantum theory into the conversation.

'Most people who want to chew ice, chew it in the form of an ice pop,' I repeated. 'It's a refreshing summer treat. Seems a bit weird to just munch plain ice cubes.'

'I think it's just a habit, helps her concentrate or something,' Sean said, a little sharply. 'Or maybe it's stress. Do you think it's stress?' And with that he went shooting back to his desk, where a relaxed-looking Xanthe sat picking the last of the ice cubes out of her drink.

Somewhat concerned, I took my worry dolls into the corridor for a serious chat about why Xanthe was still looking so healthy. I took the pin out from the bottom of the case and pierced them all.

At home that evening I went down to the guinea pigs' hutch and told them about my day. About my concern over Sean's failure, so far, to seek me out and have a proper discussion about our relationship, even though he kept reassuring me with his little comments: 'shake that booty for me, Jools,' 'imagine, Jools, you and me on a desert island.' Which were always followed by peels – no howls – of laughter, presumably to hide his discomfort at saying what was really on his mind. I asked the guinea pigs if they thought I should take the initiative. After all, this is the twenty-first century: anything boys can do, girls can surely do better. They looked at me blankly with their glassy eyes, but I was coming to a conclusion by myself.

I turned to go back into the house and nearly jumped out of my skin when I saw, leaning over the fence – Bert Jackson. He must've been watching me! Maybe listening to me.

'Evening,' he said.

'Evening,' I replied, rather tartly, I had to admit.

'You can feel autumn drawing in now,' he said.

'You can,' I said. 'There'll be less time in the garden soon. Less time chatting with your neighbours.'

'That there will,' he agreed. 'Mind, you choose some funny times to be gardening, don't you?'

'I beg your pardon, Mr Jackson?' I had no idea what he was talking about.

'I seen you that time, remember? Gardening in the night-time.'

I remembered now, an incident many years ago when, under a certain amount of stress, I took myself into the garden to do some work in the night. Unfortunately, Bert Jackson had seen me and refused to let the matter drop.

'I find gardening relaxing, Mr Jackson.'

He looked thoughtful for a moment, the way he did when he was about to ask an awkward question. 'Do you still have that budgerigar?' he asked.

Why did he want to know that? I thought back to our previous conversation, trying to remember what I'd said, but most of it was lost to me.

'Tweety sadly passed away,' I told him. Bert nodded solemnly; for a moment I thought he was going to make the sign of the cross.

'I'm very sorry to hear that,' he said.

'Thank you.'

'I know what a blessing a pet can be, even a budgerigar, to a girl on her own.'

'Yes, yes,' I said, 'he was quite the character. But pets come and go. C'est la vie.'

He nodded and seemed to be about to say something, but I cut him off at the pass. 'Well, it really is rather chilly out here,' I said, 'I must get myself back inside.' And with that I hurried back in.

The next day I watched Sean for the whole morning, joking with The Lads, hovering over Xanthe. I was finding it hard to concentrate. Sean is my man: we have a connection that is so much more than physical. Sparks flew from the first moment we met and I don't know if even Romeo and Juliet experienced a passion to match the one we share. Sean and I are in love and all the Xanthes in the world could never change that.

I spent my lunch break in the sandwich shop round the corner, considering how I was going to approach the task of taking the initiative. I started to feel nervous, although I wondered why I should. After all, I had to do this one thing, just one thing, and afterwards we would both be happy forever. If he wasn't going to be brave, I would be brave for both of us. When you thought about it, it stood to reason that it would be me to take the lead. I was the older by around twenty-five years. It was only fair that I was the one who was courageous sometimes.

Perhaps he was shy because he couldn't quite believe a woman of my maturity would be interested in someone like him. But Sean was wise beyond his years: he had suffered loss, he had conquered adversity and he was ready for the reward of an older woman. Sean and I had been tiptoeing around the issue for a long time and I believe he felt as I did, that although previous loves had come and gone, this was something different that neither of us wanted to get wrong. I headed back to the office to find Sean sitting on Xanthe's desk, the pair of them with their heads thrown back, laughing like donkeys. My blood boiled.

Hardly any work was done that afternoon. Not by me, at least. I barely looked at my PC. I looked at Sean, which most of the time meant also looking at Xanthe. Couldn't she tell her advances were unwelcome? I was worried that Sean was going to repeat a mistake he had formerly made and surrender himself to the vapid charms of Xanthe as a way of avoiding the depths of emotion that were his true feelings. It was time to break that cycle and bring matters out into the open. I would have to grasp the nettle.

I think Gareth noticed something was afoot. He started humming 'Every Breath You Take'.

'You know that's a song about a stalker,' I told him.

'I know,' he said.

The afternoon dragged slowly on, but eventually Sean left the room to go to the loo. I knew I had to take action, so I followed him out and waited in the corridor, pretending to chat to someone on my phone. I didn't have to pretend for too long, though.

Boys being famously quick in the toilets, he was out almost as soon as I had assumed my nonchalant stance.

Thinking I was deep in conversation with a close friend, Sean merely nodded at me when he came out of the lavatory and turned to go back into the office. I halted the pretence: I removed the phone from my ear and spoke loudly and clearly.

'Sean,' I said. He turned around. 'We need to talk.'

He looked uncertain, but said, 'Yeah, course, Jools. Later though, I'm right up against it at the moment. Yeah?' He started to walk away, but I called his name again.

'There's no need to be scared, Sean,' I said. But he looked pretty scared. 'Only fools would deny what's in their hearts. Isn't it more frightening to think of spending your life without the one you love than to endure a moment or two of honesty?'

He didn't seem to quite know what to make of that, so I clarified it for him.

'Isn't it best to be a bit uncomfortable for a minute or two, in order to be happy for the rest of your life, than to never face your fears and live in loneliness and despair?' I said. He seemed to be thinking. 'Well, isn't it?'

'Yeah,' he said. 'I suppose so.' He started to turn again, I had to get to the point.

'So, this is your chance,' I told him. 'Our chance.'

He looked at me, slightly puzzled.

'To declare our true feelings,' I explained. 'I know these aren't the most auspicious surroundings, but what are buildings, but walls and a roof?'

He nodded uncertainly. 'Shall I go first?' I volunteered. He nodded again and surreptitiously reached a hand out towards the door handle. I took a deep breath and was about to utter the words that would change our lives, when . . .

'Mate, did you see the football last night?' Mike appeared from the lift area and addressed himself to Sean.

'Yeah,' he said. 'Heartbreaking.' And off they went, discussing the merits of some refereeing decision, Sean hurrying so much he nearly smacked his face on the door as he went.

'Sean!' I pleaded just before the door closed.

'Yeah, Jools,' he said. 'Laters.'

Well, it hadn't gone quite as I had hoped, but 'later' was his verdict. I realised as I sat back down at my desk that he had obviously been overwhelmed by the power of his feelings and had been trying to control them, denying them, fighting them back down.

Selfishly, I had caught him off-guard and forced him to confront them, just as he thought he had control over them. Mike had given him a way out and in a panic, he had taken it. But his reprieve would not be for long. Meanwhile, he and The Lads were all gathered around the drinks machine, laughing hysterically at something.

Yet, Sean was now in possession of the facts and as soon as he'd had time to calm down and think things over, I knew he would come back to me: a little bashful, perhaps, embarrassed by the way he had lost his grip on his emotions, but knowing without a shadow of a doubt that there was no risk of rejection. He would come back.

I idled the rest of the afternoon away, dreaming up ways in which I could murder Xanthe:

A daddy-long-legs is full of cyanide on the inside; I wondered if I could crush one up and put it in her lunch. Would it be doable? Would it work? Was it actually a fact, or a myth?

Maybe I could shove her under one of the buses that came thundering along the road outside our office. But that relied too heavily on no one seeing me push her and the bus driver not braking in time.

It must be pretty easy to hold someone's head down in water, but how was I going to get her into a situation in which her head could be immersed? In the toilets? No, too high a chance of someone walking in, and I wasn't sure her head would go down far enough to drown. Those toilets are quite narrow towards the bottom and the water level is not very high. It would be embarrassing to get her within a few inches of her death then have to apologise and give it up as a bad job.

There was a sudden rush of scanning to be done before Gareth and I went home, so it became a question for another day.

But, how long to wait for Sean to gather his thoughts and recover his composure? I didn't know, but I'd had an idea to help hurry him along.

After work, as I waited for my evening meal to cook, I went to my bedroom and experimented with some sultry make-up and a short nightie.

Then I did something daring: I stretched out on the sofa, nightie hitched suggestively on my thigh, cleavage temptingly visible, expression seductive. I posed, I aimed the camera, I clicked . . . Perfect first time! Before I lost my nerve, I uploaded it to the Facebook.

'Wine breathing, pizza baking, me simmering . . . what's missing from this picture?'

I waited, I poked at my meal, I checked the Facebook. No change. He hadn't known I was cooking tonight, so maybe he was catering for himself. He tended to get a takeaway on a Friday night. And Saturday, Sunday, Monday, Tuesday, Wednesday and Thursday. Maybe it hadn't occurred to him that I'd be cooking on a Friday. Or that it wasn't too soon for him to start inviting himself round.

Then the doorbell rang! I'd been about to give up hope.

I rushed to the front door and flung it open, the widest smile spread across my face.

'Evening! Nothing serious!' some kid with a handful of leaflets said to me, before he felt the full impact of my attire. 'Just wondered how long it had been since you had your windows replaced,' he stammered on.

I explained, in no uncertain terms, that I had no need for new glazing and told him I was waiting for someone. I almost had a tear in my eye as I closed the door behind him: to have my hopes raised like that, then dashed. Back in the lounge, I opened up the Facebook. I wanted to write something about how I was feeling, but I couldn't put it into words.

Still, excitingly, in the top right corner was the red circle, around a number one, indicating there had been some activity. I clicked on it and up came the announcement 'Sean O'Flannery has shared your post'.

CHAPTER FIVE

2009

Oh Sean! Sean! Sean! In the giddiness of youth, he had hurried to share his happiness without a thought for the consequences. In the two minutes since he had shared the picture – the picture meant for our eyes only – it had been shared again five more times and received numerous comments, not all of them kind:

'Rosa Klebb's still alive?' some unthinking brute had said.

'It's not Halloween yet, is it?' someone else asked.

I received a fair few personal messages as well, all of them from strangers, all of the strangers men.

'Would you like to tie a girl up with me?' one of them said. And 'I also like kinky sex, preferably after breaking into a locked building.' I couldn't work out how to delete them. I thought about replying and explaining I was already in a committed relationship, but I didn't really want to open a discussion. So, I sat and watched them mounting up in my inbox.

The office fell silent as I entered on Monday morning. I walked with my head held high; Sean and I had done nothing to be ashamed of. It was just a photo, alike to those taken by couples all over the country. There were probably many in that very room who had done the same, even this weekend. It was a sign of a healthy relationship. The only differences between us and them was that theirs were probably kept within the privacy of their own home. Of necessity, I'd had to deliver mine via the Facebook and Sean had made one small mistake and let the cat out of the bag. And who among us has never made a mistake?

Sean, as usual, was hard at it, eyes glued to his monitor when I walked in. Concentrating so hard, in fact, that when I bade him a cheery 'good morning!' he just slunk further down into his seat. I continued down the office to my desk, the sound of sniggering echoing in my wake.

Gareth was already at work. Physically at work that is, he wasn't doing anything; the spreadsheets had crashed and when that happened, I was the only person who could sort them out. He glanced at me, about to voice his relief at my arrival, but then his face contorted and he swung back round to address his task.

'Good weekend?' he asked at last, having regained control of himself.

'The usual,' I replied. 'You?'

'So-so,' he told me.

'I only have thighs for you,' someone flashed by my desk singing, but so quickly that, by the time I'd located them, they were running down the aisle. It wasn't someone from our department, I knew that. Gareth stared hard at his monitor.

'It was an old photo,' I lied. 'At least twenty years old.' I don't know why I lied, but for some reason it seemed better to pretend it was a photo from years ago, rather than the previous Friday.

'You haven't changed much,' Gareth remarked. He was peering at the picture. 'Your hair was like that twenty years ago?'

Yes, it was. 'It's a classic style,' I said.

Gareth gave a brief nod, he was probably thinking the same thing about his own short back and sides.

It seemed better to pretend I hadn't been on my own either. 'It was taken by an ex-boyfriend. Not ex at the time. He caught me by surprise.'

Gareth was quiet for a moment, tilting his head as he viewed the picture. I wished he'd put it away. 'So how come,' he asked, 'there's an IKEA print on the wall behind your bed? Did they have IKEA twenty years ago?'

I peered over his shoulder, daring to look at the photo for the first time since I'd posted it.

'That's not IKEA!' I said.

'Yes, it is, my mum has the same one.'

'It was my student flat,' I said, pleased with my quick-thinking. 'The landlord decorated it.'

'I didn't know you'd been a student.' Gareth said. 'What did you study?'

'I was a student nurse.'

He wanted to know, then, why I was now an admin person in a financial services office.

'Because I didn't complete the course,' I told him. 'Circumstances conspired against me.'

But with every cloud comes a silver lining: nothing was ever proven, and I had a rather large out-of-court settlement. Which is why I live in an affluent street in one of the most desirable parts of Caerphilly.

CHAPTER SIX

1981

I can't say I always enjoyed the placements on my university nursing course. By my final year I was starting to wonder if I was really cut out for shift work and the patients were more impatient than I'd imagined. They didn't care that we were students; they gave no quarter if you couldn't get the needle in right first time.

The quiet of an intensive care unit was a relief after my previous roles: I had experienced the chaos of a mental health ward; the extremes of a cancer ward; the bewilderment of a geriatric ward and, finally, the hush of intensive care.

That was the last nice thing I had to say about it. I'd met some snotty nurses during my training, but these ones took the biscuit.

They didn't acknowledge me when I arrived, they just carried on with their conversations. Except for when they didn't carry on their conversations and instead went quiet, glancing at me, glancing at each other. Sometimes whispering.

'Of course we're whispering, this is intensive care,' they said if I mentioned it.

Sometimes they were pointedly silent.

When I asked for some learning opportunities, I was told to 'create your own opportunities'. Were they suggesting I damaged the patients myself?

There were times when I wondered, had these people never been students themselves? Were they all placed here by a divine hand, already experienced and world-weary? The disdain with which they treated their trainees suggested so.

I counted myself better than that. I had never cared for the frivolity of cliques, the lure of ganghood, the safety of the crowd. I had always been proud to stand alone. I had enrolled in this university to become a nurse. To nurse, to heal, to deliver hope. To see my own hand hovering over the button or the needle, that meant life or death, day after day after day.

If the nurses on my placements weren't going to help me willingly, what did I care? They were ships passing in my night and soon I would leave them far behind, finding my own harbour, and anchoring.

But the intensive care placement was something else. This, I reflected, was more than a disdain for students, it was an attack on them.

'Morning, Julie,' one of them said as I prepared myself for my shift. 'Ready to poison a few more patients today?' She was referring to an incident where I'd nearly got two very similar-looking, but very differently acting, tablets mixed up.

Behind her, her friend giggled. 'Come on, anyone can make a simple mistake.'

'Accepting a tablet from Julie is like playing Russian roulette.'

Thrilled with their analogy, they went off to tell the world what a death-defying feat of bravery it was to take a tablet from me.

Word got around and I was frequently asked by the other nurses, 'Have you brought your wheel, Julie?' as I was preparing the medicine trolley; the fact that Russian roulette is played with a gun notwithstanding.

By anybody's standards, this was bullying. And I didn't mean to put up with it. I vowed to wreak revenge, but I didn't have a clue how to go about it.

Then suddenly, I didn't have to: suddenly, Dr Pearson was there.

You could tell when he arrived on the ward. Everyone's demeanour changed. From the young women, wondering if a good marriage to a dashing doctor might be a better idea than a career; to the young men, feeling inferior; to the older men, feeling worse; to the middle-aged frump, kidding herself she was eighteen again. Everyone put on their best face for Dr Pearson.

Dr Pearson was quite the heart-throb on our ward. His physique was toned despite his mature years, and he only just had the beginnings of a beer belly. His face was lined solely with laughter lines. His silver-fox hair was still thick, swept back in waves, kept in place by Brylcreem, or something of that ilk. And his eyes: his eyes were wonky, so much so it looked like his whole head was misaligned. Maybe because of this, he generally had his head tilted to one side, which levelled them up a bit and made him look jaunty. When his head was straight, there was no avoiding it and I wondered if the whole world looked slightly askew to him. But it was that head at a tilt that made Dr Pearson so appealing as he moved vigorously around the hospital, never short of energy, enthusiasm or a motivating word for both staff and patients. He inspired us all.

'Good morning, Sister Nuffield,' he'd beam at the solemn ward sister. 'How's the grandson?'

'Oh, he's wonderful, Dr Pearson,' she'd simper back. 'Just wonderful.'

'Hello there, Nurse Evans,' he'd say to another. 'How's your young man? Ready to make an honest woman of you yet?' And Nurse Evans would giggle and blush.

'How are you getting on, Dr Mayer? Still giving me a run for my money?'

And newly qualified Dr Mayer would say something stupid, like 'can't teach an old dog new tricks' and everyone would roll their eyes, except for Dr Pearson, who laughed as if it were the wittiest joke he'd ever heard.

He was like the Wizard of Oz, presenting everyone with whatever they needed. When his eyes settled on me, he'd say, 'Ah, our young student, still seeing the world with fresh eyes. Let me know if there's anything I can do to help!'

Well, I smiled and nodded, of course I did, but I had no plans to tell him of my personal woes, or to make monsters of my erstwhile colleagues. No, I was not a grass: I would fight my own battles.

Yet Dr Pearson had eyes to see and ears to hear, and see and hear he did. Those madams were not as subtle as they thought.

'No, you don't do it like that, Julie,' one of the bullies was saying to me one day as I took a patient's blood pressure.

'That's how I always do it,' I said, it was one of the simplest tasks we did. 'No one else has said anything.'

But she shook her head and stood back to watch as I moved on to the patient's pulse. Out of the corner of my eye I could see her head moving back and forth as she shook it again and I heard her sigh. I knew I was checking it correctly, I'd been doing it since early in my training and had been observed and tested on it numerous times, but her sneering made me start to doubt myself. I tried to resist looking up, but it was too much when her friend arrived and they exchanged glances.

I reached for the thermometer and they steeled themselves for disaster. I trembled as I asked the patient to open her mouth. The bullies fell about, pretending they were trying not to laugh. 'Are you really in your final year?' one of them asked.

'Is she doing it wrong? Am I going to die?' the patient asked, almost as distressed as me.

'Don't worry, Mrs Thwelis,' the first bully said. 'We'll get you sorted.'

'Julie, why don't you go and tidy the computer area,' the other one said. 'If you're up to that. Oh sorry!'

Her timing was off: she said the words just *before* she tipped a full bedpan over me.

I ran from the ward, passing as I did so the watchful eye of Dr Pearson, standing only a few paces away, taking in the scene.

The next morning, arriving late for my shift, slightly hungover, I heard his scolding wrath as he warned them against their course of action.

'Bullying,' he said, 'will not be tolerated in this hospital.' He was disgusted with each and every one of them. He was ashamed of them and hoped they were ashamed of themselves. He wanted to see no more of this behaviour and if he did or if he even suspected it, a complaint would be on its way to HR and prosecuted to the very limits of his power.

They were all very nice when I 'arrived' a few minutes later.

But I didn't need their niceness then; I had the goodwill of Dr Pearson. The affection of Dr Pearson. Because it was at that time I began to notice how he smiled at me more widely than anyone else. He only smiled at the others in a perfunctory way, but with me, his eyes were aglow. His kind words to me, I realised, were from the heart; his kind words to the patients were formal and stiff. His friendly 'good morning' to me was a genuine joy of meeting, and to all others, a polite, professional greeting.

I realised for the first time that Dr Pearson was in love with me.

And indeed, it was only a day later that he sought me out while I was enjoying my break to ask if I had change for the vending machine.

I was in the staffroom, drinking my tea and reading a copy of the paper someone had left when he wandered in. He glanced at me, then glanced again.

'Morning,' he smiled.

'Good morning,' I mumbled, quite taken aback that he'd come to seek me out so soon after my revelation. He spent a moment looking hard at the vending machine, then turned back to me.

'What do you recommend?' he asked.

I had no idea what he meant.

'Marathon? KitKat? Maltesers?'

I understood! He wanted to know what my favourite chocolate was.

I think my voice was trembling as I said, 'I like Maltesers.' I imagined being presented with a huge box of them, the like of which I only usually saw at Christmas – and all to myself!

'Maltesers it is, then!' he turned back to the machine and put his hand in his pocket. He pulled out some change, rifled through it, then put his hand in his pocket again, leaning sideways as he searched for another coin. I wondered if he was buying me something now. Would he present it with a flourish? Would he drop to his knees and offer it out like a sacred treasure? Would someone come in and see us?

He turned back me. 'Don't suppose you have change for a 50p, do you?'

Clever, I thought. I reached for my handbag and took out my purse, my heart racing, hoping I was going to be able to help at such a crucial juncture.

'How much do you need?' I asked.

'18p for Maltesers.'

Eighteen pence! Someone was making a killing out of these vending machines. I placed three 10ps and a 5p on the table and started digging out my coppers, but I only had 48p.

'Perfect,' Dr Pearson said, even though it wasn't, it was 2p short. He scraped my change up and handed me his 50p piece; electricity jumped as our fingers brushed. I glanced up as he smiled down at me and I smiled back, to let him know I understood.

'I owe you 2p,' I said.

'Forget about it, Julie,' he said. 'It is Julie, isn't it?'

I nodded, surprised and charmed at his diffidence. Of course, he knew it was Julie!

He bought his Maltesers and left, smiling and nodding to me as he exited. I sat, a little disappointed at not having been bought chocolate, but in other ways glowing, feeling like Juliet after a meeting with Romeo. There would be plenty more opportunities for sweets.

'Hi, Julie. Any plans for the weekend?' One of the permanent nurses came in. They'd all been painfully nice to me since Dr Pearson's talk, but I could hear the insincerity behind it.

'Coming round to your house and killing your family,' I said.

I didn't really! I said, 'Oh, you know. This and that. Bit of housework, bit of coursework, bit of letting my hair down.'

What did I care now for their niceness? I had won the greatest prize. Now, I would have welcomed the sight of them whispering in huddles, watching as I passed. Now that the subject would be me and Dr Pearson.

Would it be a scandal? I hoped so. Something that would be spoken of for years to come, jealousy passed down like an heirloom. Years later, at Christmas parties and charity balls, I would be paraded on his arm, tall, dark, ageing wonderfully. I would be the envy of all the other guests, while these nurses I saw today, these nothings, these nobodies, would only be able to watch enviously through the windows. Standing hand in hand with their ordinary, nobody husbands, wondering what secret I held that lifted me up so much higher than they could ever dream of.

But that would be then. For now, Dr Pearson and I had a more pressing problem: namely how to get the ball rolling properly when we could never get a minute to ourselves.

He could have just asked me for my number, I would gladly have given it, but I suppose he was concerned about seeming unprofessional. Or maybe he was afraid I would come to regard him as predatory. He needn't have feared: I had seen the shining soul behind his genial eyes.

The days rolled by, patients came and went but the staff were the one constant: me, the nurses and Dr Pearson. But with every day that passed I was drawing closer to the end of my placement, and Dr Pearson and I had still not had a chance for a quiet tête-à-tête.

It was not for want of trying. We were forever following each other into the break room, starting with a bit of small talk: 'How was your weekend?'/ 'Beautiful weather today.'/ 'The patient in bed three is a chronic junkie who doggedly refuses to do anything to help himself,' you know the sort of thing, but we were always interrupted before it became anything more.

He approached me while I was gazing into the dangerous drugs cabinet, dreaming of the power within those little capsules.

'Alright, Julie?' he said, and I turned. But as he took a step closer, a gaggle of nurses passed by – ruining the moment, muttering something I probably wasn't supposed to hear about 'at the dangerous drugs again, Julie' – and when I turned back, Dr Pearson was disappearing round the corner.

That was the way in that hospital, some unwanted presence would always enter the room, make themselves a drink and sit down to read a magazine. Sometimes they even joined in the conversation! For a profession that supposedly places great emphasis on social skills and reading people, the average nurse has a very poor ability to pick up on nuance and sexual tension.

Then I had an idea. I was stuck on a piece of coursework, and it was always hard to get Sister Nuffield's attention. I laid my plans and chose my time.

I waited one morning as Dr Pearson went through his usual round of pleasantries: 'How's the grandson?' 'How's your young man? Oh dear. Still, plenty more fish.' 'How's the greasy pole?' to Dr Mayer, and finally: 'Julie! Graduation getting nearer. If there's anything I can do?'

I didn't speak up in front of the others, but as soon as they began to drift towards their posts, I made my way over to the doctor, for some reason feeling a little nervous. I stood behind him, waiting for him to sense my presence. He didn't, so I cleared my throat.

He turned round. 'Ah, Julie, what can I do for you?'

I cut straight to the chase. 'I have a piece of coursework due soon and I'm stuck. I wondered if you could go through some of it with me?'

He stared at me.

'Please?'

'Doesn't Sister Nuffield usually help the students?' he asked, keen to make sure our stories were watertight.

'Sister Nuffield is absolutely run off her feet,' I told him, moving to block his view of the sister who was usually sitting at her desk reading a Mills & Boons at this time of day. 'Overworked, even. She's doing extra shifts to cover staff sickness.'

Dr Pearson smiled and nodded. He understood as well as I did that I had just arranged the perfect meetup.

But where to go? There was no point in choosing the break room, we would have all the usual problems. As a student nurse, I was not really the person to go commandeering rooms, so I left the decision to the doctor. He came up with the canteen.

It was not my first choice of venues – it seemed rather close in nature to the break room, but it was a lot bigger and when we entered, mid-afternoon, what did we see but a huge expanse of – mostly – unoccupied tables.

We chose one and sat at a respectable distance to each other. He looked at me, his head up straight and his eyes at their wonkiest, so that I found myself tipping my own head to the side. I had expected him to start by telling me to call him Jeremy – that was his first name – but to my surprise and, I admit, my slight disappointment, he started by saying, 'So what exactly is it you're stuck on, young Julie?'

Although he must yearn to have me calling him by his given name, he knew we must remain careful in the early days. Young and impulsive as I was, there was too much risk that, in my happiness, I would forget myself on the ward and refer to him as 'Jeremy'. So I carried on with my pretence.

'Umm ... I've never really got fully to grips with anatomy and I'm worried it will be a big part of my final exams.'

'Is that what your coursework is about?'

'Mostly.'

'Well,' he said, 'Let's see what we can do.' Then, to my amazement he began singing 'Dem Bones'. That wasn't part of the learning material.

After that, however, he knuckled down and explained anatomy at length and in detail, never wavering from the subject to broach the matter of our grand passion. It was just as well I was already pretty well versed in anatomy because I was so befuddled by his behaviour, I could hardly take a word in.

'Has that helped?' he asked, coming to a stop. I nodded. 'Is there anything else?'

Realising the meeting may be coming to an end, I opened one of the textbooks I'd brought for appearances' sake and opened it at a random page. 'This,' I said. By chance it was a chapter on epidemiology, which was an area I could improve on, so this time I listened hard. He had a wonderful way of explaining matters and under his tutelage it all became crystal clear.

Better still, as we worked, our hands brushed over the textbook at every opportunity, and our heads bowed together over a diagram, closer than was strictly necessary.

He finished our session by saying he hoped he had helped, which he had, and saying if there was anything else he could assist with, he'd be very happy to do so. How else could he have finished, but with an invitation to meet up again?

Yet, I was perilously close to the end of my placement and doom was staring us in the face. I wondered if Dr Pearson actually knew how close I was to my finishing date. I had to assume he did not. Otherwise, how could he have remained so calm? I made a mental note to mention it next time we were exchanging pleasantries in the break room, although it pained me to be the one to give him such a shock.

I thought of us ditching our shifts halfway through and running out of the hospital into the park yonder. Finding an old oak tree to hide behind and expressing our feelings in a physical way. Maybe from there we would go straight to Gretna Green and make an honest man and woman of each other. I couldn't think of anything greater than to become the wife of Dr Pearson.

With this in mind, I braced myself to tell him the news at the very next opportunity. But before I could do so, a better chance came around. One of the other doctors, Dr Harris, was retiring and his retirement party was to be held on the following Friday. We were all invited.

In fact, I found out everyone else had been invited some time ago. I was only an afterthought when I overheard some of the others talking about it.

Remembering their newly found niceness, one of them casually asked me if I was going and when I remarked this was the first I'd heard of it, she said there must have been some mistake and invited me to come. 'Dress to impress,' she said.

This must have been why Dr Pearson – Jeremy – had been so calm. Not realising I was nearly lopped out of the loop, he must have been banking on that night to declare his love. Not only would it be completely normal for us to be seen together, huddling close and talking, but the truth was always easier to broach with the application of a little alcohol.

I had to look my best. I went into town with my credit card and a resolution to shop as if I were in ABBA. I returned to my student digs with a selection of dresses, glittery tights, shoes, jewellery, make-up and a tiara.

I scuttled past the lounge, avoiding my housemates, who would want to know how I could be spending money when I still owed them for the utilities, and up to my room.

I tried on the dresses, but I wasn't sure which I liked best. Should it be the pale green floaty dress, which hid all my sins, but didn't really go with my colouring? In fact, it made me look a bit ill. What about the little black dress? It was sleek and classy and could never look wrong or out of place. It narrowed my waist and flattened my stomach; it made my hips look curvy instead of wide. But I would probably just be one of many in such an outfit.

Or the blue cocktail dress? It was my favourite but had been so expensive there was no way I would ever pay off the credit card bill. It was going to have to go back whatever my decision, but if I wore it, I would spend the whole night worrying about spilling something on it or tearing it. With regret, I decided against the blue. But I could wear it for the night in my room. I sat and listened until I heard my housemates going out.

I hated my housemates. They were already installed when I moved in, my place in the halls of residence having fallen through, so I took a box room in a house with existing tenants.

I felt shy, but determined to make the best of it at first, so when I heard them all downstairs, I took a deep breath and went to join them.

The room fell silent when I appeared in the kitchen doorway for the first time. I smiled, but none of them smiled back. Eventually, one of the boys took a step to the left.

'Did you need the kettle?' he asked.

I shook my head.

'Oh.'

More silence.

'We didn't think they'd find anyone for that teensy little room you're in,' one of the girls said.

'We were told they weren't even advertising that room,' the boy who had asked about the kettle said. 'We understood it was just going to be us in this house.' He looked around the room at the other housemates, I looked as well, and they looked at each other.

'Don't you have any friends to rent with?' the girl asked, and I shook my head again.

'Would you like a drink?' I asked, making for the kettle that I'd already said I didn't need, imagining that might somehow turn the situation around.

'We're going out in a minute,' she said.

'In fact, it's time to go,' another girl added and before I knew it, they were all out the front door.

I persevered for a few weeks but gave up when I realised the very sight of me sent them either running for the hills or into peals of laughter. I got the point: they'd rented the house together and didn't want me there. After that I started avoiding them. Instead, I'd wait until the house was empty and go downstairs to drink their milk from the carton, to tip vinegar into the washing they left in the machine, to take change from the kitty they kept on the windowsill. Small revenges, but it was all that I could do.

Lately, they were becoming increasingly pushy about the gas and electricity money – even though I'd assured them I'd pay it – and I found myself actively avoiding them. I wondered what Jeremy would say if I told him of the way they were treating me. Would he come to speak to them, as he had done at the hospital, telling them, in no uncertain terms, to leave me alone? To befriend me even? Probably, I thought. Then I thought it was more likely he'd just give me the money to pay the bill. Maybe he'd give me the money to pay for the dress. But I couldn't count on it.

In my room, I cheered myself up by donning the blue cocktail dress. I would bet none of my housemates had anything like that in their wardrobes. It was rather tight. I had to stand up straight and breathe in, but it really was beautiful with its shimmering silky blue, and I had time for a quick crash diet before the party, if I dared to wear it.

As a child I'd been somewhat on the stocky side. As I'd grown, I'd been lucky enough to grow upwards more than outwards until I could describe myself as statuesque rather than stocky. But I was never going to have one of those willowy, waif-like figures you see on other girls.

I'd been unusual as well, in having a rather large nose as a child, but I'd also grown into that and now, while aquiline, it was at least in proportion to my face, framed by my deep-set eyes.

I thought again about keeping the dress. I made up my face and tried different combinations of jewellery. Some of the silver looked good, but it didn't feel right to be wearing a £5 choker with a dress that had cost over a grand. I looked closely and wondered how many people could tell, at a glance, the difference between expensive and costume jewellery.

I combed and styled my hair, then I put the tiara on my head. It was perfect! I looked like a princess, a real-life fairy tale princess. I put some gentle music on and swayed gracefully round the room, arms open as if I were dancing with Jeremy. I pictured the two of us in a ballroom, dancing an elegant waltz while the other guests looked on. I danced for what seemed like hours. When I switched on the TV and sat down, I realised that it was Eurovision Song Contest night and I was just in time for Bucks Fizz.

I jumped back up again. Bucks Fizz were fantastic! I bopped along and at the bit where the boys pulled the girls' long skirts off to reveal shorter ones underneath, I took myself off in a series of high-speed pirouettes, until—

The sickening sound of fabric ripping. I looked down and the dress had caught on the corner of the cheap desk that was provided with the room; the very same corner responsible for a hole in the sleeve of one of my jumpers.

My first thought was that it was quite a small tear and I could sew it up, but at that time I was relatively unpractised in arts and crafts. I had never been top of the class in home-ed, and the material itself began to fray beyond repair. After an hour, I admitted defeat. It was ruined.

I put my pyjamas on and crawled into bed.

My dad ended up paying off the credit card bill. I said I had racked up the debt via unforeseen expenses related to my course. The dress stayed in my wardrobe for years, waiting for the day when I had occasion to use it, a day that never came.

My spirits had revived by the night of the party. I applied my make-up and donned the green dress. I added the tiara and gave myself a twirl. Perfect!

But it was unlikely anyone else would be wearing a tiara. My confidence fell and I took it off. I looked at my make-up, and on reflection, maybe it was a bit much; I wiped most of it off. Finally, I reconsidered my dress. Green really wasn't my colour; I changed it for the black one, with just a silver necklace and matching earrings. Perfectly appropriate.

I had felt a little nervous in the week leading up to the party. It had occurred to me that Jeremy had not said anything about it. I hoped he hadn't had a prior engagement. If he wasn't coming to the party, I thought, surely he would have mentioned something by now, so we could make other arrangements.

And I must remember to call him Dr Pearson, at least until the green light was given. I knew Jeremy wouldn't mind himself, but it would be giving the game away to everyone else.

The party was only just starting when I arrived. Perhaps I should have given it another half hour. A few of the nurses from my placement were already there, looking pretty tarty, I thought. Remembering their recent telling off, they let me stand with them.

The music was not the classical style I would have expected from Dr Harris, but a series of disco hits. Evidently there was going to be dancing later. I had anticipated a more sedate affair, standing around, talking, and I had readied myself with a number of interesting topics for discussion: are we ready for a new national anthem? Are you for or against cryogenic freezing? Spurs for the cup this year? Or do you fancy City? That was a gem I'd gleaned from the tabloids my housemates left lying around in the kitchen, sports page up. Now, I saw, there would be little need for them.

The first half hour was slow. Someone was bringing around wine. I'd never really drunk wine before, but I needed something to steady my nerves, so I accepted a red. The first glass familiarised me with the fruit flavour, the second gave me a taste for more, after the third I was ready to dance and by the fourth there was no stopping me.

I kept an eye on the door, waiting for Dr Pearson and wondered if, when he arrived, he would make a beeline straight for me, or play it more casually. I'd be interested to see what he brought back from the bar: alcoholic or non-alcoholic. If alcoholic, he was clearly not on call and the night was ours to do as we pleased.

The hour grew later and guests began to pack the venue. They were pouring in through the door thick and fast. Dr Harris must have been more popular than I gave him credit for. Unless these people just didn't get out enough.

Eventually my patience was rewarded. I heard his laugh first. He, like me, must have been excited about the night ahead. Then I saw him. Tall and handsome in an evening suit. A slightly aged James Bond. My heart skipped a beat, then the blood rushed through my veins. I saw him smile that smile I'd fallen in love with, I heard that deep, bass voice ring out.

Then my heart skipped another beat before dropping right down to my shoes. So heavily did it fall, I wouldn't have been at all surprised to see it drop right out of my body and through the floor below. Seconds after I saw him, I saw a woman catching him up and putting her arm through his. She was tall and slender, with Farrah Fawcett hair and a burgundy velvet dress. I saw him cover her hand with his and look down at her lovingly, smiling that smile I thought he reserved solely for me.

'What's the matter, Julie?' one of the nurses asked. 'You look like you've seen a ghost.' She followed my gaze to the point at which I was looking. 'Mrs Pearson's really elegant, isn't she?' she said.

He never told me he was married! He didn't wear a ring!

The last thing I remember about the party was falling drunk down some stairs and onto a table full of empty glasses.

CHAPTER SEVEN

1981

'You like a good drink, don't you!' a random nurse grinned when I arrived at the hospital for my first shift after Dr Harris's party. I didn't remember seeing her there. A number of other people paused in their work to congratulate me on my performance that night. Most of us on the ward that day were still of an age where getting drunk out of our senses was a thing to be celebrated.

I had a cut below my eye from falling on the table, but the hangover had worn off. I'd had a dry day the day before and I was feeling happier than I had on the night of the party because I'd come to a realisation:

It had dawned upon me that the reason Dr Pearson had not mentioned his wife must be because he was deeply unhappy with her. If he were happy, surely he'd want to tell everyone about her. Thinking back to when I first saw her, I understood now that the way in which she had linked her arm in his was rather controlling: daring him to wander away from her. The way he smiled at her, the look I had mistaken for love – I now saw – was a means of keeping the peace. There was probably hell to pay at home if he failed to toe the party line and treat her in the way in which she demanded. My heart bled for him as I realised the life he led, the life he had kept secret, most likely to save upsetting me.

She was clearly a termagant, a fishwife, a harpy. No wonder he was always so cheerful at work; it must be a blessed relief to be away from her.

Why hadn't he divorced her? I couldn't definitively say. Maybe she ruled the roost so firmly he had hardly realised there was a way out. Maybe he was afraid. Maybe there were children he didn't want to leave at her mercy. Maybe, having until now no one else to go to, he had not been able to find the will. It was hard to imagine: this kind, friendly doctor going home to a love-less marriage every night. To a woman who made his life a misery.

But not for much longer. As soon as we could make our arrangements, I knew, he would take heart, tell her the truth and break free from her shackles.

Yet now, we were back to the old problem of how to make our arrangements. Hadn't he known on Friday she would be watch-ing our every move? Men! If you want a job done properly, get a woman to do it! Or maybe he'd only found out at the last moment she would be coming? Maybe she'd declined, then changed her mind. And he'd been forced to put on a happy face. My poor Jeremy.

I was pondering the matter on my break, when who should come in but the man himself. He seemed in a hurry. He had his wallet out, looking at a bank card and simultaneously trying to write on a scrap of paper. He went to the worktop so he could put the wallet and card down and write more easily. Once he had finished, he dug in his pocket for change and went to the vending machine, smiling and nodding at me as he did so. He bought a Mars bar, then left. Leaving his wallet on the side.

I waited, my heart racing. So, he had already thought of a plan. He was leading me somewhere, and he had obviously left his wallet there for me to bring back to him. He probably had a room ready for us and was expecting me to follow.

I took it from the counter and walked to the door. I looked left, I looked right. No sign of him. I walked down to one end of the corridor and looked both ways again. I walked to the other and did the same, but he had been too fast for me. I returned to the break room door and waited for him to realise he'd lost me and return. Then a new realisation dawned on me.

I would have to be quick: aside from Jeremy's brief visit, I had been in there on my own for about two minutes. That was unheard of. Someone was bound to come in at any second.

Carefully positioning the scene so that if anyone did appear I could pretend I'd just noticed it and was checking whose it was, I picked up the wallet and flicked through the pockets. Bank cards, bank cards, bank cards – how many did a man need? And it was hard to see what I was supposed to do with them. There was no loose paper, he had written me no notes. I was perplexed.

Then I found, tucked away in a hard-to-spot inner pocket, his driving licence. That's what he wanted me to see! A piece of tatty green paper showing his date of birth – a little younger than I had thought and – lo and behold – his address! I took a napkin and copied the street name and house number down on it. I roughly knew the area and a street map would do the rest. Then I replaced the licence and helped myself to two quid; I knew he wouldn't mind. I would have chips after work and think of him as I munched on them.

I was still unsure as to what exactly he wanted me to do with this information, but understanding came as I worked through my shift that afternoon.

It just so happened that I was going to be on lates the following week, while Jeremy would be on the day shift. A fact that had initially seemed calamitous, was now, I realised, my window of opportunity.

On the first morning I roused myself early, showered, and left the house without even stopping for breakfast – I had change for a butty and a coffee if the need arose later. Then I set off for the doctor's side of town.

It took longer to walk than I had expected, but eventually I found his street. It was, unsurprisingly, an affluent area. The houses must all have had four or five bedrooms, front rooms, dining rooms, sitting rooms, games rooms, dens, offices as well as a number of bathrooms. They had big, well-tended front gardens, and promised huge landscapes around the back. I found Dr Pearson's and stopped, standing beneath a tree on the opposite side of the road, looking at his long, flat lawn and open curtains, giving a fair view of the interior. I pulled my hood up as it began to rain.

I could see heavy old furniture, framed pictures, an open fireplace and doors into rooms beyond. I imagined myself as the mistress of the house, giving orders to the help about where to dust next, how to arrange the cushions, what Dr Pearson – Jeremy – would like for his tea. I would be a kind mistress, but I would not tolerate any backchat. I imagined my maid would be the latest in a long line of impudent predecessors.

In the evenings, Jeremy and I would relax with a G and T. Just a tipple before we went out to an expensive restaurant. Or staying in, reclining in our antique chairs, as something from Waitrose bubbled on the stove. I must learn how to cook.

I crossed the road. I wasn't sure what I was going to do when I got there, so I approached at a leisurely pace, but not so slowly that I would draw attention to myself.

Getting to the front door would be easy – there was only an unlocked gate at the end of the drive – but it was unclear as to whether or not there was anyone in. It looked empty, there were no cars visible, but there was a big garage with a closed door.

It started to rain harder, and clouds covered the sky, blocking out the sun. No lights went on in the house. I decided to take a chance and trotted through the gate, up the drive and rang the doorbell. No answer. I rang it again, just to be sure.

A car pulled up in the neighbouring drive and an elderly couple got out, her unfolding a plastic hood, him holding a newspaper uselessly over his head. They saw me and I began to panic. The woman spoke.

'Are you the new cleaner, love?' she asked.

I beg your pardon?! A surge of rage rushed up. Did she not know who she was talking to? Had she no idea what a stupid, ignorant thing she'd just said? She had a south of England accent and was well-spoken, with hints of an expensive education. Even though they were obviously a retired couple, she was fully made-up and wore a suit. I bet no one had ever mistaken *her* for the cleaner.

'No!' I wanted to shout at her. 'I'm the new wife!' But I didn't. I just said, 'Yes'.

'Felicity said to tell you the spare key's under the plant pot, by the back door.'

'Thanks,' I said.

'Good job we got back when we did, wouldn't have been great to have you standing out here in this weather. Is your stuff in your car? Your mop and bucket?'

'Yes,' I said. 'Thanks.' She took her leave and the man smiled and nodded, and they both went into their own house. Probably for some Earl Grey tea and a dose of Radio 3. I made my way to the back of the house. Felicity and Jeremy, I thought. Jeremy and Felicity. I smirked. Jeremy and Julie had a much better ring to it. Julie Pearson.

The key was going to be a mixed blessing: on the one hand it had saved me the job of breaking in, potentially cutting my hand on broken glass, being caught and arrested and definitely alerting Felicity to the fact there had been an intruder. On the other hand, I now knew there was a cleaner due soon and if she arrived, she would almost certainly find me. So, I nipped round the back, found the key, pocketed it and set off back to my house.

I wondered what would happen when the real cleaner arrived and couldn't get in. Had she been told to ask the neighbours? If not, would she wait, or just leave? What would Felicity say when she found the key was missing? Would she notice straight away? Would she phone the real cleaner, all irate because she'd taken the key? Would the house be cleaned this week? Would Felicity have to do it herself? I giggled as I swerved into a café and ordered myself a milky coffee and a bacon-and-sausage butty.

CHAPTER EIGHT

The next question was when to go back to the house. The neighbours had seen me now. They didn't get the best look at me, with my hood pulled halfway down my face, but I couldn't guarantee they wouldn't be able to point me out in an ID parade.

I waited until my day off to give time for the dust to settle and the neighbours to forget about me. We all know memories aren't what they were when you get to a certain age, and I was hoping they were no exception to that rule.

Once again when I arrived at the house, there was no sign of a car. I waited once more on the other side of the road, hiding from the neighbours' view, but they also seemed to be out. What do people with no jobs go out for? Though I didn't know that Felicity didn't work: for some reason, I'd just made that assumption. Maybe because I didn't intend to work when *I* was Mrs Jeremy Pearson.

I was ready to make my move. I dispensed with the doorbell and put the key straight in. It didn't fit. I wriggled it around and it definitely didn't fit. My high spirits dropped as I realised they must have changed the locks! So soon. It would take me weeks to get round to something like that. Then I had a thought: the key was left by the back door, so maybe that was the lock it was intended for. I ran round to the back and tried the lock. It was a perfect fit and a moment later I was standing in a large, bright, country-style kitchen, complete with an AGA and timbered beams. It was pretty warm in there, so I took my anorak off and hung it over a chair.

There were utensils hanging from the ceiling: a ladle, a slotted spoon, a medieval torture instrument. I did a double take.

I unhooked the torture instrument. In my hands I realised it was a meat tenderiser, but my goodness, they'd really gone to town. This could tenderise the hide of a dinosaur. The handle was made of hard wood, built to last; the join of the handle and the head almost invisible. The edges were metal, the spikes long, the weight heavy.

I had a go at swinging it, like a real knight of old, slamming into his opponent at the joust. I took it with me as I left the kitchen to explore the rest of the house.

The lounge – sitting room, drawing room, front room, whatever they liked to call it – was to the right of the kitchen. All the rooms led off from a large entrance hall, the front door in the centre.

The furniture looked ancient. A scuffed leather sofa, old, creaky and uncomfortable; it would be the first thing to go when I was lady of the house. The chairs and tables were dark wood, the curtains heavy velvet and the wallpaper was patterned and dark. I could smell lilies. The decor had probably cost a fortune to put together, but it would all be blitzed as soon as I got my hands on it. I made a mental note to order a Laura Ashley catalogue.

I glanced across the bookshelves filled with weighty tomes about medicine, philosophical stuff, gardening manuals, a variety of Bibles and, along the top shelf, a long row of Jilly Coopers. Ah, Felicity, I've uncovered your secret.

As expected, the furniture looked heavy and expensive. The lilies I could smell stood in a vase on a side table. I wondered if the vase was worth much: if it was from a Ming dynasty, or if it was available for £3.99 in BHS. Either way, they were going to be needing a new one. I swung the tenderiser and smashed it to spillikins. I remembered learning on the *Antiques Roadshow* once that vases tend to come in pairs. I looked around for its mate and there it was, on the other side of the room. I raised the tenderiser again but stopped myself. They were worth more as a pair; I decided to leave Felicity with the frustration of one, potentially, devalued vase and a lot of clearing up.

At the far end of the room was a dresser with a load of photos on it. There they were, Felicity and Jeremy through the years. Felicity all dolled up, Jeremy smiling bravely, head ever-tilted, with merely a grimace giving away the truth of the matter in their wedding photo. I leaned forward and looked closely for the pain behind the smile. You had to know what you were looking for, but it was definitely there.

I left the lounge and entered the dining room. Nothing of interest in there, but I put a dent in a silver candlestick anyway.

I went upstairs. I found the bedroom. I stood at the foot of the bed and tried to work out which side was Jeremy's. I guessed it was the one with the phone on the bedside table, all the better for him to answer if he was called to an emergency at night.

Standing by Jeremy's side of the bed, I stripped to my underwear, then lifted the covers and climbed in. I pressed my face into the pillows, then the sheets, hoping to breathe in the scent of him, but I only detected the scent of fabric conditioner. Frustratingly, the sheets seemed to be newly washed.

Still . . . I lay there for a minute, looking round the room that would soon be mine. Mine and Jeremy's. Then I had a thought: if this was his side, I wouldn't be here, I would need to shuffle over. I was reluctant for a moment, then I remembered, if the sheets are clean, I won't really be lying where she has lain. I moved across and lay, looking at Jeremy's spot, imagining him there, thinking of the secrets he would tell me, how I would comfort him as he came to terms with the years wasted under the thumb of Felicity the Tyrant. I drummed the tenderiser gently to and fro against the duvet, making a muffled rhythm. I closed my eyes.

I opened them to see Felicity, posed like *The Scream*, leering over me. I nearly had a heart attack! My mind was racing. Was this what Jeremy wanted? Was this going according to plan, or had I taken my eye off the ball and let him down? I didn't know.

'Who . . . ?' she said. I saw now that she was shaking a bit, whether with fear, or with rage, I couldn't tell. 'Vase . . .' she said. I nodded, then remembered my coat.

'Anorak,' I said. She nodded.

I realised I had to make a decision. I was going to lose the advantage of surprise if I lay here much longer, exchanging single word sentences. I leapt up out of the bed and her eyes widened once more as she saw I was only wearing my underwear.

There was only one thing to do. Earlier ideas of confronting her with the truth, of telling her I was the other woman and letting her take the initiative were abandoned: I raised the tenderiser and brought it down on her head.

She did not crack as easily as the vase had. In fact, she stood there staring at me for a moment, hardly dented. Then she ran and what else could I do but run after her?

I chased her downstairs, with the advantage of youth, going two at a time. I caught her by her long, blond hair and, pulling her towards me with one hand, whacked her over the head with the other. She nearly got away from me, but then we stepped, from the highly polished laminate flooring onto a rug which was not properly anchored. We slid quite a distance and finally landed in a heap near the front door. I was on top and she had no chance of getting free.

Still, it took a few goes. For future reference, meat tenderisers, even heavy-duty models, are not good skull smashers; I ended it by giving her a clunk with the cast iron umbrella stand by the door and nearly put my back out.

Eventually she lay quiet, the pattern of the tenderiser decorating her forehead. Dead, I thought and was about to check when the doorbell rang.

I froze. The door was surrounded by frosted glass and if I moved, I would likely be seen on the other side. The doorbell rang again, then a note was pushed through the letterbox and footsteps walked away. I ran upstairs and pulled my clothes back on. There was a long, dark hair lying on the pillow. I was about to dust it off when I realised what a subtle, but unmistakeable message it would leave for Jeremy. I left it where it was.

I went back down to the kitchen and grabbed my anorak, then I remembered: fingerprints.

Oh! What had I touched? What had I touched? I panicked for a few seconds, then I thought, not much. Not much more than the tenderiser, the door handle and the key. I rinsed the tenderiser in the sink and put it to drain, then I dusted around where I had been and left.

These were the days before DNA was a well-known phenomenon and I felt little concern. Jeremy and I had been so discreet, there was nothing to link me to the house. I felt a thrill of gratitude that he had ensured we kept a professional distance at work, that he remained 'Dr Pearson' in the hospital. For I knew now that if he had done differently, somewhere along the line I would surely have given the game away.

Thank you, thank you, thank you. I muttered to myself as I made a brisk march away from the house and I glowed as I realised this was exactly what Jeremy had wanted me to do.

CHAPTER NINE

2009

The day at work dragged on, with the hilarity over the photo I had taken never abating. While I was at lunch someone left a whip and collar on my desk and the messages didn't stop. I had well over a hundred.

'Don't worry about it,' Gareth said. 'In a couple of days some celebrity will flash their backside and then that'll be all they want to talk about. You're almost chip paper already.'

At home that evening, in need of solace, I went to the cupboard under the stairs and brought out Fluffy, my cat. Completed before I became good at taxidermy, she looked like the victim of a strange and nasty accident, but that is not how she passed. Now she spends eternity with legs of uneven length and fangs that, for reasons I never got to the bottom of, look like Dracula's.

I stroked Fluffy's fur and wished I hadn't posted that photo. They say you only regret the things you didn't do, but I can confidently confirm, that is not true. It hadn't occurred to me it could escalate like this. I only imagined it being between Sean and I. It was meant to bring us closer, but I don't think I'd ever felt more apart.

My phone beeped. Another message on the Facebook. I was about to ignore it when I noticed the name of the sender.

It was from Sean! It was one word, 'Sorry'. My heart soared.

I typed back, 'That is quite alright. I know you didn't mean any harm.'

Pretty calm and reasonable by anybody's standards. I added one more sentence, just to get things back on track: 'Call round for a drink when you're in the area. Xxx'

He came straight back to me. 'Will do,' he wrote. He would! He would! He would! I decided to try to pin him down to a date.

'I'm cooking coq au vin on Friday,' I sent. There was quite a long pause, then he replied, 'I'll have to see what I'm doing on Friday.'

What did that mean? Was it a 'yes, I'd like to, but I might've inadvertently made plans with the boys', or was it something less favourable?

I decided to head his doubts off at the pass. 'Or, if the weather's still good, I could fire up the barbecue, for one last time this year. You'll let me know?'

He sent back 'Yeah, I'll let you know.'

In years gone by, I thought I had been in love, but when I met Sean, I realised those affairs had been but passing fancies. They had grown from the humdrum of the everyday, kindled almost by boredom, and faded when my beau was revealed as the flawed character he inevitably was. But Sean was different. There had been electricity from the first moment we met and far from fading with familiarity, or off turned by a character trait, our passion only intensified over the years, as we came to know each other better.

We had met at a time when our stars were both on the ascendant – I was an established member of a crucial team, he was taking the first giant step in an illustrious career. We were not flailing for meaning, or hoping to fill a void. This was not the passing fling of an idle afternoon. It was true love.

*   *   *

I all but floated through the rest of the week, planning and dreaming of how Friday night would be. I even smiled and said a civil 'hello' to Xanthe as I passed her in the corridor.

On Friday, when my lunch break came and I intended to nip to the shop, I stopped by Sean's desk.

'Chicken or burgers tonight?' I asked.

'Eh?' his mind had obviously been somewhere else.

'Chicken or burgers. At my house. Tonight. And drinks.'

He looked blank for a moment, then I saw the dawning of realisation. 'Oh. Oh yeah, 'fraid I'm going to have to take a rain-check on that, Jools. Got something planned that can't be unplanned.'

'Oh,' I said. I wanted to add some choice words about how he was supposed to be letting me know and what could be so important that he chose it over our rendezvous. And in fact, which came first: our night together, or this unavoidable engagement that on Tuesday night either hadn't been arranged or was so important, apparently, that he couldn't quite bring up? But I didn't want to appear shrewish, so instead I said: 'Never mind. Another time.'

'Yeah, cheers, Jools. Great. Later.'

My zest for cooking that night left me, I went to the shop and bought a selection of cheese and crackers, along with two bottles of wine.

A bottle and a half in, I logged onto the Facebook. I was greeted with the words 'Sean O'Flannery is at Casanova, Italian restaurant and bar, with Xanthe Irving'.

On Monday morning, as I walked sleepily and somewhat later than usual from the train to the office, I wasn't quite sure if I had seen what I thought I'd seen ahead of me. I thought I'd seen Sean and Xanthe walking hand in hand into our building.

I thought. But there are many men of average height and build in this city, even this building, and many girls with bleach-blond hair. Even many of them in relationships with each other. It may have been them, it may not. It was certainly very late in the morning for Sean to just be arriving, being an early starter as a general rule.

I got a second glimpse a moment later and it was definitely him; after all these years I'd know his slightly lopsided gait anywhere. I was pretty sure it was her as well. After only a few weeks I was suitably au fait with her swinging hips and swishing hair; her tiny handbag and impractical shoes. So impractical, she could only walk at a snail's pace, and I was rapidly gaining on them.

'Morning,' I said brusquely as I marched past.

'Morning, Jools,' Sean said, seemingly unconcerned at being caught.

'Morning,' I heard Xanthe chirp as I thundered towards the lifts.

There was a wait to get in and they caught up with me there. They had the grace to unhand each other but kept up a quiet conversation while we made the ascent.

I suppose Sean was in a rather difficult position: unable to face the enormity of his feelings for me, he had fallen for the obvious, but shallow, charm of Xanthe. She was a straightforward proposition, an easy-come, easy-go kind of choice, with none of the emotional risk an entanglement with me presented. But now he'd been caught taking the primrose path, he was faced with the dual problems of knowing his weakness had been exposed and not wanting to hurt Xanthe's feelings.

Knowing he would no doubt come grovelling to me as soon as he could get away from her, I went to my desk, logged onto my PC and waited for his email.

Gareth was conducting an imaginary orchestra with my letter opener as I approached our desks. He stopped when he saw me.

'Been sucking lemons?' he asked.

'What?'

'You're looking a little sour this morning.'

Sean's email didn't come, but he was never much of a correspondent. Watching him from my end of the office I noticed he seemed more jubilant than usual. He was a cheerful man by nature, but today, from what I could see, he was all chatter and no work. Was it really jubilation, I wondered? Or hysterical guilt and fear at what he thinks he may have lost?

I began composing an email of my own: 'Sean,' I wrote – no 'dear,' no 'darling,' no 'good morning,' just straight to the point, 'Sean, I think . . .' But there words failed me and after an hour I was no further on, the stack of post was hardly touched and Gareth was muttering about having to do everything himself.

At lunchtime I nipped out for air, to be greeted on my return with the sight of Sean and Xanthe huddled together in the corridor outside the toilets.

I hurried to my desk with the intention of studying the online HR guide, there must be a section on this kind of behaviour. Maybe I could get Xanthe sacked for gross misconduct: making advances on a colleague's man must surely count.

Half an hour later, I had read all the dos and don'ts of office conduct and found nothing with which to hang her. Quite an oversight, how did they expect to keep the peace if homewreckers couldn't be disciplined?

But I did come across something of use. In a section about creating a strong password it gave some examples of common passwords that could easily be guessed, the name of a loved one, for example, with a number added to the end. When the time came to change your password, often only the number changed. I must confess, my own – 'Julie&Sean4ever!36' – updated from 'IhateDave!19' not long after Sean arrived – did fall into that category, but I hazarded a guess that Xanthe's did too. After all, it couldn't be very tricky if *she* had to memorise it.

So, I stayed a little late at work that evening and once the coast was clear, spent some time experimenting with Xanthe's log-in details. Her username was easy and no secret, it is our staff number and can be found in the email address book with our email details.

Then onto her password. I guessed Sean would be the meat of the matter and she had been here around seven months, so the number would be close to seven: security being what it is in the world of finance, we update our passwords every month. We must choose a word which is at least eight characters long and it must contain a special character. I started with 'SeanO!07' – no.

SeanO!06

No.

SOFlan!05

No, and with that I'd locked her out of the system. I made tracks and the next morning watched with pleasure as Xanthe had to phone IT to get access.

Yet a couple more days in the same vein and I was in, 'Flanners!4' was the winner. I waited again until the office was quiet, logged into Xanthe's email and typed out a fresh missive:

'You smell. Someone has to tell you.' I addressed it to Abi, who usually kept herself to herself, and set it to send at 9.30 the following morning. I arrived the next day expecting fireworks at half-past nine, but no fireworks erupted. Instead, sensitive Abi took it to heart and from then on could be found in the ladies on the hour, every hour, spraying herself with so much deodorant it was becoming hard to breathe in there.

I couldn't stay late every evening, so a couple of days later, when Gareth went off for lunch, leaving no one to see what I was doing, I logged into Xanthe's email and wrote,

'I didn't mean it, you don't smell. Stop spraying yourself, it's killing us,' and sent it to Abi.

I watched as Xanthe went for lunch, then I typed, 'You are a useless manager. Everyone says so,' and readied it for Marcus.

Just after three o'clock, Marcus's voice broke the silence. 'Xanthe, can I have a word, please?'

I had a few more days with it:

'I always think of you when I hear the song "You're So Vain",' had Gareth drawing a sharp breath.

'Dave thinks Cardiff City supporters are nonces,' I wrote to Mike and nearly caused a riot.

'But I didn't send that!' Xanthe protested when they confronted her about it.

'It came from your email,' Mike said.

'Did you leave your screen unlocked?' Dave asked her. 'While you were away from your desk?'

'No!'

They left her to ponder the situation, until the next day . . .

'Xanthe,' came Marcus's dulcet tones upon receipt of an email that said simply, 'Though I am small, I am fierce.'

I couldn't keep it up forever, it was only a matter of time until someone worked out what was happening. Xanthe was looking refreshingly befuddled, and I could always come back to it at a later date, once the furore had died down. But before I gave it up as a bad job, I opened up one more email in Xanthe's name and wrote simply, 'It's over.' In the 'To' box I clicked on Sean's name and pressed send.

At the other end of the office, I saw Sean look over at Xanthe. I saw him say something. Xanthe scooted over to his desk and looked at his screen. They both spoke at once, around them heads started to turn, they went out into the corridor. Time for me to go to the loo.

I could hear the shouting before I got to the door, but I couldn't hear the words, so I hurried through, to where Sean was saying he'd thought better of her, and Xanthe was saying she'd never send an email like that.

Disappointingly, they went quiet when they saw me, so I bustled past into the toilets and stood behind the door, eavesdropping. But they lowered their voices and I couldn't make out what they were saying. A minute later I failed to hear Abi's footsteps approaching and received quite a clunk on the head when she shoved the door open while I was still standing there. Back in the main office, Sean and Xanthe were standing by Sean's desk, talking in angry whispers, but I could hardly hover nearby, although Dave and Mike were making no attempt to conceal their curiosity.

Yet after a while, the whole department was alerted to the action, and I was able to shamelessly join the crowd huddled around her desk. Marcus went to see what was going on.

'Have you told someone your password?' Marcus asked Xanthe, towering menacingly above her. Xanthe quaked, knowing what a serious offence that was.

'No!'

'Did you write it down and leave it lying around?'

'No!'

'OK,' Marcus said. 'We'll get IT to see where the messages were sent from.'

I nearly fainted with the shock. I had no idea they could do that!

'In the meantime,' Marcus continued, 'change your password.'

And she did, to 'Flanners!5.' I checked.

Later that day, I took a risk. As I passed by Xanthe's desk, I took a sheet of notepaper with her handwriting on it. At home that night, copying her handwriting, I wrote her password on a slip of paper and crumpled it to make it look used.

On my approach to the office the next morning, I paused near the main door and bent down, as if picking something up. Then I continued on my way, up to our floor and straight over to

Marcus's desk, where I showed him the paper with Xanthe's password on it and told him where I'd 'found' it.

'Who else would have that as a password?' I asked. 'Anyone could've picked it up if she always carries it around like that. We'll never know who.' Marcus nodded like a disappointed parent.

'Xanthe,' he said, when she arrived a few minutes later. They went into one of the side offices and returned a few minutes later, both looking suitably irked.

A stern email was sent from HR to the whole company saying we had to be more careful about keeping our passwords secret, it could be a disciplinary offence if our password was found to have been compromised. Training followed, and it included our exact scenario, even up to the 'Though I am small, I am fierce' email. The summary at the end said, 'In this case, no real harm was done, the colleague was merely the brunt of a practical joke. She was warned to keep her passwords strong and secret.'

No more was said about it. Xanthe was blamed for poor security management and IT were called off in their hunt for my computer. But after all that, satisfying though it had been, was I really any further on? Xanthe still had her job, and she still had Sean. More was needed.

CHAPTER TEN

1981

On the evening of Felicity's attack, I sat down, giddy with excitement, to watch the news. I admit to being disappointed to find it hadn't made the national headlines, but I sat all the way through anyway, to see if it was one of the more minor stories amongst the major ones, but no, it didn't get a mention.

I was beginning to feel somewhat deflated as we arrived at the sports news with not a mention of the demise of a distinguished doctor's wife, but then *Midlands Today* began. My stomach somersaulted as:

'Violence in the suburbs! A woman is left for dead in a Nottingham home.'

'Left for dead?' I wondered what that meant. Had she lingered for a while after I left? I was left to wonder while Tom Coyne continued with the headlines: someone from Retford had an invitation to Charles and Diana's wedding; the junior school at Harby was doing a pilgrimage for their namesake, Queen Eleanor; Notts County had a cricket match to play. Get on with it! I howled in my heart.

Finally, he got back to the lead story.

'A fifty-four-year-old woman was attacked and left for dead in her own home today. She was found by her husband when he returned from his golf club. Police are baffled and neighbours say nobody heard a thing. Mrs Pearson is in a critical, but stable condition. Alistair Yates is at the scene.'

I reeled as the picture changed to an image of the Pearsons' house. Critical, but stable. I felt tears form and bit them back. Critical, *but stable*. I could hardly hear the rest of the report: nothing stolen, no obvious motive. Nobody saw anything. I breathed a sigh of relief, until I remembered: Felicity saw plenty. What if she wakes up?

'I'm sorry, I'm sorry, I'm sorry, Jeremy,' I muttered. I had failed and in doing so had put us both in a very precarious position. One of us was going to have to finish the job while she was in hospital. I wondered if he might do it that night, but in the morning the news was that she was still critical, yet stable. I thought he was probably angry with me for having messed things up so badly and expected me to put matters right. I cursed myself for having lost my nerve when the doorbell rang. Stupid, stupid, stupid.

In the morning, I got ready for work and, wearing my most innocent face, went out to face the day.

As you can imagine, it was all they were talking of when I arrived. They all seemed to be in shock.

I crept through to where Felicity lay and saw her all wired up, with Jeremy by her side, dishevelled and unshaven, playing the part of the distraught husband to a T. I watched, expecting him to sense me there and turn, revealing his secret elation to me and me alone.

'You'd make a better door than you would a window,' Sister Nuffield shoved me to the side and went to Felicity's bed. 'Don't you have something you should be doing?'

Jeremy looked up at us both and I expected him to say something, to tell her he wanted me there, but he said nothing. My heart sank, but even as disappointment flooded through me, I knew we still had to be careful. It would be some time yet before we could reveal our true feelings to the world and when we did, we would be wise to pretend they had not blossomed until after the demise of Felicity.

I would have preferred for him to finish the job. He had far more opportunity than I did, sat there all day, often on his own, no risk that anyone would challenge him for being there. In fact, later that day as Felicity remained stable, I felt slightly annoyed that I was expected to do all the work. Would it always be like this?

No opportunity presented itself over the course of that day. All eyes were often turned to the ward and Jeremy was constantly by her side. A part of me saw no reason why I couldn't just go in there and polish her off in front of him, but somehow that seemed a bit taboo, a breach of etiquette. So, I watched and waited for my chance, concerned as I left for the day at the news that she seemed to be on the mend.

I walked home, deep in thought, pushing myself on past the off-licence; I needed a clear head for a clear plan. Since Dr Harris's party I had developed a taste for red wine and Piat D'Or was always 3–for–2 there, but still, I resisted. Back at the ranch, my housemates were still banging on about the utility bills. Maybe I should have had a look round to see if there was any cash at Jeremy's house. In the end I wrote them a cheque which would bounce but would keep them quiet for now.

I woke in the morning without the plan I wanted, but as I showered and dressed, I thought, I did not need a complex course of action, just a window of opportunity.

Jeremy was gone when I arrived at the hospital. He was taking part in a press conference to appeal for help and when the time came, we all huddled round a TV that had been wheeled into the staffroom especially for the occasion.

I kept my fingers crossed tight, hoping and praying that Jeremy would not inadvertently give us away, but he played a blinder.

He sobbed, he stammered. 'My wife . . . Felicity,' he kept saying. 'My darling . . . Vicious individual . . .'

'Was that last bit still about Felicity?' I asked and received angry stares and shushes in reply.

He couldn't finish what he was saying. In fact, I began to cringe a bit, so over the top did he go.

The police inspector obviously felt the same as me because after a few minutes of this, he cleared his throat and got to the point.

'Sometime yesterday morning, an unknown assailant entered Dr and Mrs Pearson's property and violently attacked Mrs Pearson. We believe this was an opportunistic crime. We don't think the culprit came prepared, but found a key and let themselves in. That only deepens the mystery because nothing was taken and there was no sign of a sexual assault.

'Therefore, we need assistance from the public. If anybody saw anything suspicious or unusual that morning, if anyone you know is acting strangely, please call us on the number at the bottom of your screen. You don't have to leave your name. Help us solve this motiveless crime.'

They returned to the TV where the journalists were asking questions:

'How is Mrs Pearson now?'

'Still stable.'

But not for much longer, if I had anything to do with it.

'Do you have any suspects?'

'We have no names at the moment.'

I began a small cheer but caught myself and managed to turn it into a hiccough before anyone noticed.

'What kind of person would commit a crime like this?'

'The perpetrator is obviously a very disturbed individual.'

I struggled to restrain myself.

'You alright, Julie?' one of the permanent nurses asked, seeing my distress.

I nodded. 'Difficult viewing.'

Other than the drama over Felicity, that day was a slow one in the ICU, leaving me plenty of time for loitering around her bed, waiting for my chance. Jeremy had phoned to say he would be back in later, he was visiting her parents and brother first. To the others he seemed like the typical shocked husband, but I knew he was just making sure the coast was clear for me. And just as well because the plan I had decided on was going to be pretty difficult to explain away if I was caught in the act.

Mid-morning I had the idea of asking Sister Nuffield if I should go and make sure Felicity was comfortable, to which she readily assented. I entered her room and approached her bed, chatting nonsense in a quiet and reassuring manner, nothing to worry about, just your friendly student nurse, come to check your pillows are straight and your airways are blocked.

I stood over her. I checked that no one was looking, no one was coming. I tugged a pillow out from under her head and placed it over her face. I held it gently, so as not to cause bruises, but firmly and – most importantly – airtightly. It was difficult to know if I was getting it right. Not being conscious, she was not fighting back in the way you'd normally expect. Then I had my confirmation: the machines started bleeping and alarms went off.

Of course that was going to happen! I cursed myself for my stupidity. That should've been the first thing I thought of! In my haste to complete my work and put my earlier mistake behind me, in my eagerness to clear the last obstacle and cement mine and Jeremy's future, I'd rushed rashly into the first thing to spring to mind!

Hearing hurried footsteps approaching, I shoved the pillow roughly back under her head and ran to the door shouting, 'Help!' as Sister Nuffield came charging down the corridor, followed by Dr Mayer.

'Everything just suddenly went off,' I explained as they all set to work, hoping that would allay their suspicions, but I needn't have bothered, they weren't watching me.

I observed them from a few feet away, going through the emergency procedures, but I felt no elation or expectation. I hadn't had time to push Felicity much further towards the next world. Although, apparently I had done *some* damage. It took them the best part of an hour to stabilise her, but eventually, stabilised she was. They all stepped back from the bed, and someone went to phone Jeremy.

I wondered if he'd be cross with me for failing again so pathetically. Yet, at the same time, I thought it would have been so much easier for him to do. I thought I might say something when I next saw him.

Jeremy sat, not much later, by his wife's bedside, another doctor explaining Felicity had stopped breathing, for reasons they had not yet worked out. They said she may have brain damage, the extent of which they currently could not tell.

I took a chance and stepped into the room and they both looked up at me. Against a background of pea-green walls and bleeping machines, Jeremy sat by Felicity's bed, the covers pulled so tightly over her I wondered if that was what was actually stopping her from breathing. Jeremy looked as if he'd aged ten years overnight. His face was haggard, the laughter lines turned to worry, his clothes were crumpled.

'Oh, good lord! What did you do to your face?' As he looked up, I saw that one side of his face was covered in bruises.

'Oh, I slipped on a mat,' he said. 'Silly thing, but we have a new cleaner. She pulled it up to polish under and forgot to stick it back down.'

'Yeah, it's a real peril,' I said, remembering Felicity lying there, and speaking before thinking. They both looked at me with more interest than anyone had ever looked at me with before.

'We had one like that when I was a kid,' I said. They looked less interested. I sloped away, hoping out of sight would be out of mind and busied myself with my work, keeping my eyes to the floor, as if not seeing other people would stop them seeing me.

But in my peripheral vision I saw the other doctor come out of Felicity's room and speak to Sister Nuffield. She looked in my direction and picked up the phone. Not long after that I saw police officers wandering around, speaking quietly to the senior staff.

Mid-afternoon, Sister Nuffield approached. 'Julie,' she said, 'the police would like to speak to you.' She gestured for me to follow her.

'There's nothing to worry about,' the police officer lied as I sat down opposite him. He looked young and keen to make a name for himself by pinning this on someone. 'We're speaking to everyone.' He consulted his notes, 'Have you ever met Dr Pearson's wife before?'

'No,' I said. 'Yes.'

'Which is it?'

'She was at the party. Dr Harris's party. But I didn't meet her. So, no.'

'Thinking back to yesterday, or the weeks before, did you notice anything unusual? Anything that seemed strange? Did you see any strangers hanging around the hospital?'

I pretended to think hard before telling him it was a hospital and it was full of strangers at any given time.

'Anyone who looked out of place?'

'There are usually a few people who look lost. Physically or spiritually.'

He nodded and wrote that down, then rifled through his notes. 'I'm told you made a very interesting comment earlier today. Dr Pearson said that when he mentioned he'd slipped on a mat, you said, "Yeah, it's a real peril."'

Jeremy said *that*? I opened my mouth to speak, but words wouldn't come, confusion addled my thoughts. Why would Jeremy say such a thing? Didn't he know he would be pointing the finger straight at us?

'Did you say that?' the police officer asked.

'Umm, I did. But I explained at the time I was referring to a mat we had at home when I was growing up. It brought it all back to me. Maybe Mrs Pearson slipped on a mat? Do you think that's what happened?'

'Not unless she slipped on it several times at about fifty miles an hour.'

I tried not to smile as I imagined that scenario.

'Where were you yesterday morning?' he asked.

'In my student house, in my room, reading a book.' I had practised that, just in case.

'What were you reading?'

He'd caught me there. It seems obvious now, but I was young and inexperienced in the ways of creating a false alibi. '*Great Expectations.*' I instantly regretted it: I should have named one of my text books. At least I knew what was in them.

'And your housemates will back that up?'

As soon as my shift finished, I dashed around the bookshops of Nottingham until I found a copy of *Great Expectations*, and then I sat down to read it. Half of it anyway. I hadn't said I'd finished it and to this day, I still haven't.

My housemates were of the view that, if I said I was in my room, I probably was in my room. That's where I was most of the time I wasn't at the hospital. They said I was a loner and a drinker and all I did was sit in there and drink; they didn't think it was likely I was reading a book. It was neither a watertight alibi, nor a ringing endorsement, but there was nothing they could prove.

The police came back a few days later and asked the same questions about the mat in a variety of different ways – my old

English teacher would have been infuriated at the number of words they used to ask one simple question. But in the end, they were clutching at straws. They didn't know the neighbours had seen me, the neighbours thought they'd seen the cleaner, who presumably had an alibi. They didn't ask for my fingerprints and I took that to mean either I wasn't a suspect or they hadn't found any. The local news bulletin indicated they thought it was a burglary gone wrong and that's where they were concentrating their efforts. Eventually they went away and the longer they stayed away, the safer I felt.

There was another consequence of the episode, however. A few days later I received a phone call from my dad.

CHAPTER ELEVEN

1981

'There's a letter come for you from the university,' my dad said. 'I don't know why they've sent it here when you're only down the road from them.'

Neither did I. 'What does it say?'

'You want me to open it?'

'Yes, please.'

I heard the envelope tear and a minute later, he said, 'The dean wants to see you. It doesn't say why, just asks you to present yourself at his office at 11am on the 17th. It says your personal tutor will be there and you can take a friend, a family member or the union rep.'

'Right.' I felt a thrill, the dean had singled me out for something. After three years of hard work, I'd been noticed!

'Your mother says wear something smart,' was my dad's parting shot.

But what were my options? Maybe I was supposed to go there in my student nurse uniform and they would present me with my qualified nurse uniform at the meeting. There would likely be a screen for me to change behind, and I would disappear a mere caterpillar and emerge a fully fledged butterfly-nurse. I imagined the dean's jovial face as I reappeared.

Then, with some disappointment, I realised that the whole year would probably be invited to do the same; it was hard to concoct a scenario in which I would be singled out for such treatment.

I didn't really have anything else except for the little black dress I'd worn to Dr Harris's party.

Eleven am seemed a bit early for a cocktail dress, but the wording of the invitation: 'The dean cordially invites you . . .' suggested a champagne reception. So, on went the dress. I tried to make it more business-like with a smart jacket one of my housemates had left over the back of a chair.

And so it was that on the day of the meeting, I made my way regally down the stairs, housemates open-jawed – 'is that my jacket?' – and out of the house for the short walk to the university campus.

I'd forgotten, in all the excitement, that my personal tutor would be there. I had no idea who that was and was thrown off-kilter for a moment when, outside the dean's office, I was greeted by a creature from the 1960s, delighting us all with a psychedelic two piece. I wondered if my outfit was too conservative after all.

The dean's office was not what I imagined. It was not full of ancient old books, stacked to the ceiling, with half-melted candles on a huge oak desk. There were no cats or owls present. Instead, the desk, chairs and bookshelves were cheap, functional office furniture, the books surprisingly scant, and there were some drooping spider plants on the windowsill.

Yet the dean himself didn't disappoint, he was white-haired and genial, with wire-rimmed spectacles and a skew-whiff tie. He waved me to a chair but offered no champagne. Just a jug of water and an empty glass were nudged my way. I tugged my dress down my thighs as I reached for the glass.

My personal tutor sat alongside me, facing the dean, who sat between the head of my course and the head of faculty. Quite an illustrious gathering.

'Are we waiting for anyone?' the dean asked. I shrugged and he pointed at the empty chair on the other side of me. I shook my head.

'Very well, I'll cut to the chase. You may be aware there have been a number of complaints made about you.'

The dean paused as I shook my head. He looked at my personal tutor.

'Do you ever check your pigeonhole, Julie?' my personal tutor asked. The answer to that was no, but I now learnt that had I done so, I would have found a number of invitations over the academic year, to go and discuss various matters with him. They'd written to me at my student house as well, where it went astray amongst the general debris. My failure to reply had forced them to write to me at my parents' address.

'Your housemates have complained that you don't contribute your share of the bills,' the dean said. 'More pertinently, you haven't paid your rent and you're living in a university-owned house, which means you owe the university money. The staff at the campus shop say that whenever a certain student is in there, things start to go missing. The description they gave matched yours . . .'

'What was their description?' my personal tutor asked.

The dean looked at his notes. 'About twenty, average height, average build, shoulder-length dark hair, long nose, beady eyes, shifty disposition. Do you want me to go on?'

'There are more girls of that age, of average height and build with shoulder length dark hair around here than I can count,' my tutor said, and I realised he was there to be on my side. 'And I don't think "shifty disposition" is something that could be easily captured on a photofit.'

A photofit? Were they putting me on a 'Wanted' poster?! Dead or alive, presumably.

'The rest of it?' the dean asked.

'What exactly do beady eyes look like?' my personal tutor said. They both stared at me.

'I'll go on with the allegations,' the dean said. 'Your colleagues on the wards have complained of a certain . . . lurkiness about you.'

'Lurkiness?' my tutor interrupted. 'They have to use actual words.'

'I'm coming to it. They say she deliberately gave the wrong drugs to a patient.'

'That was an accident!' I interrupted. 'They know that. I was new.'

The dean ignored me. 'Another patient complained that he was scared of her.'

My tutor sat back in his chair. 'I'm not sure what the point of his complaint is. Unless he had a reason to be scared of her, it's regrettable, but not something we can act on.'

The dean shrugged. 'They say she seems enthralled by the dangerous drugs cabinet. They say she tries to follow deceased patients down to the mortuary.'

'That's not true!' That last one was a total fabrication, although it was an interesting idea.

'Dr Pearson says he's noticed a smell of alcohol around you,' the dean finished.

Jeremy! The traitor.

The dean was still talking, something about my failure to engage with the faculty: I think he meant the notes in my pigeon-hole. A lack of interaction or cooperation with my peers, a drinking habit. An uneasiness around me in the hospital . . . unsuited to the role . . . they wished me the best of luck with whatever else I chose to do—

'What?'

'I'm afraid they're terminating your place on the course,' my personal tutor said, and I wondered if he was in on it after all.

'But I've nearly finished,' I said. 'I'm almost a nurse.'

'All the more important we act promptly,' the dean said. 'If we let you loose on a ward . . .' He didn't finish the sentence, he just looked down at his notes while my tutor, the head of course, the head of faculty and I waited futilely for him to clarify.

'But I've passed all my modules,' I said. 'I've had good marks.'

'No one is disputing your academic capabilities,' the dean said, and after a long silence, he added, 'We have to have every confidence that the nurses we send out into the world are suitable for the job, not just academically, but also in their personal qualities. There is a lot more to nursing than the science and we think you would be happier in another profession.'

'There you go, Julie. You could easily pick another science-based job,' my personal tutor said, trying to drag a silver lining from this great big grey cloud. 'Maybe experimenting on animals?'

'Do you have any questions?' the dean quickly jumped in.

If I were treated in this way now, with my years of life experience behind me, I would indeed have many questions and the first would be about how to appeal. But back then at the age of 21, thinking the dean's voice was the law, I did not fight. Instead, I rose unsteadily, noticing for the first time how very short the dress I was wearing really was and how low it was cut at the bust. Trying to keep my head held high and my eyes dry, I tottered my way out of the office and into the rest of my life.

CHAPTER TWELVE

1981–2

When my dad heard the reasons the university had given me, he went straight to a lawyer.

'She might be a proper weirdo,' he said, 'but they can't just get shot of her on gossip and hearsay.' The lawyer was of the same view and off they went down the warpath.

Well, as you can imagine, it wasn't quite as simple as that. A few facts came to light: my enjoyment of fine wines, an overdue credit card bill and a few more comments from Dr Pearson.

I'd heard that it was a fine line between love and hate, and now I understood the truth of that saying. There was no in-between stage. I loved him, then in the blink of an eye, I hated him. I wondered if I should have attacked him instead of Felicity; I wanted to go back and do exactly that. But it was too risky. I had no legitimate reason to be in the hospital and I wasn't supposed to know where he lived. I hated him all the more when I realised I'd sacrificed my entire nursing career for a knave like Dr Pearson.

Eventually the university agreed to settle out of court. I had enough for a sizeable deposit on a house and some time to think about how to spend the rest of my life. Not a care in the world, other than a vague concern about an unseen witness coming forward or my falling ill and shouting out my guilt in my delirium.

Although it was impractical, I still dreamed about returning to the hospital and making Jeremy pay for what he'd done. I lay awake at night and imagined him weeping, begging for mercy and pleading with me to believe his declarations of regret. I imagined him seeing himself, the cowardly being he was, and mewling in shame at his own weakness.

But as the days went by, I began to think less about Jeremy. I noticed first that there were moments in the day when I forgot about him. Then whole hours when he didn't cross my mind. After a while he was no longer my first thought when I woke in the morning, nor my last thought at night. As time went by, he encroached on my reveries less and less. I went a day and then a week without recalling him and when I did, sometimes it was just in passing: 'Oh, him. Who cares about him and his dreary life?' He had been a flash in the pan, the fickle fancy of a young girl.

As time went by, I found another love.

While the dispute between my dad and the university had been going on, I'd been following a TV drama that was popular at the time. It was a detective series in which the handsome young detective always saved the damsel in distress at the last minute. He had an on-and-off relationship with an ambitious journalist, but when he looked into the camera – into my room – at the end of every episode and smiled that intimate smile, I knew that it was me he wanted to be with.

His name was Ieuan Prosser and, reading an interview with him in my mother's *Radio Times,* I learnt he was from, and still lived in, a town in South Wales called Caerphilly. Once my settlement came through, I called a local estate agent, booked in a few viewings and headed out to Caerphilly.

After I'd seen the houses, I had a look around the town. It was the most picturesque place I had ever seen, with its castle in the town centre, opposite a small shopping mall and within easy reach of a few pubs and the train station. I jumped on a train and had a look around nearby Cardiff, which also had a striking, although very different, castle in the centre, and shops enough for any shopaholic. With its hilly landscape in between, it was idyllic. I bought my house.

I spent the summer decorating – I found I had quite a talent for it. At first, I'd been minded to hire a professional, but then thought it might be fun to have a go myself; I'd never wielded a paintbrush before, but I'd seen some real idiots make a success of it.

So, I set to, and the result was a triumph. A different colour in every room and not a missed spot in sight.

Next, I decided to make my own curtains. The results of this were more mixed. The first set I made were terribly wonky, but having nothing else and being fed up of having to sit in the dark after sunset in case anyone should look through the window and see me, I hung them anyway. I tried again and they were worse! On my third attempt they were straighter. Encouraged, I had another go, and another and another, until I had a whole house full of perfectly straight curtains, hanging uniformly in their rooms. Although I'd ended up spending more on material than I would have done if I'd just bought them ready-made in a shop.

From decorating, I went on to try a whole array of crafts: I experimented with weaving, sketching, pottery, crochet, papier mâché, clay modelling, origami, taxidermy. Some were more successful than others. I did a photography course, I began to teach myself to cook: I was twenty-two by then and a woman, I couldn't live my whole life on toast and Pot Noodles. Now that I had a bit of money, I experimented with different wines. I matched them to my meals and found a wine for every dish, even Weetabix – all self-taught!

Once my house was adorned with as much homemade decoration as it needed, I found myself in the market for a companion and began traipsing the streets, expecting at any moment to run into Ieuan. At the same time, my thoughts turned to other forms of company. I considered a lodger but dropped that idea pretty quickly after a dream about muddy boot prints on the carpet and washing-up in the sink. Instead, I chose, of course, a cat.

Fluffy came to live with me that autumn. She soon made herself at home, clawing at the carpet, leaving hairs on the soft furnishings and waking me in the morning with a dead mouse on my face. Messing on the carpet and returning to the scene time and time again; gobbling her food too quickly and throwing it back up on the sofa.

It was not quite what I had envisaged when I had chosen her. I imagined feeding her in the mornings, then seeing her off through the cat flap as she went to do her catty work and I set off to do mine. Then in the evenings we would both return, tired but content, to eat our suppers and sit together in companionable silence, watching TV or reading, painting, weaving, whatever.

That was not how it panned out. The cat was cantankerous, never content to sit still apart from when she was sitting on me and I wanted to get up. Otherwise, she would spend her evenings meowing to have the door opened and then not wanting to go out; meowing for food and then not eating it; meowing for me to play with her toy and then walking away when I picked it up. She would ask to have her chin stroked, then bite me as soon as I looked away. She had a magnificent scratching post, but she would scratch the furniture.

Indeed, the cat-owning experience was not what I had expected at all. I thought about taking her back to the cats' home, but I didn't want to admit defeat. So, on we went, at odds with each other, knowing this could not continue for long.

Meanwhile, I decided to give myself a new image and off I went to the hair salon where they chopped and shaped my long locks into the same style as Princess Diana who, at the time, was a recent addition to the royal family. It has been my style ever since: the look just never goes out of fashion.

I took walks through the town, getting to know my new home. I walked around and around and around the castle, the sight of it reignited a love of painting, which had rather been forgotten during my student days. I took my watercolours and my easel and painted the ruins over and over. I painted the leaning tower from several different angles: the classic tilt from a distance that you see on postcards; closer up where it's harder to notice; and right beneath it, where it leans menacingly over you.

I began to take a little flask of vodka with me and I sipped from it as I painted. My brushstrokes became more extravagant and less precise as the buzz went to my head, raising my spirits and fuelling my inventiveness. I painted the castle with the tower almost on the ground, as it one day will be, and I painted it with all the walls upright, as it once was. Then I swayed my way happily home where I lined the pictures up along my lounge wall: castle past, castle present and castle future.

My parents came to visit. Their heads tipped one way, then the other, as they viewed my art.

'It's very good,' my mother said. 'Is it meant to be like those unrealists? Those melting clocks and things that couldn't happen?'

'Surrealists,' I said. 'It's Caerphilly Castle. I experimented with the tilt of the tower.'

'The one on the end's the best,' my dad said, referring to the tower at the sharpest angle. 'That's what it looks like.'

'The tower's nearly touching the floor,' I pointed out.

'Is that not right?' he asked. I turned and saw he wasn't even looking at the paintings, he was watching Bert and Mabel getting into their car, loading their picnic basket into the boot.

'Do you see much of your neighbours?' he asked.

'This and that. Why?'

'Just wondered how you were fitting in. It's a nice neighbour-hood, this.'

When they'd taken themselves and their art reviews back to the East Midlands, my thoughts returned to Ieuan. I tried finding him on the electoral register, but there was no trace. It was as if he really did only exist on the screen. I wondered if Ieuan Prosser was his professional name and he was going under the radar with something less recognisable. But if you were choosing a professional name, wouldn't you choose something better than that? Something a little more romantic? Jet, or Fleet, or Dartanian?

Meanwhile, although I made economies – to this day my phone is a pay as you go – my bank account was not getting any bigger. I started looking for a job. I set my sights high – I was a nearly qualified nurse after all – but nearly, it seemed, wasn't near enough; the only job in the caring profession I was offered was as a day care centre dogsbody.

As a temporary measure, I turned towards the more mundane, and set my sights on becoming one of the rat-race. One of the nine-to-fivers, trudging despondently to the train station every morning, gazing soullessly out of the train window.

Except I wasn't one of the soulless ones. I was just marking time before Ieuan came for me, before my real life began. Meanwhile, I was watching him every night on the TV.

I landed an entry-level admin job at a big financial company that had recently set up offices in Cardiff. I marched in for my induction day alongside a batch of new graduates, also starting their first jobs since university, although possibly under slightly different circumstances to me. I looked at them with pity.

They were young, they were bright, they were clean, they were fresh. They smiled, they chatted, they talked about their uni courses and what they aspired to do in the future. I was itching to tell them, 'I'm only here for a while – just until I marry Ieuan Prosser,' but I decided not to spoil their fun.

While all this was going on I'd come to admit to myself that adopting Fluffy had been a mistake.

I actually realised this pretty quickly, it just took some time to admit it. The funny thing was, what made me realise was quite a minor incident really: I woke one morning to find Fluffy washing her privates on my bed!

I thought of the times I'd come home tired but had to move Fluffy from where she was sprawled before I could rest. For a small animal she took up a lot of space. And how many times had I put my hands round her body, ready to lift her, to be rewarded with a hiss, a scratch or a bite? It hurt my feelings, as well as my skin, to be thanked for my charitableness with such violence. Then she'd stalk off to the bedroom, as if she were the injured party.

I was bored of feeding Fluffy, I was bored of vacuuming up her hair. I was bored of shifting her out of my space and if ever again I had to plaster up one of her scratches . . . I thought back to my dreams of having a quiet companion to sit and watch TV with in the evenings and I thought of the reality of the situation. I realised I did not want a cat. At least not like this.

I was still a learner at taxidermy, although I was coming on in leaps and bounds. I would be taking a break from it over the winter; it's not the kind of thing you want in the house and my garden shed was unheated. I reckoned I had time for just one more project before calling it a day for the year.

CHAPTER THIRTEEN

I had been in my role for twenty-five years when a nervous young Sean walked in – and it was fireworks from the word go. With previous affairs it had always taken some time for the object of my affection and I to realise our feelings for each other but with Sean, sparks had flown from the first 'hello'.

I was, by that time, a very senior figure in the department and the first-aider for my floor to boot – albeit half the population stuck 'do not resuscitate' signs to the back of their chairs when they saw my name on the noticeboard.

Sean was to be my new assistant, the previous one having found herself a place in the civil service, leaving us all rather in the lurch. He was the answer to our prayers. He soon proved himself a very quick student, picking up even the most complicated parts of the job, and our instant chemistry meant we were soon working like a well-oiled machine.

Over the following weeks, Sean and I fell into quite a routine, and it must have seemed to anyone who saw us that we had been at the coalface together for many years, so neatly did we complement each other.

After a couple of months sitting side by side, soldiering through the days, dealing together with the perils and pitfalls that regularly beset the admin crew in a busy office, Sean and I were deeply in love. The days flew by in a blur, so infatuated we were. We wiled away our time chatting: all those little conversations that deepen a connection.

'Can't wait for the weekend,' I began one morning, although, in truth, weekends at that time were things to be endured, keeping Sean and I apart as they did. 'What are your plans?'

'Watching the football in the afternoon tomorrow, then out until I get back in. We'll probably have a lie-in on Sunday – morning after and all that. We usually get up around eleven, have a bit of breakfast. Then we tend to head out. There's never a definite plan: family, shopping, a trip, occasionally we work-out on a Sunday, if we're feeling up to it. That sort of thing.'

I sat there, flabbergasted. He looked at me, probably looking as if I'd just seen a bomb go off. In the end I spoke, but all I could say was, 'We?'

'Me and the ball and chain.'

'Ball and chain?'

'Only joking. Susannah, my other half.'

I was struggling to process it. 'You have a twin?' I asked.

'What? No. My missus, my girlfriend. Susannah. What's wrong?'

I think I spasmed. I think my heart stopped. 'I need a drink,' I said and I stood and ran to the fountain. There, I gulped down water I didn't really want while I waited for my heart to restart and my head to stop spinning. A girlfriend? How could that be? My hands were shaking as I refilled my cup.

'Not diabetic are you, Julie?' Dave approached from behind, making me jump. I stared at him blankly. 'An unquenchable thirst. You're glugging it down like you've just done forty nights in the desert. Or are you hungover?'

'Neither of those.' I dropped my cup into the recycling and stood up straight, my shoulders back. I walked serenely back to my desk.

'Seriously, Jools, you're not ill, are you?' Sean asked when I returned; he was already calling me Jools by then. 'It's just with the weekend coming up, I could do without catching anything.'

'I'm not ill,' I said. I turned to him, trying to keep a poker face. 'So, tell me about Susannah.'

They lived together in a rented flat, walking distance to the office. He said it was a pretty small flat and originally the idea had been to get houses with their respective friends in their first year out since graduation. Sean and Susannah had been a couple for well over a year by then, but it had all seemed a bit sudden, and a bit grown up, to move, in one fell swoop, from studenthood to professionalism and from houses of multiple occupation to a one-bedroom flat. But, for various reasons, the houses had fallen through, and they had found themselves together in the one-bedroom flat. 'And the rest is history,' he said.

I understood, then, what he was telling me. They'd been thrown together by circumstance, not desire, and it was proving to be too much, too soon. The job must be a blessed relief to him: a chance to be rid of her for a while. After all, he had referred to her as 'the ball and chain'. What more needed to be said?

But things were about to take a turn for the worse. The company had been on a very aggressive recruitment drive recently. There was a big project starting up which required a significant intake of admin staff. They had gone around the city and surrounding areas, all but hauling people in by their necks.

One morning I was in early, fixing a few spreadsheets for our neighbouring department, when there was a kerfuffle at the end of the office. I looked up to see Sean throwing open the door, holding it and then gesturing to someone beyond to enter.

In walked a female. Medium height, very thin, yellowy blond hair in large curls that she'd pinned back from her face with clips decorated with bows. She wore a frilly pink blouse, a skirt that was shorter than an office skirt needs to be and shoes that told us all that she hadn't walked to work.

'So, this is it,' Sean said, waving his arms around the room. 'Your new office.'

The female stood, her hands clasped together, looking around the room as if this were the office of her dreams.

'I'll show you around.'

I watched as they made their way amongst the early birds. 'Hi, this is Susannah, she's starting here today,' he said as they moved from desk to desk. My fist gripped the letter opener harder and harder as they came closer. I watched her smile and sway her hips and flick her hair. I watched everyone else break from their work and smile back and tell lies, such as 'nice to meet you' and 'looking forward to working with you'.

Eventually they came to me.

'Jools, this is Susannah,' Sean announced. I took a closer look at her. Too much make-up and too much perfume: my eyes began to water.

'Hi, Jools, I've heard loads about you,' she said and fell about giggling.

Well, she wasn't what I'd expected, I can tell you that! I'd thought she'd be prettier for a start. I suppose she was in a way, if you like that sort of thing, but it was the kind of pretty a man with any depth would get bored of easily. The lights were on, but I don't think anyone was home.

And I was surprised she had blond hair – I'd been given to understand Sean was more enamoured by darker tresses.

And she was so sullen! Oh yes, she laughed, flattered and fawned when people were talking to her, but as soon as they turned away – as soon as she thought no one was looking – her phizog turned foul and her true self floated to the surface. I mentioned it to Jayne when she brought the post, but somehow, it had escaped her attention. Which was unusual for Jayne, being partial as she was to gossip and nosiness.

Jayne passed it off as being just how Susannah's face hung, 'You can't expect her to sit there grinning like an idiot when she's concentrating on her work.'

I wondered where the point of no return had come for Sean. When had it become too difficult to say, 'No! I don't want to live with you! Go back to Yorkshire.'

And once my attention had been caught by that accent it was all I could hear all day, all over the office.

Seeing Sean's misery a few weeks later as he slunk back to our den after a run-in with her at the drinks machine, I asked him how long the tenancy agreement on their flat had to run. They were on the home straight, it transpired, just another six weeks.

'And you'll be moving out then?' I asked. He looked surprised.

'No,' he said. 'It's handy for work and it's handy for town. Pretty cheap too, all things considered, we couldn't afford much more.'

I almost had a tear in my eye. He was so controlled by her, he hadn't even realised there was a way out. Money should never be a barrier to happiness, and I saw where I could help.

'I have a spare room at my house,' I told him. 'It's quite spacious.' He looked surprised again. I suspected that no one had ever shown him the kindness he deserved before now and he didn't know how to react.

'Yeah, um, thanks Jools, we'll bear it in mind.' I could see he was going to need a bit of time to come round to the idea, to readjust his thinking to the possibility of freedom, but I had six weeks. I'd give him a few days to let the notion take seed, then I'd throw it back in the ring.

The intimacy of 'Jools' had not escaped me. I didn't think we were going to be needing the spare room for very long!

* * *

Susannah's grip was stronger than I imagined though. The six weeks came and went, with me dropping ever heavier hints, but still he stayed on in the flat with her. The good news, however, was that he could walk away soon:

'Yeah,' he said. 'Twelve months minimum, then we can move out anytime, with a month's notice. Why do you want to know so much about our tenancy agreement?'

Yet, the weeks rolled on, becoming months and still he came and went from the office with her – you could almost see the tight leash she held. Still he dwelt in the flat that was walking distance from town. Still her voice rang like a foghorn across the office and still Sean and I grew closer and closer, but with him not having a clue how to disentangle himself from Susannah.

Then one day, her claws dug sharper. They were having a reshuffle across the aisle and she was coming over here! She was no longer to be a temp, hired only for the convenience of a project, she was to become permanent staff and take a place in our long-standing and well-bonded team.

I could see it wasn't going to go well. I knew she wouldn't fit in when she brought cakes in on her second day. She'd made them herself and they all had that lopsided look of homemade produce.

I suppose she had to buy her friends and you could see why when, standing over the cake display she had set up, she began regaling people with tales of her ill-health.

'Now that I'm coming to work here, I have a number of allergies I need to make you aware of,' she said, pulling out a list from her bag. 'I've got so many, I have an A–Z here!'

People turned, curious as she began to read out: 'Almonds, animals, celery, dust mites, dairy . . .'

And on it went, each allergy, apparently as dangerous as the last. And it only took a molecule to get near her airways to put her in mortal danger. It was a miracle she didn't have to walk around in one of those hazmat suits.

'I've been in hospital five times. Did I say five? I meant six, at least six.'

'And that time on holiday,' Sean said.

She nodded. 'That was terrifying.' She reached into her bag and pulled out something the size and shape of a marker pen. 'This is my EpiPen. If anything happens, this is what you do. Are you listening?' Her tone became sharp and those who had been drifting away dutifully returned. 'It's pretty easy, but I might not be in a position to do it myself and Sean might not be around. First you take the safety cap off, then hold the tip about ten centimetres away from my thigh, at ninety degrees.' She demonstrated like an airline hostess. 'Then jab it in and hold for three seconds, until you hear a click. Then call an ambulance. It really could save my life.'

Indeed, she proved her point within a month when she had a run-in with a latte, landed herself in A&E and had to take a week off work. Sean came to the office with a boring tale of how she had collapsed while out shopping and he had been the one to administer the pen. A missed opportunity if ever I saw one.

She pinned her list to the noticeboard. I photocopied it while no one was looking, took the copy home and memorised it.

CHAPTER FOURTEEN

2007

I went home that evening in a bad mood. Of course I did – having to watch that display all afternoon. I was only surprised that everyone else seemed unruffled.

I consulted the worry dolls. I took them out, told them my concerns, and then I stabbed Angela through the heart. Angela was hard-hearted, which, in fairness, wasn't something you'd say about the real Angela, my dearly beloved sister, who shuffled off this mortal coil rather earlier than expected. The pin bent when it should have penetrated. But it didn't matter, they had put me on the right course. The only thing to do was to tackle the problem head on.

I needed the right approach. I dug out a notepad and pen and began. Several hours later I had the perfect speech and I began committing it to memory. By Monday morning I was ready to orate; I waited for my opportunity.

It didn't take long: Sean, slightly hungover from a pub quiz the night before, was in a listening mood. When he was sitting comfortably, I began.

'There is a time in a man's life,' I said, 'when he needs to be self-sacrificing. For example, when he really wants the last cake, but the lady in his life wants it more. Or when he'd like to stay and have another pint, but he promised he'd pick the kids up from swimming . . .'

'Was he driving there?' Sean asked.

'What?'

'To swimming. When he wanted another pint, but he had to pick the kids up, was he driving? Because if he had a few pints down his neck, he might not want to be driving. That might not be so sacrificial if he involved the kids in a drink-driving incident.'

I hadn't thought about that. Was he driving? I didn't know. 'He'd only had one,' I said in the end. 'He was a big man, he could handle his drink. It was fine.'

'OK. But technically, I think he's still over the limit.'

He'd broken my train of thought and I found it hard to pick it up again. In the end I skipped a few lines.

'But there comes a time, when a man must do what's right for himself.'

Sean was nodding sagely. 'And so saying,' he said, 'I need to siphon the python.' And off he went to the loo.

I watched them carefully, Sean and Susannah, over the following weeks. I watched how they interacted. She clingy, following him around the office, always wanting to spend their lunch break together. He, keeping a professional distance, polite, but at arms' length between the hours of nine to five. Except the hour of lunch, when he did tend to go off with her.

Unlike Sean, Susannah was not someone people took to their hearts. I watched her day in, day out, chatting away while people hid their faces in boredom, totally disinterested in anything she could think of to say. Sportingly, they would try to keep up their end of a conversation, now and then they would even bellow with false laughter, kindly keeping up her spirits. But every conversation would end, inevitably, with her companion taking refuge in their work. Dull though the job can be, it was not duller than Susannah.

And really, I had no idea what she could be talking about down there, vacant and inane as she was, but empty vessels make the most noise. Not like Sean and I, as we put the world to rights time after time. The subjects we didn't cover aren't worth mentioning! It must have been a pleasure for him to have a real conversation, after evenings full of *I'm A Celebrity* and *The X Factor*.

That autumn turned to winter with Sean still unable to break his chains. I was starting to wonder how many months – or even years – of his life he'd waste under Susannah's tyranny.

I was even starting to wonder if maybe she'd saved his life at some point and he felt beholden to her. Maybe she'd risked everything to drag him from a blazing building; maybe he was wandering around with one of her kidneys. Something was keeping him there, however much he longed to be free.

As spring sprung, when Christmas was just a distant memory – although Sean was still wearing the festive socks Susannah had presented him on Christmas morning – we were no further on. I was wondering how I could make the point; what would it take to save him from himself?

One sunny morning I came in somewhat later than usual to find Susannah – in my seat! – next to Sean, who was sat some way back, holding my letter opener and using it to point to his screen. I approached silently from behind and there on his computer were pictures of houses. And not just any old houses – houses for sale.

I stood and watched as they clicked on the images and the maps – no, too far out of town; no, the second bedroom was too small; no, absolutely no way. One after another, the houses were dismissed. Until they came upon one in Danescourt.

The house was lovely, someone had obviously put a lot of work into it, but why were they looking at it so closely?

Susannah nearly jumped a mile in the air when she saw me, her knee knocking satisfyingly hard on the desk. 'Christ, Julie! You made me jump!'

'Morning, Jools,' Sean looked round at me, clearly glad of the interruption.

'What are you looking at houses for?' I asked him.

'We're buying a house,' he beamed.

'Buying one?' I said. 'Isn't that a bit of a commitment?'

'Well, maybe, but we're always going to need somewhere to live and we may as well spend the money on a mortgage instead of rent.'

'We could be mortgage-free by the time we're fifty,' Susannah chipped in, grinning at Sean. What is wrong with this generation? Why can't they just live in the moment? Twenty-somethings shouldn't be dreaming of paying off their mortgages.

'And now that we have a deposit ...' Sean said and they looked at each other again and grinned. He tapped her arm and I tried not to retch as I wondered how they came to have a deposit. Had they robbed a bank? Laundered some money? Been compensated for being accused of a crime they did commit, but no one could prove?

'Susannah's great aunt died and left her some cash in her will,' Sean explained.

'And I don't want to squander it. That would seem like a bit of an insult to Great Aunt Agnes.'

'Well, that's very lovely,' I said, 'but it's gone nine o'clock and we really should be getting to work.' They both nodded and Susannah slunk away saying 'see you at lunchtime'. To Sean, not to me.

This was a disaster hitherto undreamt of, I thought, as I dropped into my seat – still warm from Susannah. How could Sean have let this happen?

'You know, you're not committed until contracts have actually been exchanged,' I told him.

'I know,' he said. 'It's a bit nerve-wracking already, I've heard of sales falling through at the last minute. Everything all packed-up and suddenly nowhere to go. At least we don't have to wait for a buyer.'

Brainwashed.

To celebrate their news – although I would hesitate to call a vague decision to do something sometime in the future 'news' – Susannah brought in more of her nut-free cakes. Although I didn't see how any environment containing Susannah could truly be considered 'nut-free'. When I mentioned that to Sean, he didn't think it was very funny.

It was time I made some cakes of my own. There had been an era when I brought them in every Friday; I was considered the master baker of the financial services world. Then as the weeks went by the enthusiasm I received for my efforts began to dwindle, and so too did my enthusiasm for baking them. I reduced my output to once a fortnight, then to the last Friday of the month and then only for special occasions. Of which there was only really Christmas, and we were all stuffed up to the eyebrows with chocolate then, so eventually it stopped altogether.

Yes, it was definitely time to resurrect the tradition. After all, most of the current staff weren't here in my baking heyday.

I brought a batch in that Friday. I'd forgotten what a hassle it was, carrying them on the train in the rush hour; everyone grunting and muttering at you because of the space they took up. I did tend to make a lot.

The cakes were well received in the office, although Susannah's deposits of earlier in the week cast something of a shadow over them. Susannah, of course, couldn't just gobble one quietly at her desk.

'Do these contain any nuts?' she asked me.

'No,' I said. 'They're all sponges.'

'Did you have any nuts in the area while you were making them?'

'No.'

'Did you use any utensils that had been in contact with nuts?'

'No.'

'Have you ever, in your entire life, been in the vicinity of a nut?'

I made that last one up, but she didn't stop far short of it.

She ate one eventually, while I watched her, wondering if at any point I'd forgotten about a huge pile of cashews on my worktop. Sadly it seemed I had not. She finished her cake, and her day at work, without a trace of an adverse reaction.

Elsewhere in the office they were more gratefully received and, I believe, I was considered the better baker. I resolved to make more for the following Friday.

Once again it became a regular event and colleagues would start making comments about them on Thursday, eagerly anticipating their arrival on Friday morning.

Then one Friday, as I set out my wares, Sean and Susannah walked in with an extra cake. It was covered in white icing with extravagant decoration, quite out of place on an office cake, and topped with purple lettering bearing the slogan 'Just Engagged!'

'That's not how you spell "engaged", mate,' Marcus pointed out to Sean. Although 'engagged' might be a better description, I reflected, as I bit back tears.

'What's the matter, Jools?' Sean asked as he noticed me. 'You look like you've been sucking a lemon.' As if he had to ask! I cheered up a bit when I noticed he looked as pained as I did. I struggled for words for a moment, torn between taking a stand and ending the whole Sean and Susannah charade there and then.

'*I* bring cakes in on a Friday!' I blurted in the end. In years ahead, when scholars muse over the course of our romance, they'll compare our shared inability to take action to that of Hamlet.

'Oh, I'm sorry!' Susannah lied as she waved her (cheap) engaggment ring in my face. 'We didn't think you'd mind. It's only a small one, it'll be gone in a few minutes,' she said. And that was true.

'Are we all getting an invite?' Mike asked, downing a slab of cake in one.

'We're keeping it very small,' Susannah said. 'Very close friends and family only. We're on an incredibly tight budget.'

'I can help you with the flowers,' Dave said. 'Well, my sister can. She's just opened a florist – she'll do you mates' rates if you let her take photos for her website.'

'And I can help with the dress,' said Abi, who we didn't hear from very often. 'My cousin has a bridal-wear shop and I can do the alterations for you. I was a seamstress before I worked here.'

By the end of the morning most of the wedding had been arranged on charity and the guest list had subsequently grown in proportion.

Back at our desk I grappled with how to broach the subject with Sean. How had he got himself into this situation? I was starting to lose sympathy; I could understand not wanting to hurt her feelings, I could understand getting in a little deeper than you intended, but this was starting to look like spinelessness.

'Did she pop the question to you?' I asked Sean, once we were safely ensconced at our desk. He shook his head.

'No,' he said. 'I asked her.'

I admit I hmphed.

'What?' he said, and he sounded rather snappy.

I was tempted to say, 'As if you didn't know,' but I believe men dislike this kind of cryptic comment, so instead I hmphed again; let him make what he would of that.

'You need to take a chill pill,' Sean said. 'You seem to have been slapped with the grumpy stick this morning.' And I was stung by his tone, especially when he knew I was still dealing with the engaggment cake scene.

We sat pretty quietly for the rest of the day. I was annoyed, but you can only do so much to help someone, then they have to take some responsibility for themselves.

Briefly, I toyed with the idea of abandoning Sean to his fate. Would it be better to cast him adrift to make his own way through life? To work out in his own time, a divorce down the line, the mistakes he was making in his youth? Then I recalled the electricity that sparked the first time we met, the deep understanding we had as we ploughed our way through the week's work and the unspoken messages we sent each other with every glance.

We beavered away, morning, noon and afternoon, Sean and I, over those next few weeks. He unusually quiet, me expecting him at any moment to blurt out his true feelings and ask my advice on how to extricate himself from this situation.

But it didn't come. If anything, Sean became more distant as the weeks wore on. Probably trying to lessen the impact when he finally tied the knot. I found myself faced with a situation I didn't know how to deal with and, to my shame, I dealt with it by doing nothing. I left Sean to his fate.

And the inevitable upshot of that was that a date was set. It was in a little under a year, which was not my idea of a long engagement, but I suppose time seems to stretch for longer when you're younger.

On hearing the news, I took a bold decision: with all the offers of help, the flowers, the dress and so on, they were still without a cake, and so I offered to make one. If Sean was going to make the biggest mistake of his life, I was at least going to be there for moral support, or more. As with the other offers of assistance, I was sure my hand would be duly bitten off and an invitation to the big day would be winging its way to me.

For some reason Susannah wasn't keen. She muttered something about the guest list being very full as it was, she just couldn't squeeze another one in.

But that was before she looked into the price of a wedding cake. 'Jesus!' she told Jayne from the post room. 'It's more than the dress.'

Not long after that she came shuffling over, eating humble pie, and accepted my offer. A wedding invitation, I was assured, would be mine.

'You do know I'm allergic to nuts, though, don't you?' Susannah bleated, unable to stop herself from spoiling the moment.

'I know,' I said, hiding my disgust behind a smile.

'You'll be really careful, won't you? You'll read the ingredients on everything?'

'Of course I will,' I said.

'It's just that Susannah could die,' Sean piped up.

'I know,' I said. 'I know how serious it is.'

'If you have any doubts about anything, do give us a shout,' he said.

When I had a moment alone, I went online to order a book about icing and was amazed, and somewhat dismayed, to see the range of tools you could buy for the job. In all my baking days, I had never really dabbled in icing, and I realised I had something of a mountain to climb. I ordered a piping tube and an angled icing spatula to get me started.

I spent the weekend practising and as I did, I chatted to my new companion, hoping for a bit of conversation in return. I'd learnt from bitter experience that a cat was not the pet for me, so when I once again felt the urge for animal company, I'd invested in what I thought would be a simpler pet: I had bought a budgie, Tweety.

I'd imagined owning a budgie would be something akin to having wildlife in the house. I thought I would hear birdsong in the morning. Then later we would chatter away, me bringing it up to date with the goings-on of the day and it responding in kind, even though we would only have the vaguest gist of what the other was talking about.

But, no, if ever you've thought a budgie might make a nice companion, think again. Tweety was sullenly silent all day, until the time came when I wanted to put the radio on or watch TV. Then what a squawking he would create! Without fail!

It was not what I expected of him, but if I was learning one thing about life it was this: things are never how you imagine they'll be.

I hadn't presumed to be an independent career woman in my middle years. Never in all my dreams had I thought I'd be such a vital cog in a multi-million-pound company, seeing that business flowed smoothly through our hands, working as master of the spreadsheets and training up the next generation of workers.

And as for my life partner, I'd assumed he'd be a stable, solid worker, not too exciting, but reliable, predictable. From my humdrum beginnings, how could I have foreseen the passion I was to experience? And only one obstacle to overcome before our glorious future could begin.

I thought I'd have the icing nailed by Sunday afternoon, but despite my natural flair for all things artistic, that little piping tube was a devil to get the better of. I didn't panic: I had several months left.

Monday was gloomy. I wandered past Susannah's desk and over-heard her complaining she had a headache. Someone offered her paracetamol and she recoiled and pointed to her list of allergies pinned to the noticeboard. I already knew it: paracetamol, in between mustard and peanuts.

The team meeting that morning was not all I dreamed of. In it, a list of the candidates for next year's financial exams was read out and on the list were both Sean and Susannah! I was giddy with the horror of it as we left the room, my legs would hardly carry to me to my desk.

'Just six to twelve months, Jools, and I'll be away from here and sitting over there.' Smiling, Sean waved to where the case reviewers sat, only twenty metres distant from our desks but, metaphorically, light years away. 'Doing the cases instead of just handing them out.'

I huffed. 'To be honest, I never hear anyone with a good thing to say about the exams,' I told him.

'Yeah, but you only have to do them once,' he replied. 'I can live with that.'

'The job's not up to much either,' I said. 'Just think of all the moaning and grumbling we hear. I believe "bored" is the most common word over there, closely followed by "stressed".'

'I'm sure it's not that bad, it's a step up. Anything's got to be better than this – you know that.'

I believe I had to catch my breath. Someone had certainly been dripping poison. 'This is the most important job in the department,' I reminded him.

'That's not really reflected in my pay.'

As if on cue, Mike wandered over, nodded at Sean and rubbed his fingers together in a gesture I understood to mean money. 'Good choice,' he said. I moved my curser from the nice easy case I'd been about to give him and sent him over a tax-planning nightmare from the sixth circle of hell.

I returned home to a screeching Tweety. Still no words, although I'd been patient and had tried talking to him about a variety of subject matter, in different tones and at different volumes. Meanwhile, I was missing all the programmes I enjoyed on TV, thanks to his squeaky frenzies, from which there was no reprieve. Am I not entitled to enjoy the peaceful use of my own home, I mused. The home I have bought and paid for through my own labours.

I thought back to my dreams of happy, if slightly shrill, conversation I'd imagined with him perching on my finger while we sang a duet. Then I thought of the reality of the situation. I realised I did not want a budgie.

All I had to take my mind off the situation was my icing practice. I couldn't say I was really in the mood, but it would be the means to an end and would eventually take the sting out of Sean's potential move to the wider department. I stopped in the super-market on the way home and bought industrial amounts of baking supplies.

Soon my house looked like a patisserie – and smelt like one. I ate a large slice of cake and began the icing practice, artfully incorporating the gap I left when I cut a slice into the design, so it became the open mouth of an iced sea monster. Then it became the gaping mouth of an iced sea monster when I took a second piece, and the dislocated jaw of an iced sea monster on the third. I sung Susannah's list of allergies to the tune of 'Stayin' Alive' as I worked.

My bins were overflowing with discarded cake and there was a limit to how much rubbish the council would collect. I needed another way to dispose of them, so I took a couple round to the Jacksons. I knew, from noisy experience, that they had grand-children who often visited, so they shouldn't have too much trouble offloading them.

I'd never been inside Bert and Mabel's house before and I was surprised by how untidy it was, quite a contrast to their well-tended garden. They had a visitor that day, a man in his thirties, or perhaps his forties. He was quite short and slim, wearing baggy, grey corduroys and a blue sweatshirt. He had medium brown hair, a bit too long to be tidy. When he smiled, I saw he was slightly snaggle-toothed at the top right incisor.

'This is Frank,' Bert said, nodding at him. 'Our son. Have you met him before?'

I shook my head.

'Frank, this is Julie, our neighbour. Are you sure you haven't met? You've lived here a fair while. You've never brought us cake before, mind. Have you had a knock on the head?'

Frank and I looked at each other and shook our heads, but I noticed now the similarity to the young boy who appeared in pictures around the room, captured at various ages. Sometimes he was alone in the pictures, sometimes he sat beside the daughter, Debbie.

'Well, it's not all that often I get to visit,' Frank said. 'Duty calls and all that.'

As we spoke, Mabel, solid and dour, shuffled in and out with plates and knives. She cut the cake and insisted I stay and join them for a slice.

'Have to check you haven't poisoned them,' she said.

'She's just having a joke,' Bert said, sheepishly.

'Your garden's looking lovely, Julie,' Frank said.

'Thank you,' I said. 'I like to keep it tidy, the house as well.'

'The residents at yours have been a bit of a mixed bunch in the past, haven't they?' He turned to look at Bert and Mabel to verify his statement. They both nodded. 'Those ones in the late seventies were the worst.'

'Weren't right for this street,' Bert said. 'Should've been up Lansbury Park.' He was referring to a local estate that had seen more than its fair share of trouble and strife.

'Steady, Dad,' Frank said. 'The folk on the Lansbury wouldn't like to hear you say that. What happened to them anyway?'

'No one knows, they just packed all their stuff and vanished one night. After that was the couple that looked perfectly nice but turned out to be vampires.'

'Not actual vampires,' Frank helpfully explained to me. 'Dad means they were night owls. And they liked a good party. They were noisy; nearly ruined my A-levels.'

'Then it was rented for a bit, had a bit of a mix coming and going, but no problems and then it went on the market and young Julie moved in. Must've been a good twenty years since. Maybe more?'

I nodded.

'Anyway, it's been plain sailing since you've been there.' Bert concluded the story with this happy ending.

'Just a pity we haven't met before,' Frank smiled at me and I felt a little frisson of excitement. I shuddered to shake it off.

'Are you cold, Julie?' Frank asked.

'No, no,' I said.

'Someone must've walked over your grave, then,' he said.

'I'm not dead yet.'

'It's a saying. If you unexpectedly shudder it means someone has stepped in the spot where your grave will be.'

I stared at him, horrified by the idea that people were tramping over my future grave and sending me supernatural messages about it.

'That's a bit macabre,' Bert intervened. 'Shall we dig in?' He waved his hand at the cake. 'We should put the kettle on as well,' he turned to Mabel. 'Seeing as Frank's back and we're having a bit of a celebration.'

'Have you been away?' I asked Frank and they all nodded.

I waited to hear more about where Frank had been, but further details were not forthcoming. Instead, Bert turned the conversation to me.

'So, where are your parents, Julie?' he asked. 'What do they do for a living?'

'My parents are in Derbyshire,' I said. I was pretty sure they were retired, I vaguely remembered an invitation to a retirement bash a few years before that I was far too busy to attend.

'Is that where you're from?'

I nodded. 'Originally.'

'Do you see much of them?' Bert asked.

'Now and then,' I said, although the truth was, no. From time to time, they would phone me with some news: Petra Rigby from two doors down has been in hospital; Jacqui Hartnell from Angela's class at school is a grandmother now – a grandmother, could I believe it?! And so on. Occasionally I'd be invited to some event, the village fete, the opening of a community building, Christmas, but I was invariably too busy to make the journey.

'Any brothers or sisters?' Bert asked.

I looked down at the floor before I said, 'One sister, but she died.'

The mood in the room changed.

'Awfully sorry,' Frank said.

'It's quite alright,' I replied, hoping my tone and body language were appropriate. 'It was a long time ago.' Then, in a moment of inspiration, I added, 'My parents never really got over it.' And with that, I saw off anymore prying questions.

I finished my cake and made my excuses. The Jacksons didn't try to persuade me to stay longer, so I left to continue with my icing, and to muse over the chequered past of my house.

All morning and well into the afternoon, I iced calmly away, chanting Susannah's list of allergies as I did so, like a mantra, to keep the creative juices flowing. I was so inspired, I took up the piping tube again on Sunday.

*   *   *

I suffered a slight setback on Monday morning when Susannah waltzed up to me with her design for the cake. I watched her making her way across the office, a tatty piece of paper clutched in her hand, stopping at every desk and showing it to whoever was there. Everyone smiled and nodded, except Mike who held it at arms' length and tilted his head to the left and then to the right, looking puzzled. I was soon to understand why.

'I've brought the design for the cake,' Susannah said as she finally arrived at my desk. She and Sean made eye contact across me.

I took the design from her. It was somewhat more elaborate than mine. She wanted not just a few hearts and flowers, but an entire meadow: butterflies and bees flying over daffodils, blue-bells, sunflowers, dahlias, snowdrops – flowers from all four seasons – a rabbit hopping about in the background and love hearts cascading all around. I probably visibly paled.

'You know you don't get snowdrops and sunflowers out at the same time of year?' I said. 'The clue is in the names, "snow" and "sun".'

She glared at me. 'You don't get love hearts lying around on the ground in real life either,' she said. 'It's representative. Representative of all the good things in life.'

'*All* the good things?'

She nodded.

'Fine wine and music are also good things in life.'

'They'll be available at the reception, but you can put a treble clef and a champagne bottle on there if you really want.'

No, thank you, there was quite enough to be getting on with.

Every evening that week I worked away over a row of cakes. I was starting to get some strange looks in Tesco and the offer they subsequently sent me with my loyalty card was generous, but focused.

Susannah's design was unrecognisable on my first attempt. The delicate blue butterflies she had sketched looked like ptero- dactyls making their way across the top, the love hearts looked like anatomical hearts, and the sunflowers towered triffid-like over the snowdrops and bluebells. If the wedding design didn't work out, I could sell it for Halloween. But I didn't despair. I had done a fair amount of marzipan work in the past, I knew it was easily within my abilities and soon the decorations began to improve.

CHAPTER FIFTEEN

2008

The seasons rolled around, Sean and Susannah both passed their exams and Sean moved out into the wider department.

I slumped into something of a depression. I'd done everything I could to make sure Sean failed, encouraging late-night drinking, drawing his attention to the cream of prime-time television. The exams were not fun things, I'd seen plenty start down that road and fall by the wayside. Susannah had the look of one who would fall, if ever I saw one, but even she passed first time and before I knew it, the pair of them were out there amongst the case checkers, several desks away, but still in my eyeline, chatting and jabbering the day away together.

The wedding approached with Sean still not finding the strength to be honest with Susannah and confess that his heart lay elsewhere. Bravely, I soldiered on with the cake preparations. By now my execution of the design was almost faultless and I could recite Susannah's list of allergies as naturally as the alphabet.

The bride and groom were to be shop-bought and plastic, so all that was left for me to do was perfect the little love hearts.

My invitation did indeed arrive, a traditional six weeks before the wedding. It surprised me somewhat by stating the venue as a five-star hotel when I had been imagining a church. But maybe Susannah was concerned she'd get a lightning bolt if she stepped onto holy ground. Maybe she was concerned *I* would be struck and my charred remains lying in the aisle would spoil the ceremony.

It included the option for a plus-one. Strangely, I thought immediately of Frank, whom I had met briefly at the Jacksons, but I pushed that thought down as quickly as it had risen up; I had no idea what had come over me. Anyway, since I would be leaving with Sean, I didn't need to bring a companion.

I spent some time looking at the venue online. It was a renovated castle some way to the west of Cardiff, at the far end of the Vale of Glamorgan. Set right on the coast, its grounds ran to the edge of the cliff and provided views of the sea beyond. Tight budget indeed.

Not being a motorist, the venue was too remote for me to drop the cake off in person. In fact, it was so remote, the happy couple were laying on a bus from Cardiff for those of us not booked into the hotel.

Susannah's mother was staying at the hotel and she was going to call by on her way there in order to pick up the cake. Sure enough, the doorbell rang at the appointed time and I opened it to find a last-generation version of Susannah grinning on my doorstep.

'Julie?' she said. 'I'm Sonia.' She paused. 'I'm here for the cake.'

'I'll go and get it,' I told her and turned back into the house, supposedly leaving her on the doorstep, but she had other ideas.

'Can I come and have a quick look? Before it's all packed up for the venue.'

I turned and she was already standing in the hallway, looking around her. 'Lovely house,' she said.

'Thank you.' I felt a thrill of satisfaction. It *was* a lovely house and I had worked hard to make it so. She took that as an invitation and followed me into the kitchen.

'Ooooooh! Is that it?' She had caught sight of the cake sitting on the counter. She hurried forwards and spent a few minutes exclaiming over it, leaning backwards and forwards, to the left and to the right, looking at it from all angles, her hands waving over it, but never touching.

If I say so myself, the cake was a sight to be seen: butterflies and hearts cascading down the sides, while the bride and groom stood, slightly tilted into each other by a tiny glitch in the baking, at the top. You could almost believe they were actually in love.

'Wonderful,' was the verdict. But then: 'What are the butterflies made of? You know Susannah's allergic to nuts.'

Oh yes, I knew. 'Rice paper,' I told her.

'And the love hearts?'

'Icing.'

At the last minute I had lost confidence in my marzipan love hearts – everyone knows marzipan is made from almonds and *everyone* knows Susannah is allergic to almonds.

There was more than one way to skin a cat.

'Perfect,' she said and helped me pack it up. She left, promising to buy me a drink at the wedding. What a pleasant woman, I thought. Almost enough to make me have a quibble with my plan.

After she'd gone, I made my way to the corner shop where I bought latex family-planning items. I put them in my bag for later.

I was nearly late catching the train to Cardiff. I got carried away doing my make-up, plastering it on, then losing my nerve and redoing it with a lighter touch, all whilst feeling slightly lightheaded; but who turns up to a wedding entirely sober? I checked I had everything I might need: purse, tissues, phone, comb, compact mirror, mints, and soluble paracetamol.

As we waited to go in for the ceremony, I scanned the room for people I knew. There were a few there from work, lads Sean's age, come to lend moral support. I wondered how many of them knew about the predicament he was in. How many nights had they spent over a few manly pints telling him he didn't need to sacrifice himself, he had to do what was right for him and his mystery woman?

I wondered if they knew it was me. If, when they saw me here, there was going to be trouble. Or excitement. They noticed me and nodded a greeting.

It crossed my mind, briefly, that if Sean had carried on the charade this long because he didn't want to hurt her feelings, he was unlikely to deliver the insult in front of all their friends and family. But then again, as he saw time running out for him, he could be driven to desperate measures. I felt a thrill. One way or another the Susannah problem was sure to be solved that day.

The room they had hired was nothing if not flowery, you could hardly see down the aisle. Pollen seemed to be the one thing Susannah was not allergic to, however I was not so lucky. I felt my nose tingle as soon as I stepped through the doors, and I cursed myself for not having brought antihistamines. In all my imaginings, not once had I factored in a hay fever attack.

Suddenly, the chatter among the guests hushed and Sean and his best man – someone I didn't know – hurried up the aisle to the front of the room.

There, they whispered to each other. I tried to lip-read, but I'm not trained, plus Sean had his back to us and the best man was sideways on. From what I could make out, though, the best man was saying something along the lines of, 'You don't have to go through with it. We could nip out now and tell Susannah in private. You don't have to humiliate her.' Then Sean said something and the best man said, 'Is she here? Your one true love. Can you see her?'

Yes, I'm here, I thought. I stared harder – definitely something about 'don't have to'. Sean was whispering something back, but what, I could only imagine. Then music played, something twee, a definite Susannah choice and, as the congregation looked around . . . there she was. On her father's arm grinning like an idiot at everyone, nodding and smiling to individuals, looking like a walking meringue. I pictured myself in a classic, stylish design, not the monstrosity before us. I turned to see Sean's reaction . . .

At the far end of the aisle, he too was grinning like an idiot. The terrified, rictus grin of a doomed man. So panic-stricken did he look that I wondered if he was going to just make a run for it, but he stood his ground. Maybe he had already surveyed the room and realised escape was going to be impossible: the windows were pretty high and there was a glowering mob of Susannah's nearest and dearest close to the door.

She made her relentless way towards him and arrived, taking the place beside him, facing the also-grinning celebrant. The ceremony began.

The room was warm, the alcohol ran through my veins to my head, my eyes started to droop. The celebrant droned on for a very long time. I wasn't the only person whose attention was flagging. After all, he wasn't starting with very interesting subject matter and his dreary delivery did nothing to perk it up. I heard something from the top of the room about an impediment. I groped for the meaning, the significance . . .

I stepped out into the aisle. Everyone looked to where I was standing. Sean's jaw dropped as he saw who it was.

'Don't!' I said. There was silence, they were all waiting for more. 'Just don't. Marry the one you love, not the one you feel tied to.'

Sean's face melted into relief, his eleventh-hour reprieve had come. We stared at each other for a moment more, then he ran. He took my hand and together we flew out of the hotel, down the driveway and onto the country road beyond, where we began looking for a bus stop or a passing taxi . . .

'Stop snoring!' I felt an elbow in my ribs and opened my eyes. The ceremony was over, the happy couple were walking down the aisle, grinning as if they'd just been lobotomised. I fought back tears, telling myself that wasn't the plan anyway. The plan was better. I joined the rest of the congregation as they shuffled to their feet and followed them out.

The photos always take ages. It's easily the most boring part of the day. I waited to be called for one of the group pics – or maybe one of just Sean and I – but the call didn't come and before I knew it we were being herded in for the wedding breakfast.

The bride and groom greeted us all on the way in. 'Thank you for coming. Lovely to see you,' they said to every guest, then placed a quick kiss on each cheek. Sean hid his feelings well when he came to me, but I heard the crack in his voice as he thanked me for coming and I noticed the way he hung onto my hand just a little too long as I filed into the dining room.

They'd sat me next to an elderly bachelor uncle of Susannah's. He was flabby and mostly bald, and with what hair was left he'd given himself a lank, grey comb-over.

'Lovely to meet you, Julie,' he said. 'I've heard loads about you.'

'Have you?' I asked him. 'I thought you were Susannah's uncle?' Why had she been telling him about me? Had she identified me as her rival? Had Sean inadvertently mentioned me once too often, leading her to put two and two together? He leaned over and breathed his mothball breath into my face. He was really going to spoil the meal. But then he said:

'Can I get you a drink?' And things started to look up.

Well, the meal and the speeches passed in something of a blur. It was lucky that during the gabfests they brought round coffee. I needed a clear head for the next bit.

After the speeches, the music began and everyone started milling round. The cake was at the end of the room, displayed on a decorated table and soon they were ready to cut it.

They held the knife between them and I was taken by surprise as Susannah said she'd like to thank me for my work. It took me a moment to realise she meant the cake. For a second there I was back among the spreadsheets! There was a ripple of applause as everyone turned to look at me and I smiled and took a small bow. Then all eyes were back on the Mr & Mrs.

They cut it – no problems there, not with my light and fluffy baking. Then a member of the hotel staff stepped up to do the more complicated stuff – chopping it into even portions. Paper plates were handed out, each with a small cube of my handiwork. I stepped up for my own and hung about, checking how it had fared since I had left it.

It had fared perfectly well. I wandered round the room watching the other guests. I bought another drink, so did everyone else. Sean and Susannah had their first dance, an awkward, clumsy affair. The disco started properly; a few people got up to dance. After a while, one over-enthusiastic bopper lost his footing and ended up under a table. The hilarity seemed to spur everyone else to their feet.

Susannah walked away from the dancefloor and towards me.

'Can I get you a drink, Jools?' she asked and I shuddered at the word 'Jools'. I thought it was understood that that diminutive was only to be used by Sean. But I let it go for now, I'd be getting my revenge soon enough. 'Least I can do after that cake you made.'

'No, no,' I said, 'let me get you one.' For a start, she didn't seem to have her purse with her, and it wasn't a free bar.

'Really,' she said, 'I'd love to.'

'No,' I said again. 'It would be an honour. What will you have? Something sparkling?'

'Well, if you insist,' she said. 'Prosecco, please.'

I made my way to the bar, through the deepest part of the crowd, ignored by all as I reached into my bag and popped a paracetamol tablet out of the packet. I snapped it in half to help it dissolve more quickly and held it in my hand as the bartender made eye contact.

'Glass of prosecco and a large pinot noir, please,' I said. Smiling, he handed them over and demanded a king's ransom in return. But it would be money well spent when it brought Sean and I together.

As I turned away, I held Susannah's glass close to the rim and dropped the paracetamol in. I looked to see if anyone was watching, but frankly, I could've put everything out on the bar and done it all in plain sight: no one was taking any notice of me.

I gave the glass a shake as I watched the tablet dissolve, a little extra fizz among the bubbles. I made my way back to the bride.

'Thank you, Julie,' she said. We tipped our drinks to each other, then down the hatch.

Well, I tipped *mine* down the hatch, Susannah took a delicate sip, then another and another. The drink was not going to go down quickly, but from what I'd heard of Susannah's exploits, the merest hint of an allergen was enough to wipe her out.

'How did you get on with my uncle?' she asked.

'His breath smells of mothballs,' I told her.

Judging by her expression, that wasn't what she expected me to say, and she made her excuses and sauntered off to a gaggle of other guests.

I meandered around, trying to keep her in my sights as she moved from one table to another. The prosecco was going down, but Susannah was still up and about. I saw someone else hand her a glass of something and she knocked back the rest of the prosecco I had given her as she accepted it.

With nothing to do but wait, I thought I'd pass the time with a dance and I joined the mass, boogeying enthusiastically to 'The Edge of Heaven'. There was a group whirling around Sean and I joined it. Susannah arrived and waved her hands in the air to 'Tragedy'. As the song entered its final stages, she put her hand up to her throat. My spirits soared. She dropped her hand back down and carried on dancing. My spirits sank. She lifted her hand again and stopped jiggling. She seemed to be trying to cough.

Some of the others turned to her. Sean noticed and started to speak to her, but Susannah seemed to be struggling to breathe and didn't answer. As 'Tragedy' ended and 'I Will Survive' began, Susannah dropped to the floor.

People milled around, confused about what was going on. The music stopped – just as I was getting into the new song! – and the lights came on.

Susannah's face was blue. Sean shouted, 'Call an ambulance!' and a hundred mobile phones appeared.

Then he shouted, 'Where's her EpiPen?' It was with her mother, who had nipped out for a fag. Smoking really does kill.

In the absence of the EpiPen, Sean didn't seem to know what to do. 'Stop it!' he shouted at his sister, who was running around in panicked circles. Then, 'Help me lie her down flat!' As she lay on the floor, looking like a tragic heroine, he changed his mind and yelled, 'Sit her up!'

She was hauled into a sitting position, and he began shaking her shoulders, saying, 'Susannah, Susannah, talk to me.'

Eventually the pen arrived, as did the ambulance, but they were both too late, Susannah lay peacefully on the floor, her suffering over.

The aftermath was something of a let-down. There was some milling around, we were all ushered out of the hall. The reception was over, although it seemed to be a lot of fuss over someone who had so many allergies. She was bound to have had an accident like this sooner or later.

Strangely, I felt slightly shaky when I got home. No doubt the adrenalin wearing off from the hullaballoo that followed Susannah's collapse. It had given me a splitting headache – then I remembered, I had paracetamol in my bag.

CHAPTER SIXTEEN

2008

I was in early on Monday morning. I hadn't slept well the night before, impatient to see what the atmosphere would be like in the office following the weekend's excitement. It was disappointing to find the mood was subdued, and there were a fair few absences. We were informed of the weekend's events, in case anyone wasn't quite up to date with the gossip, and told a counsellor was available all week if anyone needed to talk about it. Other than that, it was business as usual, although business in rather hushed tones.

Keen to hear their thoughts on the demise of Susannah, I made my way towards the case reviewers with a tray and offered to fetch a round of drinks, hoping to be asked to stay and chat as I handed the refreshments around. But they barely looked up as they shook their heads and muttered 'no thank you' and 'not for me'.

The mood continued all day and the next day, but as the week progressed, I started to find myself enjoying the calm. Without Susannah caterwauling across the office, it became rather peaceful there; a peace that had been lost in the time since she had joined us. Indeed, we were well on our way to a restoration of the old order. Sean would soon be back to work and all would be as it had been before he walked her through the office doors and ruined everything. In no time at all

Susannah would be forgotten and the way would be clear for
Sean and me.

I wondered how soon I could take her list of allergies down
from the noticeboard without attracting attention.

The weather didn't match the harmonious mood. It was drab
and rainy all week and I had to skip my usual lunchtime walks.
Instead, midweek, I read a piece in *Wales Online* which posed
the question, 'Whatever happened to Parklife Paolo?' He was a
Caerphilly vagrant who had, apparently, frequented a local park
for many years, in the late '70s and early '80s, singing the works
of Barry Manilow, holding a hat out for change, before vanish-
ing without a trace.

He had been spotted for the last time in a pub in the town
centre, in the company of a woman described as in her early
twenties, stocky, shifty-looking and with dark hair. After that
the trail went cold. No more sightings, no more collecting his
benefits, but no body. Quite the mystery. Right up there with the
Bermuda Triangle, as Barry Manilow might say.

The article ended with a few statistics on the number of
people who go missing every year in the UK – one reported every
90 seconds – and the low chances of finding a vagrant adult.

1982

When I first started my daily commute for this job, I kept my
eyes out for Ieuan Prosser as I travelled to and from Cardiff and
anytime I was out and about, but he never appeared. Not in
town, not at my house, not even on the TV anymore. His show
was cancelled after the second series and he wasn't to be seen in
any others. I wondered if he'd gone over the pond to be a star in
Hollywood, but study the glossy magazines and gossip pages of
the papers as I would, I could find no trace of him. He had just
vanished into the ether.

And then, a couple of years after I arrived, I saw him.

I was walking through town one Saturday afternoon when suddenly my ears were assailed by the words 'Spare any change?' I was about to walk past when something about the way he held his head made me stop. I looked at him.

'Spare any change?' he said again. I looked in my purse, I had a few coins. I took my time digging them out and used the opportunity to have a good look at him.

He looked different. Time had not been his friend, and even after just a couple of years his hair had greyed, his skin had aged and he could do with a trip to the dentist. Yet here he was. Fate had brought us together as it was always bound to do.

'Ieuan?' I said as he was about to thank me and resume his refrain. He looked at me blankly. 'It is Ieuan, isn't it?'

He seemed to be thinking. 'You can call me Ieuan if you like,' he said in the end.

'Can I buy you a drink?' I asked. He looked hopefully at the pub across the road and minutes later we were sat inside it, our respective poisons in our hands. He drank thirstily, giving me time to observe his features and match them to the image of the dashing hero I still held in my mind. I had to admit, he wasn't quite as I remembered.

His face was longer in shape than I had thought, something of an improvement in fact, although rather than chiselled, I would have described his features as gaunt. Still, I'd only seen him on TV before and they say the camera adds ten pounds, although probably not all to the face. His skin was rather mottled, but plenty of water and easier living conditions would soon put him right.

The biggest surprise was his teeth, a real higgle-piggle, with a couple missing in the lower set. In fact, on closer inspection, he didn't look much like his TV persona at all. If you didn't know, you wouldn't think it was the same person! But I didn't worry over it too much: they can work wonders in the make-up room.

He finished his pint in seconds and looked at me expectantly. So, I chugged down my own wine and stood, already a little dizzy, and made my way to the bar for another round.

I watched in horror as he began to tip the second pint down his throat, thinking I was going to be back at the bar before I'd even had time to take a sip of my own drink, but he stopped halfway down, put his drink on the beer mat and let out a satisfied 'ahhh'. We gazed at each other and I waited for that magical 'click' between us to happen.

'Who are you then?' he asked me. 'A homelessness worker? They don't usually offer me pints.'

'No, no,' I told him, 'Just a fan of your work.'

'Ah, you like a bit of Barry Manilow.'

That sounded like a euphemism, but I had no idea what for, so I smiled politely while he sang a few lines of 'Mandy' and the bar tender, out collecting glasses, said, 'Keep it for the great outdoors, Parklife.'

Ieuan stopped singing and took another glug of his pint. I did the same with my wine.

'What brings you to be begging for change in the street, then, Ieuan? Is it a new role?' I asked. Maybe I'd interrupted him while he was getting himself into character.

He rubbed the stubble on his chin and gazed at that ceiling. 'It's a mixture of things, I suppose. Goes so far back, it's hard to remember. It starts with abuse, then I ran away from home, got in with a bad crowd – seemed like a good crowd at the time. Got into drugs. Then I became the bad crowd and so on.'

It sounded like a very intense role. 'Plenty to get your teeth into,' I said. 'Lots of social issues.'

He frowned. 'Are you some sort of psycho . . . psycho . . . psychopath?'

'I beg your pardon?'

'You know, a head doctor. Is that why you keep calling me Ieuan?'

He really was getting into character if he couldn't remember the difference between a psychopath and a psychiatrist.

'No,' I said. 'But carry on.'

'There's not much else to say, I ended up the man you see before you today. Off the drugs, more or less, got my own squat. Don't think I could've done it if it wasn't for the singing, it's what's kept me going.'

I nodded, assuming he was talking about another string to his performing talents. Maybe the new show was a musical. It certainly sounded like a tale of hope.

He was rooting around in his pocket. 'Another drink?' he asked. 'I'll get these, I've got a bit of change from my morning performance.'

Well, we had time for one last round, but by then it was gone 2.30pm and the pub was closing for the afternoon, licensing laws being what they were back in the '80s.

'There's an off-licence next door,' Ieuan said, looking at the clock. 'You could buy some cans and we could drink them outside the castle, by the moat maybe.'

I said yes to the cans, but no to drinking them by the castle. Instead, I invited him back to my house, to tell me more about the new show. The spark between us still hadn't lit, but I felt sure that once we had some privacy it would be all systems go.

Back home, we opened our cans – he declined a glass for his and made himself comfortable on my sofa. I had noticed in the pub a miasma in the air around him, but now, in my lounge, it was almost overpowering.

I opened a window, although the day was a bit chilly and asked him, 'Would you like to take a shower? I have plenty of clean towels and I could give your clothes a spin in the washing machine.'

'Nah,' he said, stretching himself out and reaching for another can. 'Thanks. I'm alright. You going to put the TV on?' He really did like his method acting!

So, we spent the rest of the afternoon, into the evening together, and I found I soon got used to the smell of him. He was fast asleep by the time the national anthem played as the TV broadcasting ended for the day. I turned the TV off and went to bed.

When I woke the next morning, I felt a thrill that Ieuan Prosser was in my house. Or had been the day before; he may well have left by now. Would he have left me a note with his contact details, I wondered? I rose from my bed and hurried to the lounge as if it was Christmas morning.

I heard him before I saw him, snoring like a beast, his head tipped back over the armrest. I was about to wake him, when I had a better idea. I hurried back upstairs to wash and change and as Ieuan snored on, I nipped out to the nearby shop and bought the ingredients for a full English breakfast. Or Welsh, seeing that we were in Wales.

Ieuan was waking when I arrived.

'Breakfast?' I asked, waving a packet of bacon in the air.

He nodded. 'Don't suppose you bought any fags with that lot, did you?'

I hadn't, so ten minutes later I found myself back in the shop asking the shopkeeper to recommend a brand of cigarettes, not being a smoker myself.

After breakfast I expected him to say he had a lot to do that day and be off. The romantic flame had still not caught, but I was sure it was only a matter of time and my stomach fluttered with nerves as I waited for him to ask for my phone number or offer me his.

But he didn't say he had a lot to do that day, instead he said, 'Might take you up on that offer of a shower.'

I jumped to it, happy to be of assistance, and happy to have the chance to fumigate my house.

A while later, showered and with his clothes washed and out on the line, Ieuan sat wrapped in a sheet, waiting for them to dry. We watched an Open University lecture while we waited; daytime TV was in its early evolution and the options were limited.

'We got any of those cans left?' he asked, even though it was still morning. We did have a couple, so we drank those and then I was persuaded to make my way back to the shop to purchase some more.

'I'll pay you back when I get to the bank,' he said as I put my jacket on. They were quite a weight to haul back to the house, I could've done with some help, but clearly Ieuan couldn't have accompanied me wrapped in a bedsheet.

And so, we spent our second afternoon much like our first.

By the following weekend, Ieuan still showed no sign of moving and our click had still not clicked. My cupboards were nearly bare and I needed to go to the bank, as I knew he did as well, so I suggested a trip into town.

'Probably best you go on your own,' he said. 'My clothes are still wet.' They had had another wash the previous morning and felt dry to me, but he insisted his jeans were still wet at the crotch and I didn't feel like handling them there to check.

'Get some more cans,' he said as I headed out. 'And fags. I'll pay you back.'

When I got home, I found, to my horror, all the downstairs doors had been taken off their hinges.

'Your doors were sticking,' Ieuan said, fully clothed now. 'I thought I'd sort it out for you, earn my keep, so to speak. But you don't have any sandpaper.'

They weren't sticking, but it was a lovely thought. 'Shall we put them back in their frames then?' I said.

'Let's just have a can first,' Ieuan said. 'Thirsty work taking them off.'

And so, our second Saturday became like our first.

The next morning I was starting to think that a short time away from each other might do Ieuan and I the world of good, but before I could suggest it, I found myself back at my local corner shop, buying lager and 'fags'.

'Thanks,' he said. 'I owe you one,' as he cracked open a can.

I made my way through the house, doors still out of their frames, and into the kitchen, where I found the u-bend on the worktop and the taps in pieces next to it.

'It was dripping,' Ieuan said when I asked him what had happened. 'Thought I'd fix it for you, but I haven't found the fault yet.'

'You just need to turn it a bit tighter when you turn it off,' I said.

On Monday morning, I lay in bed and thought things through: the fact he hadn't answered to 'Ieuan' when I first met him; the fact he seemed to have nothing better to do than hang around my house; the fact that he was always asking for me to pay for everything. I would've thought that any self-respecting TV star would be falling over themselves to flash the cash. And the click, the click had never arrived. In truth I had realised some time ago, but now I faced the fact: this was not Ieuan Prosser snoring his head off in my lounge.

I rose, showered and dressed. I spent some time practising what I was going to say. Then I went downstairs to where 'Ieuan' was just rising, from the floor this time, where he had passed out the night before.

I took a deep breath. 'Ieuan,' I said. 'I think it's time for you to leave.' There! I'd done it! My heart was in my throat, but I'd made a reasonable request in my own home and the ordeal was about to be over.

'But I thought we had an arrangement,' he said.

'What arrangement?'

'Well, you do the cooking and the fetching and I do little jobs around the house.'

'What little jobs?'

'The doors and the taps. I know I haven't finished yet, but they're on my list.'

'But they didn't need doing.'

'They did, you just didn't notice because you got used to it. Is it the money? Because I said I'd pay you back. I get my benefits at the end of the week.'

'It's not the money, it's . . .'

'Were you expecting a seeing-to? It'd be perfectly reasonable. We can go upstairs and do it now. Be my pleasure.'

'No!'

'Well, what's the issue? You're here in this nice house that's too big for one, I just have a pokey squat . . .'

'Don't you have anywhere to be?' I asked. 'Isn't anyone wondering where you are?'

He shook his head.

I inched my way towards the telephone. 'If you don't leave now, I'm going to call the police.'

'Ieuan' tipped his head back and stood, arms akimbo, feet hip distance apart, and blocked the doorway. 'I'm not sure that's such a good idea,' he said. 'See, Welsh police, they don't know me, they think I'm just harmless Parklife Paolo, but over in London, it's a different matter. In London I'm wanted for a serious crime and if the Met Police get chatting to the coppers round here it might all come to light. And you would be found to be harbouring a very dangerous criminal. Aiding and abetting I think that's called.'

Not to mention my natural aversion to the police since the incident with Felicity Pearson. I didn't really want to call the police, but more than ever I wanted him out of my house.

'Ieuan' continued. 'What's more, I've been thinking that it seems silly for me to be sleeping down here when you've got a spare room upstairs.' And so, he took his meagre possessions and made his way up to my spare room. I made my way out to work.

For a while we went on. We fell into a routine and on wash day he meekly handed over his clothes, then sat for the day in front of the TV, the sheet wrapped around his lower half. And all the time I fumed over the audacity and plotted how to get rid of him.

I tried a few more times to persuade him to leave of his own volition, but he merely reminded me he'd be daft to give up what he had here, and I'd be mad to call the police. 'The pigs' he called them.

Just as I knew he had no one looking for him, he likewise knew no one was going to call in here to check I was alright.

'Your mum called,' he said to me one day, as I returned from the supermarket. 'She didn't know you had a gentleman guest. Didn't you tell her about me? Seemed quite pleased. And surprised.'

No, on the rare occasions I spoke to my parents, I didn't mention that I was 'aiding and abetting' a dangerous criminal. That would've brought either them or the local constabulary to my door before you could say 'Parklife Paolo'.

And he was right that I didn't want to get the police involved, although not for the reason he thought.

Yet, the further we sailed from the incident with Felicity, the less I thought of the enormity of what I had done and the more I focused on the fact I had got away with it. I realised that while no one was looking for 'Ieuan', that also meant that no one knew he was here. He never left the house, and even when he went into the garden, he sat by the wall so the neighbours couldn't see him. I chose my time.

On the day in question, we had run out of lager. 'I'm just going to get some cans,' I said, and I heard him grunt an acknowledgement. I returned soon after with the cans, and with a small bottle of vodka hidden in my coat pocket.

That evening, I opened one for each of us and we sat down to drink them in front of the TV. When he left the room, I tipped a little bit of the vodka into his can and gave it a shake.

'Ieuan' happily drank down the spiked can. Then another and another.

'Got the munchies,' he said. 'Have you got anything to eat?'

I made a pile of sandwiches and he ate them.

He opened another can, but then his head started to droop.

You'd think it would be hard to kill someone in cold blood, but once you've attacked one person with murderous intent – premeditated or not – the next one is easier. I was more worried about the size and strength of him compared to the size and strength of me, and it wasn't really in cold blood anyway. I was furious; my blood was boiling.

I waited until he was, once again, sprawled across the carpet, then I crept upstairs and fetched a pillow and two pairs of tights. I tied one pair of tights gently around his wrists and the other around his ankles, then I tied them together. I didn't knot them tightly. Even if he woke up, he wouldn't feel them at first, but they would stop him having free use of his hands for long enough for me to do what I was going to do.

Holding the pillow, I crouched where I could drop it straight onto his face. He snorted and I waited until his breathing became regular again.

'Sorry about this,' I whispered. Then I pounced.

It took him a few minutes to stop wriggling and even then I was nervous to lift the pillow in case he was bluffing, but after half an hour sitting there with no movement, I considered it safe. I stood and looked down at the corpse in my lounge.

At the point of killing 'Ieuan' I had a body disposal plan, but I'd underestimated the physical effort involved. The dead body of a grown man is not an easy thing to manoeuvre out of the house. After dragging him across the lounge floor, I was knackered. It was quite the workout.

I took a short break while I went out to the shed and checked I had what I needed, i.e. a large spade. I began to dig, but soon realised that digging a grave, even a shallow one, was going to take more time than I probably had before dawn revealed to the neighbours what I was doing. So, I covered over what I had started and went back inside, where I dragged the body as far as the kitchen door. And there it stayed for the whole of the next day, with me stepping over it every time I needed anything, until darkness fell.

Then I went back out, took my spade and dug and dug and dug as if my life depended on it. Which it did, really. I dug with supernatural speed, only pausing once when the light went on in the Jacksons' bathroom window. A moment later the toilet flushed, then I froze as the window opened and Bert's head popped out.

'Anyone out there?' he said. He waited, then, 'Thought I heard something, Mabel, but there's no reply.' But before he closed the window, he looked straight down at where I was standing and I stared back, with no idea whether or not he could see me.

I finished my work, dragged the body out and, with relief, dumped it in the hole. I covered it over and scattered the rest of the soil around to avoid that tell-tale hump you see in graveyards.

I woke the next morning with every muscle aching, but with the knowledge that 'Ieuan' was gone. Then I remembered Bert and ran to the window to see if the police had arrived yet. But they didn't come that day, or the day after, or the day after that. They didn't come that week, month, or year. They simply didn't come.

CHAPTER SEVENTEEN

2008

Ffion from HR came down, looking all tragic, to announce that the counsellor would be in the building all week and that they would be sending flowers to both Susannah's parents and to Sean, along with a card. The card would be brought down so anyone who wanted to could sign it.

Dave asked if passing it round for people to sign was in very good taste and Ffion wrote his question down and bustled off, saying she'd get back to us with an answer.

Sean was told he could have as long as he wanted off work, stretching into months, if he wished, but he returned to the office after just a few weeks. He said it wasn't doing him any good being around the house on his own, thinking about things. I walked in that morning to find him sitting there, scrolling through the hundreds of emails that had built up in his absence: 'cake sale on in the foyer'; 'can everyone come out of the "pendings" spreadsheet, please,' and so on.

He didn't always complete a full day, though. He wasn't always in by nine o'clock either, and apparently this was all perfectly acceptable while Sean came to terms with his loss. When he was there, he looked tired, his eyes were red and he looked unkempt. His clothes were crumpled, he was unshaven, his hair needed a trim.

Some of Susannah's personal possessions were still locked away in her drawer and although she was no longer of this world, it turned out they still needed signatures in triplicate to be allowed to open it. Once permission was granted, Ffion came down from HR for the opening, along with someone from Facilities, with the key. She, Marcus and Sean stood and watched, along with Dave in his role as union rep and Mike in his role as nosy parker, and the rest of us from wherever we sat, as it was unlocked. It was almost a complete ceremony; I was expecting a blast of the 'Last Post'.

Once it was opened, Sean removed some bits and pieces, then he sat, clutching a scarf that had been in there and staring into space before, once again, heading home early.

'Cheerio, thanks for calling in,' I muttered, as I saw him departing.

'Julie!' Dave said. I hadn't noticed him standing behind me.

Only I knew it was all an act; he was keen to put Susannah behind him and be reunited with me.

It was a while before I had an opportunity to speak to him. I started by offering my condolences, insincere though they were.

'Thanks,' Sean said and turned back to his computer screen.

'If there's anything I can do.'

'Thanks,' he said again, obviously unsure how to approach such an awkward situation. But how much longer was this going to go on for? After about six months, which felt like six years, I decided to see if I could move things along a bit.

'Are you eating properly?' I asked him. I wasn't concerned he'd lost his appetite, I was more aware boys his age didn't always have full mastery of their cookery skills and it was something I excelled in. He nodded. I realised he was more nervous of the situation than I had expected.

'It's just that – as you know – I'm pretty handy in the kitchen. You could come round for tea. And I usually keep a cheeky bottle of red on standby. For occasions like this.'

He looked at me for a moment, there seemed to be a frown on his face.

'How many occasions like this do you come across?' he asked me. It was a fair point, you only come across a love like ours once in a lifetime.

'It's quite an old bottle.'

'Supermarket wine doesn't store as well as the classics,' he told me. 'It's probably got a best before date on it. I'd get it drunk if I were you.'

I made one more attempt. 'So don't forget, if you want a decent meal and a bit of company, I'm available any time.'

'Right, thanks, Julie,' he said.

I took a step back. *Julie?* What happened to 'Jools'?

Sean turned back to his screen, clearly overcome by the emotion. I went back to my own desk and mulled it over. I hadn't realised Sean was so concerned by appearances, I hadn't expected him to be so stand-offish, and I was hurt by the fact he'd called me Julie.

Although I suppose no one wants to appear callous, taking up with their one true love only months after the death of a wife. And sometimes people do misspeak your name, even your nearest and dearest.

Once again, I fancied a bit of company while I was waiting for Sean to observe a decent mourning period. Not a cat, I didn't want anything as fickle as a cat again. And not a bird. I didn't want another pet so slow to get the hang of things.

Instead, I went down to the pet shop and bought a hutch, a water bottle and some straw. I still had the cat's bowls; I'd never got round to getting rid of them.

'Need any help with that?' A voice came from behind the Jacksons' shrubbery, as my taxi drove away, making me jump a mile in the air and drop everything on the pavement. I looked up and saw the Jackson's son, Frank, making his way towards me.

I had been rather struggling with the hutch, but he lifted it as if it were a bird cage and said, 'Lead on.'

I led him around to the back garden, where he helped me set up the stand and place the hutch on it, chattering away the whole time. 'Exciting getting a new pet, isn't it?' he said. 'We used to have hamsters when we were kids. Stick insects as well, they were less exciting.'

I nodded, it *was* rather exciting getting a new pet if the truth be told.

'Are you putting the straw in now, or when the pet arrives?' he asked.

'When it arrives,' I said.

'Shall I put this in the shed for you then?' he asked and hoisted the straw onto his shoulder, heading towards the shed.

'No!' My taxidermy tools were hanging on the wall in there and I didn't know if he'd recognise them for what they were. While it's a perfectly legal hobby, for some reason, I didn't want him to know about it. Not on our second meeting.

'Hey-ho,' he said, putting it back down. 'I'll leave it here for you, shall I?'

I nodded and waited for him to go.

'That you back from work for the day, then?' he asked.

I nodded again.

'Any plans for the evening?

'I like to cook,' I said. 'That takes up a lot of my evening.'

'Lovely.' He stretched and rubbed his back. 'Well, I could do with a cup of tea after all that heavy lifting.'

'I'll let you get on then,' I said, slightly disappointed that our conversation was ending.

He paused for a moment, looking at me. 'I expect I'll see you around,' he said. 'I'm going to be visiting Mum and Dad more often from now on.'

'I expect so,' I said.

'Well, bye for now,' and he left.

I went into my house with a niggling sense that I could have done something differently. Maybe he could've had a cup of tea here? I vaguely remembered that when I was a girl, people would come to the house and drink hot drinks, and we would go to theirs. Frank and I could both be sitting around the table talking about . . . I had no idea what we would talk about, but I was sure he'd think of something. Then I looked down the hall and saw Fluffy, where I'd left her on the telephone table. I couldn't have brought him in to see that.

A few days later I went back to the pet shop and bought a couple of guinea pigs. I'd had them when I was small and remembered them as being pretty inoffensive creatures. Plus they didn't come indoors, so there would be no hoovering nightmares.

I picked a multi-coloured one, would you call them tortoiseshell? And a black and white one. Welcome to Bert and Mabel Jackson. Although they were both girls. Maybe Bert was short for Alberta.

They didn't do much on the first afternoon. I sat and watched them as they tried to hide themselves in the straw. As soon as you moved a pile away from them, they scurried to disappear into the next one. I took a firm hand, pulled them out and held them on my lap, and after a while they calmed down. It was all flooding back to me now, how skittish guinea pigs could be. Always running away when you opened the hutch door, playing hard to get – a bit like Sean. Once you had them in the palm of your hand, though, they were happy as Larry.

And sure enough, they started to settle. So much so that Mabel, the black and white one, sighed, sank down onto her stomach and did a wee.

I'd forgotten about that! The little blighters would gladly pee on you at the drop of a hat! Disgusted, I shoved them back into the hutch and went to have a wash. They buried themselves in the straw as soon as they landed there – probably ashamed of themselves.

Even so, we soon got into a routine. I would go down there to feed them, morning and evening, and when they heard the back door opening, they would let out a cacophony of squeaking – just in case I forgot what I was there for. As the days became longer and warmer, I bought them a pen and set it on the lawn and there we would spend the summer evenings, with them chortling away as I sketched the scene.

CHAPTER EIGHTEEN

2008–9

After eight months I was wondering if Sean was ever going to put Susannah behind him. He often looked haggard, slightly dishevelled, even. He was losing weight; he didn't always shave. I heard him telling someone he hadn't been sleeping well and every day he'd be there at his desk, tired and lacklustre.

In the early days, I admit, it took some courage to carry on with the conversation, it often seemed to be nothing but good mornings and goodbyes. I had to keep reminding myself he was just putting on an act, and it was all for appearances, so I persevered in my campaign with Sean. Little and often was the way to do it, I decided.

'Good morning, Sean,' I'd say as I passed him on my way in. 'How are you today?'

'Yeah, yeah, so-so, Julie,' he'd say.

And 'See you tomorrow then, Sean,' at the end of the day.

To which he'd always answer, 'Laters.'

Later. We were building a solid foundation from which we could develop our public association, just a few minutes together a day, not much more than anyone else really, until everyone was accustomed to seeing us together.

It was worth it eventually, when I paused at his desk after a few months, issued a hearty 'good morning!' and was rewarded with his full attention.

He stopped what he was doing, he leaned back in his chair, he looked around and he swivelled to face me!

'Morning, Jools,' he said. 'What's happening?'

'Oooh! Usual stuff!' I told him, slightly lost for words; I'd almost stopped hoping for a reply and now I was about to have a conversation! 'Post to sort, cases to allocate, spreadsheets to update! You?'

'Same old, same old,' he said. 'Cases to review, emails to send, coffee to drink.'

Of course! Coffee!

'I was just going to the machine,' I said, although I had my hands full with my bag and my umbrella and a carrier bag of veg I was taking back to the supermarket: it had gone bad before its best before date. 'Would you like me to get you one?'

'Oh, you're OK,' he said, looking at my luggage. 'I'll give you one – ahem, I meant get you one. The usual?'

I giggled at the Freudian slip – a glimpse of what was really on his mind – and nodded that I would have the usual. He strode off to the drinks machine. I hurried to my desk, I didn't want to dawdle and not be there when he arrived, and there I was, still waiting for my PC to finish going through the motions, when he reappeared.

I motioned to the empty seat beside me – these were the days before Gareth – but he shook his head, a little regretfully, I believe.

'Better press on,' he said. 'It's really piling up over there.' It was as if a weight had lifted from him, this was more like the old Sean.

I wasn't short of work to do myself – they could hardly work the cases if I didn't send them over. I started powering through the spreadsheet. After all, I was doing the work of two people while I waited for my new assistant.

I think that maybe I'd held out a secret hope that they'd find Sean irreplaceable and haul him back to my admin kingdom

– on his case reviewer's wage, of course. Or maybe Sean would decide life at the other end of the office wasn't for him and beg for a return to the heart of the department. Yet my hopes were dashed one morning when the new boy arrived.

It was around nine months after Susannah's passing that Gareth appeared. He clocked the sexual tension between Sean and I immediately. 'I can almost smell it,' he said, and I thought of *The Silence of the Lambs.*

I denied it at first. For some reason, talking about it so openly made me feel shy. I ducked my head down and tried not to smile.

'I'm right, aren't I?' Gareth said. 'You can tell me, I can keep a secret.'

I shook my head again. 'There's nothing to tell.'

But Gareth persevered. Every time Sean was in the vicinity, Gareth looked at me and grinned, or waggled his eyebrows and made a love heart sign with his hands.

'It's fine,' he said. 'It's completely normal. In my last job I had a crush on the CEO. It was quite a small company and I sat not far from his office. It used to break my heart when he came out to give us pep talks and he'd talk about his wife and family. I'm over it now, though.'

I didn't really see the relevance of that little anecdote, but Gareth persevered in trying to get the truth out of me.

'Come on,' he said, opening a packet of Love Hearts and handing me one with the words 'be mine' on it. 'I think you should speak up. If you don't ask you don't get. And you never know your luck. Stranger things have happened.'

'What do you mean "stranger things have happened"?'

'I mean love is blind.'

I stared at him.

'I mean love works in mysterious ways,' he said. 'Or is that God? Anyway, I suppose he's single now. If you don't put your bid in, someone else will sooner or later.'

'How did you know?' I asked him, although he obviously didn't know everything if he thought Sean needed to be made aware.

He sighed out a 'Weeellll . . . I'm not a body language expert, but sometimes you can just tell.'

'How?'

'Oh, I don't know. Maybe it's the way you sit up dead straight and grin like a gargoyle whenever Sean's around. Maybe it's the way your face goes red, and you stutter and gibber at him.'

'I do not!' Sean and my conversations were tempered and articulate.

'If you say so. Maybe it's the way nothing is too much trouble for Sean. Everything's too much trouble for everyone else.'

'It's not so much things being too much trouble, but people have to learn to do their jobs properly and if that means taking a hard line, then it means taking a hard line. Some of the people here never seem to have had any lines taken at all. They meander about, wandering hither and thither, never getting anywhere, never achieving anything.'

'OK! OK. It's just these little things I've noticed,' Gareth said. 'I didn't know a hard line meant a straight line.'

I decided to let it go, I had bigger fish to fry. 'So, what about Sean? What are the things he does that let you know? Is it because he calls me Jools?'

'If I'm being honest, I'm not seeing any obvious signs coming from his direction.' Gareth said.

'Eh?'

'Sean,' he said. 'I think, if you're going to make a play for him, you'll have a bit of selling yourself to do. I heard it's not so long since he lost his wife.'

So, Gareth wasn't as astute as I had imagined. He too thought Sean was grieving for Susannah and had missed the subtle, but unmistakeable signs of his true passion. In the grand scheme of things, Susannah was a very brief interlude in Sean's life. Gareth was speaking again.

'. . . can help you, though.'

'Help me?' I asked.

'With bewitching. I'm quite the Cupid when I put my mind to it.'

Gareth was not fooling around with his offer to help me. Although he was a little behind the game, he started by wanting to find out if Sean was interested – well, I've already covered that at length. But I had to admit, the signs were subtle. They'd had to be, of necessity.

Gareth began his match-making strategy by playing he loves me, he loves me not with a packet of elastic bands. The outcome was not what we expected.

'But that stuff is nonsense anyway,' Gareth said. 'We need something more scientific.'

'A lie detector test?'

'Something more subtle.'

He suggested a makeover.

'What's Sean's type?' he asked me. I wasn't sure what he meant at first, so he elaborated and I was surprised – quite obviously Sean's type was me!

'No, I mean, what did his missus look like?' Gareth said. What did that have to do with it? 'We need to establish what kind of look he goes for. Let's see if looking more like her makes him notice you.'

There was no point explaining to Gareth that Sean had already noticed me, and that the problem was getting him to acknowledge his feelings, to stop caring what other people thought.

'All the same,' Gareth said, 'it'd do no harm to spruce you up.'

I declined at first, but Gareth was very persistent. He insisted a change is as good as a break. A change of image would make everyone look up and take notice. Sean would want to snap me up before anyone else stepped in.

Sean didn't have anything to worry about on that front; I wouldn't allow myself to be snapped up by anyone else, but, as Gareth pointed out, Sean wasn't to know that. Or was he? Our love was so deep, surely he'd know that I'd never betray him.

'Would he?' Gareth asked. 'Love is fraught with insecurities and uncertainties.' It was, wasn't it. Or was it? It was getting confusing, so I consented to a late-night shopping trip with Gareth.

We headed to Topshop where Gareth believed all my imaging requirements could be met. Almost all:

'I can put you in touch with a really good hair stylist,' he said. 'Modernise your 'do a little bit.'

'It is modern,' I said. 'It's classic, timeless. It's Princess Di on her wedding day.'

'OK,' he said, sounding doubtful. 'I just thought you might like something more twenty-first century.'

I thought of the young ladies he associated with in the department across the aisle from us, and their heads, which sported long hair on one side and were shaved on the other. 'No thank you,' I said.

'If you're sure,' Gareth said, and he led the way along Queen Street, hauling me on, as I looked longingly at M&S when we passed it.

'No, no, no,' he said. 'Sean doesn't want to date his gran.'

In Topshop Gareth headed for the brightest rack. 'Let's put a bit of colour on you,' he said. 'I wonder what would suit.' He started holding gaudy offerings up against my face: orange, yellow, red, pink, lime green and electric blue. With each one he leaned back, looked at me, made a face and said 'no'.

'Which star sign are you?' he asked. I'm a Taurus.

'An earth sign,' he said. 'That explains it.' He headed for a slightly more muted patch of raiment and held up a brown and yellow top. 'We'll start with a darker base and add the brights.'

'I'm happy with the colours I have.'

'What? A base of black, layered with other blacks, only varying depending on how many times they've been washed?' Gareth scoffed. 'It's a bit monochrome.'

'It complements my black hair,' I said, it made me dark and alluring. 'I like the contrast with my pale skin.'

'Don't you think it makes you look ill?' he asked. No, I didn't. He ploughed on and I must admit, I was interested to see what some of them were going to look like: he paired a brown top with an orange scarf and jewellery; I felt quite Halloweeny. He added a bright blue waistcoat to a sunshine yellow t-shirt and a red shrug to an indigo blouse. He went a little too far, though, with a purple jumper and green jeans.

I tried them on. I looked like a different woman. Not the woman Sean had fallen in love with, but when I mentioned this to Gareth he said I wasn't doing it for Sean, I was doing it for me and I should wear what makes me feel fabulous.

I was a bit confused for the second time that day: Sean was exactly who I was doing this for, that was the whole point of the trip. The subject would never have come up otherwise. But Gareth said if I looked fabulous on the outside, I'd feel fabulous on the inside and then my life would be fulfilling and Sean would be irresistibly drawn to the beauty radiating from within me. So, we were doing it for Sean, but we were doing it for me as well. 'What's good for the goose is good for the gander,' Gareth concluded.

I bought most of the clothes he recommended, but just stopped short at pink. Susannah had been a bit of a pink girl, and it didn't suit me anyway. Gareth made up for it by buying himself a pair of neon pink trousers.

We went to one of the licensed premises for something to eat and had a drink as well. Then we went on for another drink and ambled in and out of the pubs on The Hayes and its side streets. Leaving O'Neill's, I forgot all my bags and we had to go running back. Someone had noticed and handed them in at the bar.

'That was lucky!' Gareth said and we laughed all the way to the station. On the train home, I wondered if this was what it was like having friends. Did Gareth do things like this all the time? Was shopping and visiting pubs and laughing with people just an average day in his life? No wonder he was always so cheerful. It really lifted the spirits.

And they lifted further when I turned the corner into my street to see an old Ford Focus parked outside the Jacksons' house. I surprised even myself with the pleasure I felt when I saw Frank getting out of it. He smiled when he saw me.

'Late night shenanigans,' he said, with a wink, as I reached my house. 'Dad's at his poker night and Mum wanted a cheeky burger. So, I said I'd join her in one.' He held up a takeaway bag. 'We're going to make a night of it,' he added and held up a bottle of wine. 'I'd invite you to join us, but I suppose you don't want to be drinking on a school night.'

I let out a little hiccough and swayed. Frank looked at me curiously and smiled. 'Unless you already have?' Then without giving me time to reply he said, 'You'll have to invite me along next time, I love a weeknight tipple. Say, I went to a restaurant last week and ordered a giant duck. The bill was enormous!'

'I'm sure it would be,' I said, duck was quite expensive anyway.

'No,' Frank said. 'A giant *duck*, the *bill* was enormous.'

'Yes,' I said.

'Bill is a word for a duck's bill and a bill at a restaurant.'

Oh! It was a play on words. Very clever. I laughed.

'It's a good joke, isn't it,' Frank said. I nodded, still laughing and with that, he hurried into the Jacksons' house.

The encounter with Frank had lifted my mood even further and inside I continued the party. I woke up the next morning with my face on the carpet, the rest of me half on, half off the sofa. When was too much to drink really too much, I wondered. When did it stop being fun? My bags of shopping were in a pile on the chair. I looked at the clock – I had to be at the train station twenty minutes ago! I was already more than an hour behind with my normal routine.

Gareth looked at me in horror as I sat down at my desk.

'Where are your clothes?!' he shrieked. I looked down at what I was wearing: the same outfit I always wore on a Wednesday. 'I've been telling Sean you'll be a new woman when you arrive.'

'They're still in the bags,' I said. 'I overslept. I didn't have time to co-ordinate.'

Gareth turned away in disgust. I looked down the office to where Sean and The Lads were peering over their monitors towards me. They all looked disappointed. Sean stood up and headed towards the drinks machine; a moment later he was on his way towards Gareth and me with drinks for all three of us.

'Morning, Jools,' he said to me.

'Morning,' I stammered.

'You're in late today. Got yourself a man?'

I didn't know how to answer that. In fact, I'm not sure I've ever been so confused in my life; why would Sean be asking me that?

'He's joking, Julie.' Gareth stepped in. 'You never heard anyone say that before?'

No. I never had. What was funny about it?

'Is that a new top?' Sean asked me.

'No,' Gareth said. 'She overslept. She didn't have time to co-ordinate her new gear so she decided to wear black. Black is much easier to match with.'

'Yeah, I find that,' Sean agreed. Did he? I'd never noticed. Usually he wore a shirt – various colours, but mostly quite pale – and dark trousers. Same as all the men in here. Except Gareth, who that day was sporting a pair of bright red trousers – the neon pink ones were to be kept for special occasions – and a royal blue shirt. I looked at him again. It was a little hard on the retinas. Could he be the reason I'd been getting a few headaches recently?

And I'd let him choose me a wardrobeful of clothes! I thought about what was lying in the bags at home and did an inventory of the colours: blues, greens, oranges, yellows, a splash of red over a foundation of brown.

For a moment I pictured us – Gareth and I – as others would see us, as they looked upon the muted tones of the walls and carpets, the business-like blacks and greys worn by our colleagues. Then, at the end of the row, Gareth and I, looking like an explosion at the paint factory.

I stared at him as Sean made his excuses and returned to his desk.

'What's wrong?' Gareth asked.

'Am I going to look like you?'

Gareth laughed. 'I don't think so. Are we related?'

'My clothes,' I said. 'Are we going to match?'

'You ain't stealing my style bi-atch,' he said, which, to my mind, was no answer at all. I continued to stare at him. 'Of course, you're not going to look like me,' he said. 'I chose your clothes for you, not for me. *We* chose clothes for you.'

I wasn't convinced. I thought about taking them back on Saturday.

'Try them on again when you get home. If you don't like them, you don't have to keep them. Think of what you'd be losing, though. A fabulous new you. Feeling marvellous on the inside and looking marvellous on the outside. If you have any worries give me a ring.' He wrote his phone number down on an empty envelope and gave it to me. Then he cast his gaze down the office to where Sean was deep in concentration. 'Cast those old drab-rags away!'

He'd told Sean about the new look. Sean had asked me if I was wearing a new top. He'd been disappointed not to see the new image. I remembered how I'd felt the night before: new clothes, a few drinks inside me and a masterplan for a new, fabulous me. I kicked myself for losing my nerve. Yes, tonight I would experiment with a few of the more muted outfits and tomorrow would be a fresh chapter.

CHAPTER NINETEEN

2009

Back at home that evening I started with those items most like the clothes I already had; the dark, long-sleeved t-shirts, the tailored trousers and the blouses, but they were only ever intended as a base for something more flamboyant. Over them I tried on the t-shirts, colourful waistcoats, scarves and chunky necklaces.

I chose an outfit for the next day, folded the clothes up and put them on the chair in my room. I shovelled the rest into a corner and dropped into bed.

A few minutes later, I got out of bed again. Determined to avert a failing of confidence, I took all of my old work clothes out of the wardrobe and wash basket, carried them downstairs and took a pair of kitchen scissors to them.

'You're owning that look, girl!' Gareth said when I arrived at the office and took off my coat. He couldn't stop staring! More importantly, nor could Sean.

'I said it yesterday and I'll say it again today,' he said, making his way over, 'is that a new top?'

'Do you like it?' Gareth asked.

'I . . .' Sean began. My heart sank.

'Love it!' Gareth finished. 'That's what you were going to say, isn't it?' Sean nodded slowly.

Maybe he didn't like my top, I wondered, watching his thoughtful nod. I thought of ditching them all and returning to my former wear. Friday was dress down day, but, in truth, I kept the same dark and mysterious look on all seven days of the week. Then I remembered the slashed heap on the kitchen floor and that going back was no longer an option.

I hoped Sean was just surprised by the change; it often takes time to get used to something new.

The ladies in the department were less flattering. Jayne from the post room said it looked like I was wearing all my clothes at once.

But it was a real hit with the gentlemen. They came from far and wide to ogle and marvel. One even came down from the fifteenth floor! Some of them wandered to and fro around our little pod, some of them marched right up and stared at me. That was a bit unnerving if truth be told, but they were probably too shy to speak. Not everyone is as eloquent as Oscar Wilde.

One gentleman in particular couldn't keep away and he brought a number of colleagues down to show me off to. Flattering though it was, I did feel somewhat exposed. Time was, I'd wondered if I might go into modelling, but I realised now I would have been too modest; I was sweating like a pig under all the attention. And all the clothes.

For the first time in ages, I thought of Angela and how there was always so much fuss around her – everyone full of admiration – when we were young. If only she could see me now.

When Angela first joined the saints, I was rather shocked: who wouldn't be, to one day have a brash, noisy sister and then, in the blink of an eye, to have a vegetable for a sibling, a vegetable who soon became just a photo on the mantelpiece, a mound in the graveyard.

At first, every year on Angela's birthday, on *my* birthday, at Christmas and on The Anniversary – which was never spoken of as anything other than 'The Anniversary' – I was made to traipse down to the grave with my parents, lay down flowers and relate some of my memories of Angela. Although, it wasn't long before they stopped asking me to choose my own recollections and took more of a 'Do you remember . . .' approach.

And if ever I wondered where my mother was, when before she'd have been cooking my tea, I need look no further than the churchyard; the area around Angela's grave was better tended than our garden ever had been. Even in her absence, Angela still dominated our family.

On my eighteenth birthday, I declined to attend the requisite grief-fest. My refusal was greeted with, 'Well, you're eighteen now, it's up to you.' But if I'd thought that was the end of the matter, I was very much mistaken. Eighteen, it turns out, is the age at which you can no longer be compelled by the simple fact that you are a child and they are adults; instead you are compelled with little digs, verbal twists of the knife, emotional blackmail and guilt tripping.

'I'm really disappointed.'

'It's the only thing we still have as a family.'

'Sometimes I think you didn't love your sister.'

'If the shoe was on the other foot, Angela would never have missed a visit.'

'It's such a small request.'

'Angela would be so hurt.'

So I went, grudgingly. But when I got to university, I seized my chance and in the run-up to what would have been Angela's 21st birthday, I phoned to tell them I was sorry, but I had a training session at the hospital I couldn't possibly miss. After all those years hammering on about how much I needed my education, I thought they'd be all for that, but it turns out Angela's imaginary birthday is more important than my future. They dug, they needled, they whined, but the distance gave me the strength to stand my ground. I hung up the receiver exhausted, but aware of a significant and permanent power shift in our relationship.

As Angela's birthday came and went, I experienced a niggling sense of guilt and a strange expectation of doom. But nothing happened, time passed and the guilt eased. It raised its head again at Christmas, when the conversation started with, 'I suppose we can't persuade you . . .' but I stayed firm and after a while, they stopped asking. I stopped feeling uneasy about it and before I knew it, it was normal for them not to ask and for me not to go.

I was free.

I celebrated my freedom by mixing cider with vodka and learnt, the following day, why it is a very bad idea to do that.

Gareth was very quiet. Most days I could hardly hear myself think for his gabbling and singing, but today, in the glow of his shopping success, he hardly said a word. Rather generous of him, really, to take a backseat and let me hog the limelight.

I wondered if this would be the day Sean overcame his reservations and declared his true feelings. In fact, when I saw him approaching my desk, with just ten minutes to go to the end of the day, I felt butterflies stirring in my stomach.

But all he said was, 'What's in the dressing-up box for tomorrow?'

'Wardrobe!' Gareth almost screeched. 'It's called a wardrobe!'

'Are you alright?' I asked Gareth as Sean beat a hasty retreat.

To be honest I was annoyed at the tone he'd taken with Sean, I felt it was a little brusque, verging on aggressive, and I couldn't understand why.

Back home, I went upstairs to choose an outfit for Friday. And dreamt of the time Sean would finally put his fears aside and let the world know how he felt about me. How he intended to live the rest of his life.

There seemed fewer clothes to choose from than the night before. I noticed, as I peeled my layers off to try the new ones on, just how many of the clothes I'd put on. No wonder I'd been slowly roasting from the inside out.

The fuss had died down somewhat by Friday morning. In fact, the only comment was Sean's 'nice outfit'. I felt a bit disappointed, despite the previous day's slight discomfort. Now that everyone's attention was once again with their work, I found myself missing the limelight. But then again, Friday's outfit was significantly more subdued than Thursday's had been. I resolved to experiment with my new look over the weekend and return on Monday, a diva once more.

Gareth had left a couple of fashion magazines on my desk when I arrived that morning, blazing the headlines 'Less is More with your Office Image' and 'Overstate your Case with an Understated Look'. He was clearly as excited as me about the stir we'd caused the previous day.

CHAPTER TWENTY

2009

I arrived in the office on Monday to find that Gareth and Sean had had a sword fight with a ruler and my letter opener, and Gareth had subsequently been told off for playing with knives.

'We've been fighting over you, Jools,' Sean said and walked away laughing, leaving me with a warm Monday morning thrill of happiness. After all, I would fight for him over and over again, and I couldn't say that for any of my former loves.

And as I was rejoicing over that, another blessing dropped itself into our email inboxes. Its arrival was heralded by the chorus of bings that echoed round the office whenever a department-wide missive is sent, followed soon after by an 'oooohh!' from Gareth.

I looked round at him; departmental emails don't usually attract a lot of oooohhing. Maybe there were to be redundancies. But, no, when I clicked my copy open it was an invitation to the annual summer ball.

'Are you going?' Gareth asked. I had been on a number of occasions, but I didn't have any plans to attend this one. 'I think you should,' he continued. 'It says it'll be in a marquee – so no chance to stray from the crowd.

'I'm not doing a show that week,' he said. 'We could go shopping for outfits again. And . . .' he leaned in towards me, 'you never know who's going to be there.'

I knew what he was getting at. The last time I went Sean was there – with Susannah. I remember seeing them dancing together, she hopelessly drunk, he looking over her shoulder, clearly embarrassed and desperate to get away, trying to make eye contact with anyone who could help.

But Susannah wasn't going to be there this year. Or any other year. I looked at who the band was to be: Insanity, a Madness tribute band. I imagined Sean and I ripping up the dancefloor to 'Wings of a Dove', or 'Our House'. Would that be easy to dance to?

Gareth zoomed off on another of his adventures. It took him some time, but it was worth it because when he did arrive back it was with the news that Sean and all the other lads were indeed going to the summer ball.

'Come on,' he said. 'Let's be the first to book tickets.' And book them we did. The ball was only six weeks away. It didn't seem long, especially when Jayne from the post room said she needed to lose two stone by then to fit into her favourite dress.

Soon, the night was upon us. The venue was huge, with several rooms in which to lose the people you came here with. We were amongst the first busloads and as we entered the main tent, I could see immediately that this was not the tent Sean was in. The room was set out as if for a wedding reception, with tables on which we were to eat our meals and a dance floor towards the stage.

I collected my complimentary drink at the bar and set about exploring the venue. It wasn't as big as I had first thought: just the main marquee, a second smaller marquee with a bucking bronco and various other games, and a third marquee playing different music to the main room. I bought a bottle of wine and took one glass. The complimentary drink had been a mere mouthful, so I filled my glass to the top. I hardly noticed the first glass going down, but halfway through the second I began to get that little buzz, my hips began to swing in time to the music, the world blurred at the edges, I felt the urge to drink more.

In this third marquee I found Sean at the bar with The Lads, laughing like hyenas. They had the air of folk who had been drinking for quite some time before they arrived here. There was an addition to their gang, a bloke from the department at the other end of the floor we worked on. I didn't know they all knew each other.

The group headed towards the main tent and I followed them. It was filling up in there and I realised most of the people were strangers. Weaving my way through them, eventually I came across Gareth and his merry band of friends.

'Got a thirst on, Julie?' he asked, and I noticed my glass was almost empty and the room around me seemed distant.

They set out the buffet and Gareth grabbed my hand and pulled me towards it, advising me to get some down my neck to – his phrase – 'soak up the alcohol'.

I did as he bid and not long afterwards, I was fresh as a daisy again.

As the others finished their food, I scanned the room for Sean. The tables were large, the places were not set and there were seats free at ours, so this would have been an ideal time for him to make his way over to me. After all, Gareth was right beside me, he would have been the perfect cover if prying eyes had tried to pry. But, I remembered, Sean probably didn't know Gareth was our ally, that he was helping bring us together.

I rose and started making my way round the wall of the tent; the room was packed with more people than I knew existed. If Sean had not yet found me, it could well be because he simply couldn't. Yet, like a beacon at the top of the room, unmissable in its neon glow, was the bar.

Great minds think alike, or was it just that Sean had the sense to realise what I hadn't – if he waited long enough at the bar, eventually I would have to appear!

I swayed seductively up to his group and stood among them. I smiled.

'Hi, Julie,' I heard Mike say.

'Hi, Julie,' Dave said.

'Hey, Jools,' Sean said, not surprisingly, more casual and intimate than the rest.

'Who's this?' the bloke from the other department asked.

'This is Jools,' Sean said. 'She's the admin bird in our department.'

'Hi, Jools,' the bloke said.

'Julie,' I said.

'You getting enough to drink, Jools?' Mike asked me. I looked at him blankly. Was he offering me a drink?

'Are you going to be allowed on the shuttle home?' Dave asked.

'There'll be loads like her, it'll be alright,' said Sean, ever the gentleman, although I hadn't quite understood the question.

'Oh, are you the one who always smells of alcohol?' the bloke asked, as if he'd had a sudden realisation.

'Steady!' Sean yelped.

'Well, is she?'

'No,' I said. 'I'm very clean.'

'Yeah, but my uncle was an alcoholic and it's—'

Sean cut him off with a 'Mate!' but he seemed to be more amused than annoyed: I could see, as before, that he was a fair way down the barrel himself which probably explained why he didn't stage a stauncher defence. A moment later they staggered away from the group, before the bloke abruptly changed direction and headed for the dance floor.

As I turned myself, I caught my stiletto in an uneven patch in the flooring and staggered backwards. Mike pushed me back upwards with a 'whey-hey!' He steered me towards an empty seat and Dave brought me a pint of water. They recommended I sit quietly for a while and headed off together. Suddenly I was desperate for the loo.

Coming out, having successfully cleaned the last remnants of vomit from my dress and rinsed my mouth, with my head clear and my stomach settled, the first person I ran into was Gareth.

I thought I'd been feeling alright, but for some reason, the sight of him brought the heightened emotions of the evening to a head: I burst into tears.

'What's happened?' Gareth asked, ever in the mood for a drama, but I couldn't really explain. It was all just becoming too much. Gareth looked thoughtful.

'I think this has gone on long enough,' he said. 'I think you should tell Sean how you feel. I know it's not easy, but faint heart never won fair gentleman. And if he's not going to do it, then who else?'

There was some sense in that.

'But first,' Gareth said, 'a drink.' He led me to the bar and ordered a single shot of tequila for each of us.

Tequila drunk, we went together to look for Sean. 'If he's talking to someone, I'll siphon him off for you,' Gareth assured me.

But as luck would have it, he wasn't talking to anyone. He was sitting by himself, having a breather by the looks of it.

'There you go,' Gareth said, and gave me a shove in the back.

I made my way slowly towards Sean, swaying slightly from the music and the nerves. Sean didn't see me until I was nearly upon him. He looked up, unfocused, probably due to the disco lights glaring in everyone's eyes. It took him a minute to recognise me.

'Oh, hi, Jools,' he said and turned his attention to his phone, shy as ever when a moment of great emotion was upon him. I hesitated for a second. Maybe this loud and busy room full of drunken revellers wasn't the best place for one of the most important moments of our life. Then I realised, I was only making excuses, looking for reasons to allow myself to be cowardly.

I knelt down in front of him, a bit like a suitor proposing. He glanced up at me and back to his phone. I was overwhelmed with love for this man who even now was too shy to say what was on his mind. I took his hand in mine. He looked me in the eye; it's instinctive, the way we react to a human touch. I took a deep breath.

'Sean,' I said, 'we've known each other for a long time now . . .'

'Yeah, yeah,' he said. 'I suppose we have. Three or four years probably, which is longer than some of my friends.'

I nodded impatiently, he was spoiling my train of thought. I ploughed on.

'. . . a long time now and I know the depth of our feelings has run both ways while all this time . . .'

Sean was nodding along, still looking at his phone.

'I think that life is short –' Susannah could have told him that '– and happiness can be fleeting and now that we're both free, it's time to declare our true feelings!'

'Sean,' I said, ready to spell it out. 'I love you. I always have done, I always will.'

He looked at me, his eyes bleary with the emotion – I swear I saw tears. He peered at me, his face getting closer to mine, then further away. Eventually he spoke:

'Do you fancy a shag?'

Did I?! We hurried, hand in hand, out of the marquee. He began pulling me towards the row of portaloos.

'We'll jump the queue,' he slurred in his haste. 'They won't mind.'

'No, Sean, no! Not there.'

'Where then?' he looked around. Beyond the field were empty factory buildings and sports facilities.

'Call us a taxi,' I said. 'I have a bed at home.'

'How far is it?' he asked.

'Caerphilly.'

'Oh, OK,' he said. 'Shall I ask it to wait and drop me back here afterwards?' Ever the joker! I suggested it would be cheaper to just call another one after and he said he didn't usually take more than two minutes.

Laughing our heads off, we waited for our chariot.

CHAPTER TWENTY-ONE

2009

In my boudoir, Sean couldn't tear his clothes off quickly enough. Shoes, socks, shirt, trousers and pants were discarded to his left and to his right, faster than I could pick them up and fold them neatly on the chair.

He flung the duvet back and sprawled across the mattress, his manhood pointing at the ceiling, his hand covering his eyes. 'Hop on, then, Jools.' He reached towards the bedside cabinet, feeling for the lamp switch and turned it off. 'That's better.'

I hadn't expected him to be shy, but I had other plans. I reached forwards and turned the lamp back on, it threw a gentle glow across the room.

I pressed play on my stereo and the Sex Pistols blasted out. I'd forgotten that was on there. Hurriedly, I turned it off and scrambled around for the Lionel Ritchie I knew was around there somewhere. Failing to find it, I settled for *The Hit Factory: The Best of Stock, Aitken and Waterman*.

To the tones of Pat & Mick, I began to sashay towards the bed, reaching behind me for the zip on my dress.

'Just jump on,' Sean said, peeking out at me from between his fingers. 'I'm losing the will.' He turned the light off again and it may have been for the best as I had to jiggle a bit to get out of my dress, but eventually, all garments were gone. I stumbled slightly against the bed and Sean's hand wrapped around my arm.

He tugged me towards him, I shuffled across and knelt beside him. He pulled my leg over so I was straddling him.

He didn't waste much time. Suddenly, I felt a sensation I hadn't known for some years, a young stud bucking and thrusting inside me. I let out a little squeal. I opened my mouth to declare my undying love, but Sean was muttering something. I leant forward to hear what it was. It sounded like a list of female celebrities, all young, all glamorous.

Belatedly, I remembered the condoms I'd bought ahead of Sean and Susannah's wedding, I leant forwards and down, reaching my hand out for the drawer. He put his hands on my shoulders and pushed me upwards. I felt for the switch for the lamp and turned it back on. Our eyes locked.

'Oh god,' he said. He put his hand over his eyes, just peeking out at me. 'Wilma Flintstone, Wilma Flintstone, Wilma Flintstone! Ooooooh!'

Overcome by the emotion, he pulled himself out from under me, turned over and began to snore.

The next morning, in sync as ever, Sean and I awoke together. Sean's head thrashed to and fro, looking around him. He turned towards me, and his eyes widened.

'Jesus!' he said, sitting up. He swung his legs out of the bed, and I saw his head turn left, then right, left and then right again. He dropped to the floor and crawled around, looking under the bed, under the drawers, under the wardrobe, his movements becoming increasingly frantic. 'Where are my clothes?'

'On the chair,' I told him, moving into the warm space he had left. I patted the mattress beside me and smiled, hoping he would abandon the search for his clothes and return to our cocoon. But he was already half dressed.

'You don't have to rush off,' I told him. 'There's no check-out time here.'

'Got an early start,' he said. 'Got to umm . . . got to . . . going to see the cricket. What time is it, anyway?'

It was just gone five.

'Yeah, it's in London,' he said. 'Got to shoot.'

And before I could tell him there was still an hour to wait for the first train, he was off down the stairs and out the front door.

I floated through the morning. I rose almost as soon as Sean had gone, too wide awake to lie in. At six o'clock, my headache receding and my energy high, I switched on my stereo and turned up the volume for the Madness medley I'd practised my dances to and bopped around the house as I vacuumed. I kept looking at my phone, anticipating the call or text I was sure would soon arrive.

When it didn't come in the first couple of hours, I understood Sean needed to get back to Cardiff and catch his train to London for the cricket. He probably needed to nip home first to change – I doubt he wanted to attend in his finery. He'd be on a tight schedule and he'd have more time once he was aboard the train.

But he didn't call after those first hours and my mood began to flag, until I realised, I didn't *know* he was on a train, I just assumed. He could well be on a coach, a minibus, or merely in a car, subject to the banter and boisterousness of the other cricket fans. It wasn't an atmosphere that leant itself to intimate phone calls.

So, I relaxed, wondering how long it took to travel to London, find the cricket ground and get settled in. Once the match was underway, he'd find a quiet spot and be in touch.

Later I realised it must be a particularly gripping match; he clearly couldn't drag his eyes away from it. I had a look online to see who was playing whom in the cricket that day, but I came away none the wiser. The only match I could find for either Wales or a local county team was just down the road in Sophia Gardens, but that clearly wasn't the one he was attending.

That evening, my spirits started to flag as there was still no word. Had he lost his phone? Had it been stolen? Had he been attacked? Was he in hospital?

Sick with worry, I wandered amongst the shadows of the house as the sun went down, with no heart to switch the lights on. Until I realised – we hadn't exchanged phone numbers! And with all the barking up the wrong tree I'd been doing that day, I'd probably missed all the telepathic thoughts I knew were always toing and froing between us.

I laughed out loud with relief.

After such an auspicious start to the weekend, Sunday turned out to be wet and chilly. The guinea pigs needed cleaning out; they stank if it wasn't done properly. And frequently. When nature calls, guinea pigs just go, wherever they are.

'You're brave.'

'Eh?' I looked around. A man was peering over the fence at me in the spot Bert usually occupied. It took me a moment to recognise Frank, he was dressed for the countryside.

'Out here in this weather,' he said.

I looked at the lawnmower behind him, the electric cable curling through the puddles. 'So are you.'

'But I suppose you don't really get a day off with pets,' he said. 'Quite a commitment. Unless you get a snake. I don't think they need feeding every day.'

I thought about letting a snake loose in my house and shuddered.

'I know,' Frank agreed. 'Soulless animals. It'd eat your gerbils.'

I opened my mouth to say they were guinea pigs but closed it again. I didn't want him taking any further interest in my pets.

'Anyway, I thought I'd get a few jobs done for my parents while they're out,' he said, nodding his head at the lawnmower. 'Some of the chores my dad doesn't like.'

'Is it Father's Day?' I asked.

'No, but they've helped me out a bit recently.' His expression changed as he said that, and he began to back away from the fence. 'Well, I'll leave you to your pet care,' he said, and he vanished from my sight. A moment later I heard the lawnmower start up; he was going to have the devil's own job cutting that soaking wet grass.

But it was true, I was fed up with the hassle of the guinea pigs: there's a lot of work involved and not much in the way of reward.

This pair involved a trip outside twice a day, come rain or shine. All through winter – you can't just batten down the hatches and leave them with supplies until spring. I'm not sure there is a more miserable activity on earth than cleaning out a guinea pig hutch on a freezing winter's day.

Holding them and stroking them became a pretty boring activity pretty quickly, truth be told. And they can last five or six years! I thought of the reality of the situation. I realised: I did not want guinea pigs.

CHAPTER TWENTY-TWO

1973–4

When we had guinea pigs as children, my sister always cried for weeks at their passing. It was the reason my parents refused to get any more pets, not until Angela learnt a bit of grief management.

Angela was older than me by two and a half years. Taller than me. Blonde. Blandly pretty. Noisy and self-absorbed, she was always the one people remembered, always the one they asked about.

It might be hard to believe now, but I was something of an ugly duckling as a young girl. Before my hair turned from mouse to mahogany, before my frame grew from stout to statuesque, before the rest of my face developed to suit my nose. Before all this, people thought of Angela as the pretty one. People referred to her pale, lacklustre hair as golden, her scrawny physique as svelte. They said how bonny she was in her lovely summer dresses. They remarked on how she was always laughing. Of course she was always laughing, she was a half-wit. It was her default setting: she'd laugh at the sun coming up in the morning, she'd laugh at the kettle boiling.

The people who favoured Angela were shallow people, but they were the majority. In fact, they were more than the majority – they were one and all. They were my parents as well.

'You always look so serious,' my mother said when I complained about it. 'Why don't you try smiling now and then.' But when I did it just seemed to make people uncomfortable.

Angela never finished her homework and was never in trouble about it. On the rare occasions I didn't do mine and my parents found out, there was shouting, there was no TV when I got home, there was no ice cream after tea. The homework was done in full view of both parents and checked for completeness. My homework diary was scoured for outstanding tasks and an inquisition held to make sure there was nothing I hadn't jotted down.

'But Angela never does her homework; she laughs about it on the school bus,' I said. 'Angela goes out whenever she wants and I hear her coming in hours after you said she could. Angela's always tired in the morning. Angela's going to fail her O-levels, she laughs about that as well.'

My parents weren't moved.

'Don't you worry about what Angela's doing,' my dad said. 'You just keep your eye on your marks.'

'But what's Angela going to do without so much as a maths O-level? She won't even be able to prove she can count to ten.'

My parents exchanged glances.

'Can she count to ten?' Now that I thought about it, I realised I'd never heard her do so.

'Angela's not as academic as you,' my mother said. 'She'll get her maths and English, then she'll go in a different direction.'

'What direction?' I asked.

'You'll need to get yourself a good job,' my dad said. 'Have a career.'

'Why won't Angela need a job?' I asked. With a sudden thrill, I wondered if she was dying, if there was a secret they'd been keeping from me, wrongly imagining it would break my heart. But no, my mother sighed.

'Julie,' she said, 'Angela's pretty.'

My parents were of an age where getting a good husband was a career goal in itself. Plus, Angela was good at drama, she was a good singer and a good dancer. That's where they really thought she was going, one way or the other, or some kind of hybrid.

'Don't you need your O-levels for drama school?' I asked.

'Julie, give it a rest,' they said.

Whenever my parents had visitors, Angela was always called on to give them a song, maybe a dance or a tune on the piano. Conversation would circle for a while around how talented she was, how bright, how vivacious. What a ray of sunshine.

Conversation directed towards me was along the lines of: 'You must be really proud of Angela, with that lovely voice and hair.' 'Are you going to be her assistant when she's famous?' Or, 'Looks aren't everything, you'll find your calling.'

One thing Angela and I did have in common was a love of painting. From an early age we would both sit for hours with paper and paintbrush.

Predictably, Angela's most used colour was yellow. She painted huge, bright suns and figures with yellow hair, standing on a thin line of green to represent the grass, a line of blue sky above them.

'Charming in their simplicity,' people said about the fact her painting hardly developed from ages five to fifteen, and 'Monetesque' about the lack of precision in her lines. Angela frequently ran out of yellow and helped herself to mine, which, for once, I didn't mind; my need for yellow was very limited.

My artwork was more in-depth. While Angela splashed out vapid representations of our garden, the park, the Peak District, wherever – they all looked the same – I painted from the imagination, my own interpretations of the world around me. I expressed myself in hues of black and deep blue, with magical and mythical creatures climbing out from abysses, eating people who, coincidently, looked like my family, their friends, our neighbours, my classmates and so on.

At the end of a session, I would stand back and compare and contrast our styles. They were certainly both messages to the world, Angela's: 'Hey, look at me, exciting as a glass of water.' Mine told of intensity and secrets.

Yet, it was Angela's work that went up on the wall. 'It just fits better with the décor,' my mother said. She picked up a particularly powerful piece I'd created just that morning. 'We can't really have that out on display. Paint the garden, or a dog or something. Paint a portrait of Angela.'

So I did. But it was a portrait of the real Angela, I drew her shoulders and neck, wearing her favourite blouse and cardigan and on top of them I added a big round head, with yellow hair that she might have painted herself and a blank, empty face. By that, I mean just an empty circle: I used the outside to represent what was on the inside. Angela cried when she saw it and I admit, getting her to pose for hours had been a waste of time.

'Do you think we should speak to the school?' I heard my mother ask my dad. That was a good idea, the art teachers would understand the meaning in my work, maybe I could have an exhibition in the school hall.

The exhibition never came, I don't believe they even spoke to the school, so no one ever heard the impetus behind my paintings, how infuriating I found my family and everyone else around me. How Angela could never do anything wrong and I could never do anything anyone even noticed.

I raged at the injustices.

CHAPTER TWENTY-THREE

1973–4

When you're a child, or a teenager, you think life will be as it is forever. It's impossible to imagine a time when the tables will be turned, fortunes reversed. The ugly ducklings, the misfits, the misunderstood, all tramp through their childhoods, surviving day to day, not realising that this is such a fleeting time, soon to be forever forgotten, left behind by whatever we metamorphosise into.

Eventually, I metamorphosised into a very different creature. A creature that was wolf-whistled and catcalled – from a distance – and propositioned by strange men on trains; in short, a veritable sex siren.

But all that was still ahead of me when Angela met Billy. She was a member of the local amateur dramatics group. Of course, she always had a part, always something good. When I went along they were doing *Charlie and the Chocolate Factory* and they made me Oompa Loompa Twelve. Angela, needless to say, gathered her lank, 'golden' hair into a cap and trod the boards as Charlie. Billy was Willy Wonka.

Billy always had all the newest clothes, stylishly cut hair, all the recent single releases and many of the albums. He came round to our house on a brand-new Chopper, then later a moped. He seemed so sophisticated, you didn't notice at first his huge forehead and long chin, and his incredibly narrow face that made him look like his head had had a good squeeze at a crucial moment of development. Yet, if the ever-sought-after Angela thought he was a good catch, then I was happy to assume he was a good catch.

She and Billy first met as Nellie and Emile in *South Pacific*, and life imitated art. He started coming round to our house to practise and over the course of the summer holidays I could hear them belting out 'Happy Talk' at all hours of the day, even though that wasn't one of their songs. Then it went mysteriously quiet, until one day I heard my mother heading up the stairs and moments later a shout, the like of which I had never heard from her before. Followed by more shouting. Then I heard someone running downstairs, the front door slammed and through the lounge window I saw Billy, running down the drive, trying to put his trousers on as he did so.

Yet Angela was still in *South Pacific* and she was still seeing Billy at rehearsals, and as the weeks went by, my parents began to thaw. Especially when they learnt he lived on the new estate on the other side of town where everyone was a doctor, a lawyer, a headteacher or similar. So Billy was invited round for tea where, over time, we were all charmed by him. But he was never again allowed upstairs, although many would say that was shutting the door after the horse had bolted.

The moment I fell for him was when he winked as he handed me a plate of biscuits. An intimate, conspiratorial wink that said, 'this biscuit-eating is just between you and me.' I knew then that Angela was not the sister for him.

There was no winking at her, no handing over biscuits, no looking at her curiously when he thought her attention was elsewhere. It was me he really wanted.

After all, I was the sister of substance, not the vapid, air-brained thing Angela was. These visits to our house, this courting of the older daughter, was only a way to get to the younger one. In all my childhood stories of castles and princesses, it was always the youngest the hero wanted, even when betrothed to the eldest. With that wink he said it all: he and I were destined to be together.

That night, as I waited for sleep to come, I thought of him, wondering for how long he had been trying to get my attention, trying to get me to notice him. He'd been hanging around with Angela on and off for a good six months now. Had he been smitten from the start, or had the revelation dawned slowly on him?

I preferred the idea that it had been me he wanted from the outset, I didn't like to think he may actually have had feelings for Angela. Even better, maybe he had loved me from afar and seen Angela as a way into the family.

Yet even then, at the age of fourteen, I was something of a realist. Where would he have come across me, if not for Angela?

He would have had to have seen me close up to appreciate my dark, intense eyes and the endearing expression I held when I was thinking hard. He would have had to get to know me to appreciate my inciteful comments, my rapier wit.

But how was our union going to come about? It was not going to go down well if we suddenly declared our love around the tea table. He was a couple of years older than Angela and our parents had already had their concerns about that, they were not going to sanction a man of nearly nineteen ditching their 16-year-old daughter for their 14-year-old one. It seemed likely that when we did get together, we would have to keep it secret for quite some time.

That night, waiting for sleep, I imagined Angela falling off a tall building; Angela floating out to sea on a Li-lo; Angela being trampled by stampeding buffalo. And Billy and I comforting each other, before putting the whole thing behind us, buying a house, and living happily ever after.

*   *   *

In the end Angela stuck around – as Billy's ball and chain – for quite some time. She turned seventeen. Billy turned nineteen. I turned fifteen. On my fifteenth birthday she bought me something I'd never heard of before: a set of worry dolls. Six tiny little dolls in a small wooden box.

'Whenever you're worried about something,' she told me, 'just take them out, one at a time, and tell them your cares. They will make them all fly away.'

'Do I look worried?' I asked her. She shrugged.

'Not necessarily for now, for any time in the future. Everyone is worried sometimes. Aren't they?'

I was dubious. This had no basis in any of the science we'd learnt at school. Still, the deep-seated, prehistoric, Sunday School part of me was drawn to them.

We had a tea party for my birthday – me, Angela, my parents and Billy. Billy took a photo of us with the Polaroid – strictly for birthdays and Christmases only. After it was all over, I took the dolls upstairs and tipped them out on my bed. They were all girls.

I picked up the prettiest one first. I named her Serena, my favourite name for a girl. Then down the line: Maria, Kate, Lucy, Diana and finally Angela. I took a pin from my sewing kit and stabbed it five times through Angela's heart.

I whispered to each one of them 'Give me Billy' and then I put them back in their box and into the cupboard in my bedside cabinet.

The worry dolls may or may not have supernatural powers, but they are not fast workers, I reflected a few days later, as Angela remained unaffected.

I wondered if Billy were as tortured as me. Was he lying awake at night wondering how long he'd have to carry on the pretence? He must be planning an announcement on the day I turned sixteen, I realised. He must be counting the days until then – there were quite a few – when it would be safe to declare our love.

It was surprising, though, how no one else noticed and to add to the confusion, Angela and Billy were talking about going on holiday together. My parents had vetoed the idea for the time being, but Angela would be eighteen the following year and they accepted that they were powerless to stop them then. Instead, the four of us, the family, were going on holiday for what may be the last time. We were taking the car ferry for a fortnight's camping in France.

Summer term came to an end and our trip to France approached. A foreign holiday was a once-in-a-decade event in our family. Angela and I had only been abroad on one former occasion and the sight of my dad unfolding and frustratedly trying to re-fold maps gave us a taste of what was surely to come.

Holidays always began on a Saturday for us. With *Family Favourites* blasting out of the radio, my mother ran around the house, manically packing last-minute items.

As she ran, she shouted out orders: 'Angela, make sure the windows are closed; Julie, check the swimming costumes are packed,' before checking herself that we'd done it correctly. She reminded my dad any number of times that we needed to leave time to get petrol.

Angela and I went out to the car first. I had an open bottle of apple juice, and I dropped it as I was shuffling over Angela's seat to my usual spot.

'Julie! For god's sake!' Angela shouted. 'I'm not sitting there now!'

I reached for a tissue from the box on the back window and wiped it over the spilt juice. 'There you go.'

'It will still be sticky. It will get on my clothes. I'm not sitting there.'

Magnanimously, I moved to let her sit where I had been and took her seat myself. In that way, the first argument of the holiday was averted.

But not for long. In the days before air conditioning, we roasted under the sun as we drove along, until someone wound a window down and someone else found that too chilly and the starter argument ensued.

We got as far as Watford, which was quite some way, before it emerged that one of the tasks my dad had been given was packing the sunscreen my mother had left in the kitchen. He denied all knowledge of having been asked, but she distinctly remembered asking him to fetch it, so that was the end of the discussion. It was expensive stuff, and my mother did not want to have to buy new ones once we arrived.

'They always bump the prices up at these places,' she said. 'They know they've got a captive audience.'

'Well, you asked me to remember so many things, something was bound to slip the net,' my dad said.

'Why didn't you write it down? Would that have been so difficult?'

'Can you pipe down now, please, Rosemary?' my dad said. 'This is a really tricky junction and I need to concentrate.'

'I'm only saying that it was a simple request, I would've thought you could get that one thing right.'

'You should've made yourself clearer. You were giving orders all over the place, how was anyone meant to know what they were doing? Oh, look at that! You've made me miss my chance.'

The cars behind us were tooting impatiently.

'All I'm saying is . . .'

'I know what you're saying!'

With his head turned to the right, but not looking to the left – not looking towards my mother – my dad pulled out. There was a screech of brakes, a scream, the smashing of glass and crunching of metal. A lorry had been ploughing along on the wrong side of the road, manned by – we learnt later – a drunken driver. It hit the back half of the car, seriously injuring Angela.

She lingered a few days in the ICU and that was where I had my first taste of critical care. I watched the nurse; a check here, an adjustment there; one wrong move – or one right move, depending on your point of view – could send someone on their merry way.

I watched the machines keeping Angela alive and thought of the damage I could do with a flick of a switch.

Then the doctors pronounced her brain dead and for some reason my parents didn't bother telling them that was normal for Angela. No, they just stood there and watched them turn the power off. Not literally. I imagined my mother saying, 'Do you want to pull the plug out, Julie?'

Ironically, the campsite we had booked had floods of unseasonable rain over the following two weeks, so we wouldn't have needed the sunscreen anyway.

Back at the house, I overheard them talking:

'Didn't Angela and Julie usually sit the other way round in the car?' my dad asked.

'I wonder what made them swap. On that day of all days.'

'Hmmm.'

I'd always known Angela was the favourite, but to hear it spelt out was something of a shock. I was never really able to look at them in the same way again and I wondered who else was having the same thoughts.

Days later I took out my worry dolls, forgotten for some time until now. I dug Angela out and stared curiously at her with the pin rammed right through. Coincidence? I took the pin out and put her back in the box. Of all the times I'd daydreamed Angela dead, I had never really expected it to actually happen. It was a long time before I consulted the worry dolls again.

Dear Billy was heartbroken, or so he said when he came round to pay his respects. Then he came round after the funeral. Then he came round again and again and again. My parents were saying he really wasn't getting over it very well, but I knew there was a different reason.

I'd come home from school sometimes in the afternoons to find him sitting in the lounge with my mother, face streaked with tears, talking about how he'd had his life mapped out and didn't know how to cope, now that it had been snatched away. My mother would sit, slightly uncomfortable amongst the teacups and tissues, listening politely, waiting for a break in the monologue.

Eventually, Billy would look up and ask, 'Can I see her room?'

To which my mother would say 'I suppose so' and would lead the way to Angela's room, where they would both stand in the doorway and survey the David Bowie posters vying for space with Marc Bolan, the double denim left where it had been dropped across the bed and the *Teen* and *Jackie* magazines in a fallen tower across the floor.

'Can I sit in here alone?' Billy would ask and my mother would hum and haw and decline.

'It doesn't seem right,' she'd say. 'Not since I had to ask you to leave that time.'

'You're not thinking of changing it?' he asked.

My mother tipped her head to the side. 'Hadn't thought about it.'

'Please don't,' Billy said, a hint of desperation in his voice.

'What would we change it to?'

Whenever I arrived home to find Billy visiting, I'd sit myself down on the sofa, a cushion or so's distance away, and feel the electricity between us, even as he pretended to grieve for Angela. Now and then he would glance over at me, and I knew I had not been mistaken, it was me he was really coming to see.

If I felt brave enough, if I thought my mother wouldn't notice, I'd shuffle myself a few inches nearer. But I needn't have worried, my mother obviously suspected nothing, or if she did suspect, was all in favour of it, because she began collecting up the teacups and saying, 'Oh Julie's here now, she'll keep you company for a while.' Then disappearing into the kitchen, not to be seen again until he'd left.

When she was out of the room, I'd inch a little nearer.

'I can't live without her, Julie,' he said. I was a bit surprised, we were on our own, he could be honest now. I waited for him to go on. 'I thought we were going to be together forever.'

I breathed a sigh of relief, now he was talking about us. But I wasn't sure what to say. Should I tell him that, yes, we were going to be together forever, or should I keep it more casual, play it cool? Maybe even play hard to get? I'd heard that mentioned in the magazines Angela used to leave lying around. It was a conundrum: I didn't have much experience in these matters.

'It will all be fine,' I said tentatively.

'Will you show me her room?' he asked.

'Hasn't my mum already shown you it?'

'I need to see it again.'

We made the pilgrimage upstairs and as before stood in the doorway, surveying the chaos.

Billy brought his hands to his face and bit back tears. 'Can you leave me for a bit?'

'Hmmm . . .' I knew my mother had said no and I didn't make the rules in that house, I was merely the recipient of punishment when they were broken. 'I don't think my parents will allow it.'

'You could stand outside,' he suggested, 'keep watch.'

If we were caught that would be worse than me going downstairs and leaving him to it. It would make me complicit. I shook my head. 'Maybe another time.'

'Tomorrow?'

'I was thinking a year or so.'

'A year?'

'Maybe not a year. But not soon.'

Billy's shoulders slumped and for a moment I nearly relented.

Then he trotted back downstairs muttering, 'Have to think of something else,' and in the wake of that non-sequitur, I followed him.

The next day when I returned home from school, there he was, as ever, a thorn amongst the rose-print chintz.

This time, when my mother departed with a 'Julie's here now,' he reached down to his rucksack and took out an orange squash bottle which seemed to be filled with water. 'Do you want a swig of this?'

He glugged back a mouthful and offered it to me. Well, we had more water than we could drink in the taps, and he would have been welcome to a glass if he'd asked, so, no, on the face of it I did not want a swig of that. But I understood, he was not asking if I was thirsty. This was the first step on the road of our new relationship.

So, I nodded and took the bottle from him, ensuring maximum hand-to-hand contact as I did so. I took it in a slow, sensual way and maintained eye contact as I lifted the bottle to my lips, tipped it back and drank in a long draft. I just had time to notice his eyes widen in surprise before I spat the drink across the room, gagging and coughing back up what had gone down my throat.

'You don't like vodka?' he asked.

CHAPTER TWENTY-FOUR

1975–6

Apparently, Angela had very much liked vodka. It had been a ritual of theirs to take a shot before they did anything else, every time they met.

Billy told me this as we mopped the lounge floor. He said it was a relief to get it out in the open. He said he felt the need to talk about Angela all the time, but the subject matter of this, one of the most secret parts of their relationship, was not something he could broach with my parents. I suspected it wasn't the only part he couldn't broach.

He offered me the bottle again.

I had never really been a rule-breaker before. Rules and I had lived largely parallel lives: my day-to-day activities had been uncontroversial and I was rarely in trouble. But now I was nearly grown up and it was time to take rules on head-to-head. I unscrewed the cap, sniffed the top briefly – because vodka is not an odourless drink – then I took a mouthful and swallowed.

For the second time, Billy looked surprised. He watched in fascination as I fought against the urge to spew it back out again, as it made its way down my throat and burnt into my stomach. Eventually all was peaceful, other than a slight buzzing in my head. I turned to him and smiled.

'Wow, Julie,' Billy said. 'You drank that like a pro. Is there something you're not telling me?'

'Nothing,' I beamed. He reached over, took the bottle from me and drank. I took it back and slugged another swig. He quaffed some more, and so on and so forth until I couldn't gag down another mouthful and Billy, keeping a weather-eye out for my mother's reappearance, helped me make my unsteady way up to my room. 'This one,' I giggled – suddenly everything was very funny – as he tried to veer off towards Angela's room-slash-shrine.

He put my bin next to my bed and I vaguely remember him saying something about not leaving my room until I was sober, but I didn't know what he was talking about. He was about to leave, saying he'd see me tomorrow, when we heard my dad's footsteps on the stairs. So, we hid until he'd gone into his room, then Billy tiptoed along the landing, pausing by Angela's door, but presumably thinking better of it when he heard the creak of a floorboard in my parents' room.

As he crept downstairs, I retreated to my bed. The last thing I remember was him shouting something to my mother, the sound of the front door closing and swearing under my window; I think he'd tripped over something.

I was asleep when my mother came to tell me tea was ready. When I opened my eyes, the light was like daggers into my brain. My head was hammering.

'I'm not feeling well,' I told her.

'Really?' she said. 'You seemed fine a couple of hours ago.'

'It came on very suddenly.'

I felt pretty queasy as well. I told her that but omitted the great thirst I felt; even in my addled state, I had a feeling that would send her down a road I didn't want her to go down.

She left surprised, but not suspicious, and I lay in bed wondering what had possessed Angela to do this more than once. Eventually I fell asleep in my school uniform.

And that was how I woke up the next morning, my uniform looking exactly as you would expect it to look if you had slept in it. So, with that in mind and the need to make my illness look authentic, I went downstairs, in my pyjamas, and said I felt ill. Which was true.

When Billy came round again a couple of days later, my stomach was settled and my interest was piqued once more. I took the bottle when he held it out and sniffed the top, remembering the taste, wondering how people ever got used to it.

I lifted the bottle to my lips and took the tiniest of sips.

'Have a bit more than that,' Billy said. 'I can't drink it all by myself.' I drank a bit more.

The taste was foul, and it really lingered, but I took another mouthful.

'That's more like it,' Billy said. 'More in the spirit of Angela.' I scowled. I had always been in Angela's shadow: I did not want to continue in the shadow of her ghost.

I think Billy thought I was scowling at the taste. 'It does take a bit of getting used to,' he admitted. Between us we worked our way well down the bottle, our swigs interspersed with tea.

'Listen,' Billy leaned over. 'You're going to have go and eat with your parents as normal, you can't say you're ill and go straight to bed again. They'll know something's going on and that's the last thing we want.'

Our evening meal was a carefully balanced affair. From my point of view at least. When I was called, I walked slowly to the dining room, being sure to walk a straight line down the hall. At the doorway to the dining room, before either parent noticed me, I paused and straightened my posture, I looked at where I was heading and strode a purposeful line towards it, not a stumble in sight, just a slight fumble a moment later when, once seated, I tried to spoon potatoes onto my plate. I soon found it was a job easier done by hand and, suddenly finding myself incredibly hungry, I grabbed the lion's share as my parents watched in bemusement.

As I stood, all the better to spear the chicken, my dad leaned closer and started sniffing the air around me. Straight after tea I retired to my room and immediately fell asleep. When I woke, it was once more to a banging headache and queasy stomach. I closed my eyes and wished for a few more hours' sleep. I thought about claiming illness, but I remembered what Billy had said about arousing their suspicions. There was nothing for it but to go downstairs and act as if nothing was wrong.

My dad was watching me as I took my place at the table that morning. As I poured myself a cup of tea and buttered a slice of toast, he went to the kitchen and brought back a glass of water which he put down in front of me. I couldn't help myself, regardless of my desire to play it cool. I grabbed the water and drank it down in one. He fetched me another which soon became a glass half empty.

'You feeling alright?' he asked. I nodded. 'Nothing wrong with your head?' I shook my head vigorously and it felt as if a thousand nails were rattling behind my eyes. 'Did you have anything to drink last night?' he asked. 'Anything other than tea and water?' I shook my head again, more gently this time. 'So, that great thirst wouldn't be the result of a hangover then, would it?'

I held up my hand in a stop motion. 'No.'

'In that case we should probably get you to a doctor. Rosemary!' he shouted to my mother. 'I think we should get her to a doctor.'

'What, today?' my mother asked.

'Best not to hang around with these things.'

'I don't need a doctor,' I said.

'I'm not sure we should leave that decision to you,' my dad said.

'Really,' I said. 'I'm fine. Maybe if I'm not quite right tomorrow we could think about the doctors.'

'Well,' he said. 'If you're sure.'

That afternoon, when Billy called round he was politely, but firmly, denied entry.

I spent that evening plotting. I knew Billy lived on the top estate. There were a lot of houses there and even if I knocked on every door, it could take me years to find him. But, if that was what I had to do then that was what I would do. I'd start on Saturday morning.

Satisfied with my decision, sleep finally began to overtake me, but just as I was nearly gone, I was frightened out of my skin by a tapping at the window. My first thought was that it was Angela, come in revenge, but I realised quickly that was just the sleep talking. In fact, I wondered if I'd dreamt the tapping as well, but then it came again.

I stood up and pulled back the curtain. There was Billy, standing in the front garden, holding a long stick tied to another long stick. He was waving it at the window, preparing for a third tap. I opened the window. The previous year in English we had studied *Romeo and Juliet,* and this was every bit as good as the balcony scene. Better, really, because Billy was a real-life, stunningly gorgeous man and Romeo was a self-obsessed, rather stupid boy.

Billy was mouthing something at me, but I couldn't make out a word. I whispered, 'I can't hear you.' He hissed something in reply, but I didn't know what it was. We went back and forth like this for a few minutes until I had an idea. I took a pen and a piece of paper and I wrote: 'I can't hear you. What did you say?' I shoved it into a pair of tights, weighted it with a paperweight and lowered it down to him, along with the pen and some more paper.

He wrote back, 'Your mum wouldn't let me in today. Do they know? What did they say?' He shoved it into the tights and slung it up.

'They didn't really say anything,' I wrote.

'Can you meet me at the rec tomorrow night?' he replied.

'I can come while they're watching *Coronation Street*.'

'See you at the rec at eight then.' And with that he was gone.

After that I lay awake for very different reasons. My first love, my last love, my only love, I thought. Angela had been nothing compared to the place I would take in his life.

I finally fell asleep dreaming of Billy and I running across the rec and out of town to live in a treehouse we would design in the woods beyond.

The following evening, as I heard the music for *Coronation Street* start, I yelled that I was heading out and set off to meet Billy. When I arrived, there he was, sitting on a low-hanging branch of an old oak tree, looking like James Dean. He was the only soul in sight: most teenagers in my town went to the main park to hang out; it had swings and climbing frames for them to vandalise. The rec was only really used for Sunday morning football, after-school sports and now, for our clandestine trysts.

As I neared him, he reached down behind the tree and pulled out an Asda carrier bag. From this he produced a large bottle of cider.

'Thought it would make a change from vodka,' he said. Then he produced a bottle of blackcurrant cordial and some plastic glasses. 'If you prefer it sweeter,' he explained.

Well cider and black was a real revelation. How easily it went down, how sweet on the tongue. After a couple of hours, I didn't even care that I had to pee in the bushes every five minutes. My head started to swim and I needed to lie down. I lay on the grass and closed my eyes.

I felt something over me and when I looked up, Billy was lying beside me, his face just above mine. Without saying a word, he leant down and kissed me gently on the lips. And again, but this time he poked his tongue out and tried to push it between my lips. I resisted, startled.

'Just open your mouth,' he said. To my surprise, he sounded a bit annoyed, so I did what he said and the next thing I knew, I was having my first proper snog.

Things moved pretty quickly after that. We met most nights at the rec. The night after we kissed, Billy put his hand inside my top and a moment later, undid my bra. I wasn't sure and I pushed his hand away, but he just moved it back and said, 'You do like me, don't you?'

'Yes,' I said. 'Of course I do, it's just that . . .'

'You don't want us to stop meeting like this, do you?' he said. Well, no, I didn't.

The next night he put his hand in my knickers and tried to push my legs apart. I wriggled away in shock and he looked hurt and said he'd thought we'd had something special.

I said we did, but no one had ever done that before and he said he'd hoped not, but now that I'd met him this was what was supposed to happen. So, it happened.

The next night he unzipped himself and I admit I was surprised at the size of him. I'd imagined it would be closer to the size of a tampon, considering the logistics of the matter. He made me stroke it until he juddered and sperm, or something, came out. Then he zipped himself up and poured another glass of cider. 'Tomorrow night,' he said, 'wear a skirt.'

I hadn't realised Billy liked to see me in a skirt. He'd never mentioned my clothes before, although I always made an effort for him.

The following night at the rec, wearing my school skirt and after he'd kissed me for a minute, he unzipped himself, pulled my knickers down, climbed on top of me and tried to shove himself in.

I froze. I said I wasn't sure, I didn't think I was ready and he said, 'You're sixteen, aren't you? For god's sake.'

I said 'Yeah, but . . .'

And he said 'You're not frigid, are you? It's really hard to love a frigid girl.'

'No,' I said, 'You just took me by surprise.'

He looked at me, his eyebrows raised, making me feel foolish.

'It isn't quite how I'd imagined my first time,' I said, feeling the need to explain.

'It's up to you,' he said. 'If you don't do it, Sharon Moore will. Do you want me to do it with Sharon Moore instead?'

Well, no, I didn't, whoever she was. So, I made myself unfreeze, but a few minutes later I accidently froze up again and he said, 'Wow, you're really not like your sister,' in a way that made it sound as if I wasn't as good as Angela. So, I made myself unfreeze once more.

I walked home that night wondering if I was going to have a baby.

I was a little tense the next night, but Billy told me if I just relaxed I'd enjoy it and in the end, after a few goes, I did. In fact, he told me I was insatiable.

We'd been meeting like this for a few weeks when Billy entrusted me with a secret.

'I need you to do me a favour,' he whispered one evening. 'It's really important.'

I waited.

'Is your sister's room still the same?' he asked.

'Oh yeah, it'll be decades before they get round to changing that. They've been talking about repainting the garage door for as long as I can remember.'

Billy let out what I can only describe as a sigh of relief. 'Can you go in there and get something for me? Something really important.'

'Why don't you call round and ask for it yourself? Why didn't you—' I didn't finish my sentence. Suddenly it all fell into place: his constant requests to see Angela's room, his wanting to be left alone there, his horror at the idea we might, one day, change it. 'Is this why you always wanted to see her room?' I asked.

He nodded. 'It's really important, but I can't tell anyone except you about it.'

'Did Angela know?'

'Well, it was her room.'

Then he told me to go to her room, to make sure that *no matter what* I was not seen. To go to the end of the bed, put my hand under the mattress and bring out whatever was there. Then to hide it and to bring it to him the next day.

I did what he told me, and I retrieved from under Angela's mattress a bag containing small, dark, chalky, strange-smelling rocks that I now know to be marijuana resin. I also know now that it was of a quantity significantly higher than could be considered personal use. Apparently, Billy and Angela had saved up small pieces they had bought with a view to going into business.

'Oh, Julie, you're a lifesaver!' he proclaimed when I handed it over. Then we celebrated our love under the stars.

A few days later Billy met me, looking very serious.

'I have some sad news,' he said. 'My parents are moving away, quite some way away. They're moving to Scotland.'

'Oh,' I said. 'Why are they moving to Scotland?'

He looked annoyed. 'The scenery, I suppose. Why else?'

'But we have a National Park here.'

'Been there, done that. They're moving to Scotland. And the thing is, I'm going with them.'

I managed not to burst into tears, but I felt my heart break into fifty different pieces. 'Why?' I asked him. 'You're nearly twenty, you don't have to go with them.'

'But I do. My mother's very ill, I can't live a long way away from her. You wouldn't think well of me if I abandoned my poorly mother, would you?'

That made some sense. 'Take me with you!'

He seemed to be caught by surprise by that idea: I could almost describe his reaction as a recoil. 'I couldn't do that,' he said. 'You're in the middle of your A-levels.'

'They have schools in Scotland.'

'They do different exams. You wouldn't stand a chance.'

'I could do it.'

'It wouldn't be fair on you. A different place, different people, different exams. Anyway, how would you get your parents to agree?'

That was a valid point. They were going to have quite a lot of catching up and coming round to do, to get to a point where they were waving me off with Billy and family.

'Look,' he said, 'when you've finished your A-levels you'll be eighteen and Scotland will still be there. You can come and join me then.'

Eighteen seemed a very long time away, but what Billy said was true.

'Write down your address,' I said, finding an old receipt and a pencil in my bag.

'We don't have a permanent address yet,' he said. 'But when we do, I'll write to you.'

'Promise?'

'I promise. Goodbye, Julie.' And I watched him make his way off across the rec and back to the top estate.

I waited for him to write to me, but no letter came. It was clear he couldn't remember my house number, or street name or maybe the postcode. Or his mother had taken a turn for the worse. Or he'd found a new job that was keeping him very busy. Or something. Or something . . .

I assumed that, as soon as he could, he would come back in person, but he must have been very busy helping his parents settle in because he didn't find time.

Yet, it's funny how your subconscious plays tricks on you when you're missing someone. I used to think I saw him when I was walking around town. I'd see a moped in the distance and think it was him. I'd see a boy in a biker jacket sauntering down the high street and have to stop myself calling his name.

One afternoon, I saw across the road, in the window of McDonald's, what must surely have been his doppelganger, if not his twin, with his arm around a girl made very much in the image of Angela: blonde, skinny, laughing like a donkey. Life is full of coincidences. I went home, to my parents' drinks cabinet, and took a shot of vodka in his memory.

CHAPTER TWENTY-FIVE

2009

The rest of the summer came and went without Sean acknowledging our night of passion and his failure to do so left me somewhat befuddled. I spent the first few weeks waiting for him to give me his phone number. He didn't have to make a big performance of it, he didn't have to stand by my desk and say, 'Come on then, Jools, we'd better make it official, let's have your digits.'

He could drop it on my desk on a scrap of paper with the words: 'Sean, the light of your life 07-whatever, whatever, whatever . . .' Or he could put it on an email.

But he didn't. So, I sent him an email with my number on it. No words, just my number. My email signature was below it and my name would appear in the 'From' column in his inbox, so he'd know whose it was. I waited for his reply.

It didn't come.

'Everything alright, Julie?' Gareth asked, when he caught me banging my head against the desk.

I knew he'd understand, but even so, I didn't want to tell him. 'Spreadsheets not working,' I said, and he scampered away, the green bobble on his hoodie bouncing along as he went. Hoodies are in contravention of the dress code, but Gareth always seemed to get away with it.

For the rest of that summer, I watched Sean coming and going. He rarely looked at me and when he did – because we sat at opposite ends of the office and sometimes just looking straight ahead meant looking at me – he quickly looked away.

My forehead was rather sore from bashing my head against the desk and Gareth thought I might be a candidate for a brain scan. 'Might explain a few things,' he said, but it wasn't me who needed their head read.

And then, of course, autumn arrived bringing, along with its promise of bitter weather and a wretched winter, Xanthe.

I watched Sean fall under her vacuous spell and felt despair at how close we had come to admitting our love, only for Sean to lose his nerve and follow the primrose path once more.

After work one afternoon, I took my easel and a warm coat into the garden to while away my cares with some painting. But the Jacksons had their daughter and her family round to visit so it was impossible to concentrate. The kids – not much more than toddlers – were screaming with excitement as they dashed around the garden. Had they never been outdoors before, I wondered?

The daughter noticed me and, as if it were something genetic, leant over the fence and said, 'Evening.'

'Evening,' I replied, through gritted teeth.

'Kids not bothering you too much are they? The thing is that we live in a flat, so they don't get to charge around like this very often.'

Aren't there any parks you could take them to, I wanted to ask. But I smiled and said it was fine.

'Evening.' Bert Jackson stuck his head over the fence. 'Kids aren't bothering you too much, are they?' He held a small child up to the fence in case I didn't know what a kid was.

'No, no,' I said. 'It's fine.' What was bothering me more was the gnarly old man, his grandchild and his daughter peering at me over the fence.

I could hear the shouts of another child in the garden beyond, shouting to Uncle Frank to pass him the ball and I glimpsed Frank's head and shoulders as he zipped past.

'Do you have a rabbit?' the daughter asked, looking at the hutch. 'The kids would love to see it. We can't have rabbits, living in a flat.'

I was about to say they were ill or something when Bert intervened.

'Nah,' Bert told her. 'Them's gerbils.'

'Gerbils, Dad? Gerbils are tiny, you don't keep them in a hutch like that. That's a rabbit hutch.'

'Well, that's what she told me, gerbils.'

'Are you sure, Dad? Are they gerbils?' she asked me.

Frank stuck his head over the fence and there they were, all lined up as see no evil, hear no evil, speak no evil.

'Hello again,' he said. He looked at my easel. 'Oooh! You paint. Wait there.' He ran into the house and returned a moment later with a pad, full of his own sketches.

Where I favoured views of my garden, Frank had a penchant for close-ups of leaves and flowers, the veins of a beech leaf, the wiggly shape of the oak leaf, the centre of a buttercup. Enchanting.

'Do you always paint at home?' he asked me.

'I used to go into town and paint the castle,' I said, realising I hadn't taken my easel and paints out anywhere for a long time.

'I have a few landscapes,' he said, 'I'll bring them with me next time. You can have a look, see what you think. Say, how do you inspire an artist?'

'Well . . .' I said. I'd never been asked that question before. 'I suppose you show them an image they would like to study in more detail and capture on canvas.'

'I'll try again,' Frank said. 'How do you inspire an artist?'

I opened my mouth to try a different answer but he beat me to it.

'Very easel-y!'

I frowned at him, puzzled, until he said it again and I understood. It was another joke! How do you inspire an artist? Very easel-y! I laughed, exhilarated by having understood at first, then at the clever play on words.

Like a raincloud, Bert reappeared. 'There was something I was going to ask you,' he said.

More prying questions, I shouldn't wonder. He continued anyway.

'Do I remember you once saying you used to be a nurse?'

'A student nurse,' I said. 'In the end it wasn't my vocation.'

'Ah, but you had some training, didn't you?'

'Oh yes, I was very close to the end of my course when I realised. To all intents and purposes, I am a trained nurse.' Frank looked rather impressed. I allowed myself a little smile.

'So, can you give an injection?' Bert asked.

'Of course I can!'

'Right. See, Mrs Jackson, she's got some new medication and we're not getting on with it very well. We was wondering if you could . . . if you knew how . . .'

'To give her an injection? Of course I can.'

'Dad, are you sure you should be asking the neighbours that?' Frank butted in.

'It's fine,' I told him. 'I'm a trained nurse.'

The funny thing was that as soon as he mentioned it, I felt the old adrenalin rush, the thrill of being in a hospital, someone's life in your hands . . . When does she need it?'

'Are you free now?'

Mabel Jackson's injections didn't involve the excitement of finding a vein, laying the needle tight against the skin and deftly sliding it in. It was an insulin injection, one you put into a bit of fatty tissue. It takes a bit of getting the hang of, but really, anyone can do it.

Bert and Mabel Jackson, and Frank as well, were considerably impressed though and asked if I'd mind going round again. She needed a stabbing every day and would do on an ongoing basis. It wasn't the high life of intravenous dosing, but it was a pleasure to be back in the saddle in however small a way. I promised to call in every morning before work.

Later, I clicked onto the Facebook for the first time in several days and read, 'Sean O'Flannery is in a relationship with Xanthe Irving'.

What does that mean? I wondered. 'In a relationship'? But the love hearts linking their profile pictures didn't leave much room for misinterpretation.

I pondered it for the rest of the evening and eventually, I'd come to a conclusion: it was time I started staking out my territory. I reopened the Facebook, clicked onto 'update your profile' and typed the news 'Julie Tudor is in a relationship with Sean O'Flannery'.

CHAPTER TWENTY-SIX

2009

That night I couldn't sleep. I thought about Dr Pearson and our ill-fated love. I thought about how different things were with Sean. Dr Pearson had been a mere crush in comparison, and it hadn't taken much for the passion to die. I wondered if either Sean or Xanthe had responded to my Facebook announcement. Especially Xanthe. I was ready for a fight. I checked and they hadn't. I went into the lounge and flicked through the channels on the TV. At half past five I went to get ready for work.

It may have been my imagination, but I thought I detected a strange atmosphere in the office in the days after I announced my relationship status on the Facebook. People seemed to go quiet as I passed by, and I thought I heard whisperings behind me. Very odd, when all they had to say was 'congratulations'. If they knew, that is. With Sean as my only online friend, there were limited opportunities for other people to have seen it. I logged onto my page to see if Sean had shared it, but no. Nor had he commented or 'liked' it.

Even Gareth rolled his eyes when he saw me looking down the office in Sean's direction.

Gareth paused in his work one morning. 'You know, Julie, sometimes you just have to accept it when the one you want is with someone else. You've given it a good go, but it's time to move on.' He went back to the spreadsheets, leaving me to ponder that riddle.

That afternoon, I saw Sean go into a meeting room with Marcus and Ffion. I thought nothing of it at the time, I assumed it was just time for his monthly progress meeting. But my curiosity was aroused slightly when they came out only a few minutes later, looking very serious.

Later that day Marcus took me aside and told me they had arranged a meeting for me with HR.

'That's very kind,' I said, 'but I haven't asked for a meeting with HR.'

'We've asked for a meeting with HR; we, the management. You can bring with you your union rep or any other colleague. It needs to be soon, though.'

I blinked at him. 'Why?'

Marcus bit his lip. 'They'll explain more when we get there.'

I was puzzled. Aside from killing Susannah, my behaviour towards colleagues had been exemplary. And that hadn't been at a work event. 'Can you give me a clue?'

'A Facebook post?' Marcus said, making it sound more like a question than a statement.

I shrugged.

Up in the towers of HR, it all became clear, and I was very glad I'd chosen not to bring a companion. As soon as I sat down, Ffion shoved a piece of paper under my nose. It was a screenshot of the post in which I declared Sean and I were in a relationship. Misty eyed, I smiled up at them.

'Office romances are allowed, aren't they?' I said.

'Yes, but you have to be in one to be making posts like that,' said Ffion. 'Otherwise, you can cause distress to your colleagues and those involved with them.'

'We are in a relationship,' I explained, 'but we've had to keep it very quiet. By necessity.'

'Well, I hate to break it to you, Julie, but he's having it away with Xanthe as well,' Marcus said. 'Very openly. In fact, I don't think there's a person in the office who doesn't know. Including you.'

I smiled tranquilly at them as their words hung in the air. What did I care if they all thought Sean's heart belonged to Xanthe?

'Do you like a drink?' Ffion asked.

'Who doesn't?'

'Would you say you had a problem?' Ffion asked.

'Yes, two hands and only one mouth!'

They didn't laugh, instead they came out with the outrageous allegation that there was always a smell of alcohol in the air around our part of the office. I blamed it on Gareth.

Marcus and Ffion looked at each other, Marcus seemed to have a problem with his lips, but after a moment I realised he was mouthing a word to Ffion. She didn't get it the first time either and we all sat and watched as he mouthed out DE-NI-AL.

'Gareth's on a detox diet,' Marcus said to me, apparently unaware of the little scene he had just caused.

'We can help you,' Ffion said. 'We can help you find a treatment programme.'

I waited for her to go on.

'And when you're not drinking so much, maybe you won't be so prone to fantasies. We can probably find you help with that as well.'

I opened my mouth to explain once again that we were in a relationship. We were the great love story of our time, the only reason they didn't know that was because circumstances had forced us to keep it secret. But they only wanted to hear what they wanted to hear. They only wanted to see what was put right in front of them. They only wanted to listen to one side of the story, so I saved my breath.

'To clarify,' Marcus said, 'we're not taking any formal action at the moment, but we are offering you help to get your drinking and your behaviour under control. Do you want that help?'

I shook my head.

'Very well,' Ffion said. 'I am noting for the record that help was offered and declined. That's your choice to make, but please be aware that if there are any other instances of unacceptable behaviour, we will have no choice but to take action. And change that Facebook post.'

When I opened the Facebook later, I found I had no friends.

That weekend I planned to freshen the straw in the guinea pigs' hutch before I shut them up for the winter. I knew I should tidy up the budgie cage too, but in truth I was thinking about getting rid of him. Since I'd redecorated the previous spring, his blue feathers were clashing with the new colour and he didn't sit properly on his perch anymore. Probably something to do with the way his elongated neck unbalanced him; the lightest of drafts was enough to tip him to the floor of the cage.

I found that since the last time I'd been down to the hutch for maintenance, it had started leaking. Mabel Jackson's fur was all matted around her hind quarters and it was going to need a good trim. Then she'd only have one good side to show the world.

I took her inside and reached for a pair of scissors, but as I chopped, it became apparent the rot had gone deeper than the fur. I cursed myself for doing a bad job in the first place and then not keeping a closer eye on the guinea pigs, especially when we'd had a really wet couple of weeks back at the end of August.

Defeated, I threw her in the bin.

CHAPTER TWENTY-SEVEN

2009

My mind was a million miles away from Frank when he reappeared a few days later, his head over the fence in the Jackson family way, causing me to jump out of my skin and paint a black streak across my lovely pink roses.

'Good to see you're still painting,' he said.

'It relaxes me,' I told him.

He nodded. 'Creativity is a great release; everyone should do something.' He raised his hand and produced a sketch pad. Inside were sketches he'd made and small watercolours he'd painted of landscapes. He seemed to have painted most of South Wales, most notable among them were landscapes featuring Raglan Castle, both as the subject in the foreground, and as a detail in the distance, plus Coity Castle and village.

Without an excuse to get rid of him, I took the sketch pad and flicked through it, but I soon found myself engrossed. They were very good indeed.

'You've really made use of the light here,' I said, gazing at a winter scene of Castell Coch.

'It's like that at about three o'clock in December,' he said. 'I could show you if . . .' He tailed off. 'I mean, if you wanted to paint like that, later in the year.'

I considered. It seemed a strange idea, but I found myself wanting to say yes.

'Or we could go into town and paint Caerphilly Castle. We could draw the same view and compare our results. I'd very much enjoy it, if I can be frank,' he said. 'Geddit?'

I didn't at first, but when he explained that 'be frank' was a pun on his name, I realised it really was rather clever. In fact, I was still giggling about it as I brushed my teeth that night.

'I could do, I suppose,' I said.

'Is it a date then?'

I was unsure of how to answer that. Sean was the only person I could go on a romantic date with.

'Saturday 27th,' I said in the end, just to be clear as to exactly the kind of date I meant.

Frank smiled and nodded. 'Saturday 27th.' Then he gave me his phone number, for reasons I did not understand.

We took Frank's car the first time we went to paint Caerphilly Castle, and we were lucky enough to get a parking spot by the Tourist Information building.

'It's a flippin' miracle!' he said as he turned the engine off. There were empty spaces in the car park all around us, so I wasn't sure I was in full agreement with that, but I liked the way it seemed to make Frank very happy.

We took our kit and settled ourselves with a view of the tilting tower, and there we sat in what I believe to be a companionable silence for the best part of an hour. There were times I was so engrossed in my painting I almost forgot I was in company, and there were moments I was fully aware of Frank by my side and our mutual endeavours. Yet, for the whole time it was as if we were in our own little bubble and the world around us hardly existed.

But in the end, it was rather chilly that day and reality made itself known through our cold fingers. Frank suggested we went over the road for a hot drink.

I was still trying to bring heat into my frozen fingers when Frank uttered the words. 'So, you used to be a nurse?'

'A student nurse. It wasn't for me in the end,' I said, feeling a little uncomfortable; I didn't want to go into detail. But Frank wasn't interested in hearing about the what ifs.

'What do you do now, then?' he asked.

'I work in admin. I'm the centre of a large compliance department at a major financial institution,' I told him.

He looked impressed.

'What do you do?' I asked him.

'I work in IT. Well, I did. I've had some issues and haven't been working for a while. Some years in fact, but I'm hoping to get back into it soon. I used to train people to use computers. They were usually older people and what I trained ranged from very basic skills – how to turn it on and open and save a document – to coding. It's pretty varied.'

Well, that did sound interesting. 'Tell me more.'

So, he did and by the end of our first meeting I knew that his job had been not nearly as interesting as I had first thought. Still, the time flew by and before we knew it the staff were closing up around us. We agreed to meet again, for painting and maybe coffee.

CHAPTER TWENTY-EIGHT

2009–10

After my success in poisoning Susannah, I eventually decided to put paid to Xanthe with a drink-spiking incident at the departmental Christmas do, which I was hoping would retrospectively turn out to also be Xanthe's leaving do.

In preparation, that afternoon I had taken an old glass from the back of my cupboard and smashed it. Then I put some of the fragments into my pestle and mortar, where I crushed them into smaller pieces. Then I set to work pulverising them to a powder.

It took some doing, I can tell you. After the first half hour I knew I was going to have stiff arms the next morning. Eventually, there it was, a small bowl full of a white powder that looked like sugar. And also, like salt. And also, like something you can be arrested for carrying – wouldn't they be surprised when they got the test results!

All that remained to do before I went to get ready for the party, was to decant those crystals into the empty whisky miniature I was using to transport them.

I gently tipped the mortar towards the opening of the bottle. Some of the powder went in, some spilt onto the counter. With my fingers, I swept the spilt powder back into the bowl and then tilted it into my bottle, guiding it towards the opening. Before long, I started to see blood in the powder and felt a stinging sensation in the tips of my fingers.

Damn! Damn! Damn! Damn! Damn! It's very rare I swear, but that really did call for a blasphemy. So focused was I in getting the stuff where I wanted it, I completely forgot it was designed to shred – a promising start in that direction, however.

'Four Sex on the Beaches, please,' I said to the bartender. A quick nod and off he went. A rattle here, a shake there, a shot of pre-mixed spirits and an ocean of orange juice – nobody really gets drunk on happy-hour cocktails.

With the drinks balanced on a tray and the pub packed, I walked the long way back to our niche. Hidden behind a pillar, I put the tray down on an unguarded table, checked that no one was watching and that there was no CCTV in sight. Satisfied, I undid the whisky bottle, tipped the contents into one of the cocktails – being very careful to keep my eye on which it was – and gave it a good stir with the straw.

'Merry Christmas!' I said, plonking the tray down. I made sure to hand the drinks out myself. Xanthe gave me a rather false smile as I handed hers over. Earlier that week Gareth had waited until Xanthe came to use the printer near our desks, then said:

'Xanthe, Julie, I want to speak to you both.'

I believe we each wondered what he could possibly have to say that would interest both of us, and that lured us in.

He continued. 'As you know, on Friday it will be the department-mental Christmas party and everyone is going. That means you will be in close proximity to each other, and we don't want any fights breaking out.'

We looked at each other with hostility.

'I have no intention of fighting,' I said. After all, I knew I had no need to fight.

'Wouldn't waste my energy,' Xanthe said.

'Excellent,' Gareth smiled like a wise old owl. 'Julie, you had a moment of madness on Facebook. It could happen to anyone, but I think you should apologise to Xanthe. Xanthe, you've . . . you've . . .'

I waited for him to say, 'You've stolen Julie's soulmate and partner for life,' but he didn't. He said, 'Xanthe, it would just be nice if you could be friends. If only for Christmas.'

'I'm not going to cause any scenes,' Xanthe said and walked off. She clearly felt, as I did, that no apology was needed.

'Well,' Gareth said, as we watched her sit down at her desk, 'I think we can draw a line under it all.'

But only someone as ungrudging as Gareth could think that would really be the end of the matter.

I slurped my cocktail confidently through my straw and watched as Xanthe did the same, her over-sized eyes focused on her drink. I had a sudden loss of confidence when I pictured the glass cutting, not Xanthe, but the straw, and all being revealed with no harm done to the intended victim. But soon she was done with the drink and was necking back the ice as if there was no tomorrow. Which, for her, there probably wasn't.

'Oooh!' Xanthe said, putting her hand up to her throat.

'You OK?' Sean asked her.

'Just swallowed a sharp bit of ice,' she told him. 'It'll be alright in a minute.' Sean nodded and returned to his conversation with Mike. Xanthe didn't say anything else, but she kept her hand on her throat and looked to be in some discomfort. I watched surreptitiously, but eagerly, waiting for her to fall to the floor, foaming up blood. We would all stand around, horrified as she started to convulse and someone would shout 'Call an ambulance!' With my medical training I would make a show of helping her, but it would all be in vain: the recovery position is no match for a shredded oesophagus.

But after a couple of minutes her expression returned to normal, she finished the rest of her ice and asked who was next to the bar.

Gareth grabbed my arm and pointed at a man on the other side of the room. 'He looks nice,' he said. 'Shall we go and talk to him?'

He'd been doing it all evening, trying to find random men I might like to be romantically involved with.

'You go if you want,' I told him, I didn't want to miss the drama and I didn't want to talk to any of the men he'd picked out. It was really rather annoying.

Gareth hmphed. 'You have to make an effort, Julie. I'm trying to help you here.' I looked across the table at Sean. 'That's not going to happen,' Gareth said. 'You have to get over it.'

A frosty silence descended between us. He was becoming unreasonable where the subject of Sean and I was concerned. I turned my eager attention to Xanthe.

But Xanthe lasted the whole night. She drank more. More than I could have imagined a girl her size *could* drink. She danced, she laughed, she kissed Sean. She didn't eat much; I saw her grimacing as a chip went down, then putting the rest of her food aside and reaching for her cocktail.

She outlasted me: I got a taxi home shortly after two, she was still on the dance floor, looking as if she would never stop.

Back at home, I opened up my laptop and typed in 'death by swallowing glass'. It turns out that it's very rare to die from swallowing glass. Small bits, that is. In fact, your chances of surviving unscathed are very high indeed. To put it another way: it's about as dangerous as swallowing chewing gum.

I screamed. I cursed myself. I threw my laptop against the wall and the keyboard came away from the monitor. All week I'd been planning my life post-Xanthe. Starting with the sympathy we'd all be expected to show. The understanding, the patience. I'd even bought steaks in case Sean fancied coming over. Why didn't I google it *before* I risked everything? I went to retrieve my laptop and noticed I'd left a bloody fingerprint on the sofa. I cried myself to sleep.

At the Jacksons' the next morning, they commented that I looked a little green. I was pretty quiet while I poked around the room, trying to locate the medication that never seemed to be in the same place twice. Not for the first time, I was surprised by their cavalier attitude towards Mabel's lifesaving medication. Had they put it in the kitchen? No. The bathroom? No. The sitting room? Apparently not.

'Do you remember where you were when you gave her it yesterday?' Bert Jackson asked me. I'd been in the sitting room, with Mabel in the chair by the window and me standing in front of her, the same as we always were. Bert Jackson had produced the goods from a mystery location, but I hadn't watched what he'd done afterwards.

'Don't you keep it in the fridge?' I asked Bert.

'No,' he told me. 'The doctor said they used to, but now there's no need.'

'At least you'd always know where to look. What did you do after I'd left?'

Bert sat down, looking thoughtful. 'Well, we had a cup of tea, didn't we, Mabel?'

Mabel nodded.

'Then we watched the morning programmes on the telly. A bit of news, then that nice show with all the different presenters – it's all a bit of a muddle, you never know who's in charge, but they look like they're having fun.'

'Yes, yes,' I nodded him along before I ended up with a detailed synopsis of whatever it was they had watched.

'Then we had another cup of tea,' Bert said. 'Did we have a biscuit then?' he asked Mabel, but Mabel shook her head.

'No biscuit,' she said. 'Or did we? Was it yesterday we opened the Bourbons?'

As Bert pondered the question, my mood sank. 'What happened next? When you left the room to get the tea, did you take anything with you?'

Bert gazed thoughtfully into the middle distance. 'Nah, I don't think I took anything.'

'Yes, you did,' Mabel said, and my spirits lifted. 'You took that dishcloth with you.'

'Oh, so I did! We had a little spillage,' Bert explained, 'I brought the dishcloth through. Was it your tea or mine, Mabel, which got tipped?'

I looked for a hard surface to bang my head against. 'What next?'

Bert meandered his way through the rest of the anecdote: a trip to the toilet, another cup of tea, a bite of toast and so on. I was sure he was omitting some small, but vital, piece of information. Whatever that was, no doubt it would blow the case right open, but Bert kept schtum.

It turned up in the end, on that day, in the bedside cabinet in the spare room. How it got there, nobody knew. Maybe Bert should be tested for dementia.

Back at work on Monday all the talk was of the party and how it had turned out alright considering it hadn't even been booked until a fortnight before. Xanthe seemed in particularly high spirits, happy from the weekend and looking forward to the Christmas break ahead of her.

I took the worry dolls into the stairwell and pulled Diana out for a word.

No sooner had I begun to whisper my troubles to her than an excellent idea occurred to me: here we were, seven storeys up. I could simply push Xanthe down the stairs.

Better still, I could tip her over the railings so that she plummeted to the ground.

I imagined her falling, bouncing off the sides of the stairs as she went. Maybe she'd try to grab hold of something as she fell; maybe she'd hit her head on level six and know nothing more. Maybe someone would be walking up the stairs between here and a lower floor and see her passing on her way. If that happened, I'd have to have my wits about me: I'd have to scream 'NO! XANTHE! Don't do it!' and add a 'too late', as she hit the ground.

But how to lure her into the stairwell? No one really went there unless they wanted a bit of privacy for a conversation. I'd need something convincing. But dead girls don't tell tales: my cover story needed a beginning, but it didn't need a middle or an end. I only had to get her there.

I went back to my desk and watched until Xanthe stood up and headed for the toilets. I followed and, checking the hallway was empty, waited in the doorway to the stairwell.

'Hi, Julie,' she said as she came out of the toilets, looking me askance for my strange pose.

'Come and look at this,' I said, ignoring her expression.

'At what?' she said.

'Come and look.'

'At *what*?'

'I think there's a dead body down there,' I said, predicting the future. Her expression changed.

'Shit! We'd better get Marcus. Oh my god! What if it's not dead? Who is it? We'd better raise the alarm!' and she made to head off back to the office. I grabbed her arm.

'Just come and tell me what you think,' I said.

Huffing, she pushed past me into the stairwell.

'Where?' she asked, looking around her.

'Look over the railing.'

She looked. She couldn't see anything. She leaned a bit further over. She still couldn't see anything. She stood on her tiptoes and leaned further still and I looked at her legs and wondered where would be the best place to grab to hoist her over the top.

If I went for her shins, it would be plenty low enough for me to shove her comfortably over the top, but it seemed to leave a lot of her free to bend and fight. Plus it would be hard on my back and I'd had the odd twinge in days gone by, since the time I attacked Felicity Pearson. Xanthe was a scrawny little thing, but she wasn't made of air.

If I grabbed her around the thighs, she would have less wriggle-room, but I would need a good strong heave to get her up and over. I might even need help. I imagined Gareth's face if I asked him to come and help me polish off Xanthe.

'Where?' she was saying. 'Julie, *where?*'

Disappointed, I abandoned the plan, stepped up to the railing and looked over.

'Must've gone,' I said. 'Must've still been alive.'

She stepped away then and, without speaking, left.

CHAPTER TWENTY-NINE

2010

Xanthe survived through Christmas, the New Year and beyond. By March she was set fair to survive to Easter.

One Tuesday evening, towards the end of the month, I was the last to leave the office, as I so often was, having offered to fix a couple of spreadsheets for our neighbouring department. Spreadsheets fixed, I was on my way out of the office when I noticed Xanthe had left her lipstick on her desk.

On impulse, I was going to take it and throw it away, just for the annoyance that would cause, but suddenly I wanted to try it on. I wanted to know what it felt like to be Xanthe. I hurried to the ladies.

Alone in there, I stood in the middle of the large mirror and daubed myself generously. It was very bright, I almost needed sunglasses. I stood back and looked at myself properly. It probably wasn't going to become my usual look, but I definitely wanted to try it with some other outfits. I put it in my bag.

I was about to leave, when I wondered what else she had over there. I went back to her desk and had a look. There was a sports bag underneath the desk, but I ignored that, I was more interested in what she kept in and around her desk. Nothing much on the desktop, just pens and paperclips. I shaped the paperclips into a smiley face. Then I changed it to a sad face. I went back to my own desk and fetched my letter opener. I began trying to jimmy the lock on Xanthe's desk drawer.

Believe it or not, I had never picked a lock before, and it was not as easy as I had imagined it to be. In fact, I really was making rather a mess of it, when a voice behind me said,

'Julie!'

I nearly jumped out of my skin. Xanthe was standing behind me.

I stood up, hiding the letter opener behind my back.

'What are you doing?' Xanthe asked.

'I was looking for something,' I said. 'I lost my . . .' What might I have lost? I stayed with a make-up theme. 'My mascara. I thought I might have dropped it in here.'

I rarely wear mascara and Xanthe knew it.

She looked at me and her eyes narrowed. Her gaze dropped to the desk and back to me.

'Is that my lipstick?'

I shook my head.

'It is,' she said. 'I left it on the desk. Why are you wearing my lipstick? Why are you hacking at my drawers?'

I looked at her in silence, deciding what to say. I'm not good at thinking up lies on the spot.

'What's that behind your back?' she asked.

'Nothing,' I said.

'What is it? It's something of mine, isn't it?'

'It's nothing,' I repeated.

'Show me then,' she said.

'No.'

'*What is it?*' Xanthe hissed. I shrugged. She lurched forward, reaching for it. I whipped the letter opener round from behind my back, and she careened onto it. In under the ribs and up to the organs: medical training never leaves you. She looked down in horror, her big eyes bigger than ever, realising what it was. Well, she wanted to know.

Her face contorted, the forward momentum stopped. I believe

it stabbed her right through the heart; she asked no more questions.

I felt blood on my hand. I let go and she dropped to the floor.

In the distance I could hear the sound of a vacuum cleaner making its way towards us as the cleaners began their shift. Should I come clean and explain it as the accident it was? No, it would be hard to believe someone would impale themselves to that extent and if the truth be told, I had helped it along a little.

Should I leave the cleaners to find the body? Would they be blamed? No, they would not. What would be their motive?

With panic rising, I looked around for a hiding place:

Under her desk? No, she would be seen immediately.

By the coat stand? I could cover her with the coats that always adorned the stand, even when no one was in the office. But the sight of a naked coat stand, with a heap of coats and jackets beneath it, would attract attention nearly as quicky as the under-the-desk option.

In one of the side rooms? A good idea, but there was a high risk the door would be locked and I'd have to ask reception for the key. 'What do you need it for?' they'd ask.

The cleaners were so close, I heard one of them ask, 'How's your Jim getting on at his new job?' I didn't hear the answer, the vacuum was revved up a notch at that point.

I began to panic. I was about to run, to leave Xanthe there and hope I'd be so fast, I would be just a blur to anyone who saw me, when my eyes fell on the stationery cupboard. I rushed to it and had a look inside. It wasn't too full. I shoved a couple of boxes aside and began to drag Xanthe's corpse across the floor.

Goodness me, she was heavier than she looked! I'd been right not to try heaving her over the railings. The sound of the vacuum cleaner was getting louder and louder. Someone was singing.

My heart racing, I piled her in. It was tighter than I expected, but I didn't need to worry about her being comfortable. I closed the door and exhaled my relief as I felt the catch click shut and a warning spasm in my lower back.

The letter opener was still in my hand, so I hurried to the toilets and rinsed it off. Then I poked my head into the corridor to see where the cleaners were. Near the lifts I could see the cleaning trolley, a bottle of bleach standing unguarded on the bottom shelf. Wrapping my sleeve around my hand to avoid fingerprints, I took the bottle.

Back in the toilets, I ran water over the letter opener again until every last trace of blood had vanished, then doused it generously in the bleach and rinsed it again.

When I'd finished, the toilets smelt decidedly bleachy, but holding the letter opener up to my nose, I couldn't detect a thing. I popped my head around the door. The cleaning trolley had moved, but only a little way along the corridor, and it was an easy job to replace the bleach.

I hurried back to my desk, checking for blood on the carpet as I went – just a few small blotches among a million other stains, you'd need to be looking to notice – and put the letter opener in its usual place. I took a last look around and satisfied everything was where it should be, I swung my bag over my shoulder and headed for the door as the sound of the vacuum at its loudest proclaimed the cleaner's imminent arrival.

I marched confidently towards the exit, past Xanthe's desk and – oh my goodness! – there was her handbag, sitting exactly where it had been left in the drama! I couldn't leave it there. If Xanthe's bag was at work in the morning and she wasn't, the hue and cry would be raised immediately.

Although I knew she would be found as soon as someone needed a pen or paper, my instinct told me to put as much time as possible between the event and the unveiling. Time to muddy the waters of what happened and when and who was where.

The sound of the vacuum cleaner was drawing closer. I didn't want to risk re-opening the cupboard and being seen, or worse still, not being able to get it closed again. So, I grabbed Xanthe's impractically tiny bag and hid it inside my own sturdier recep-tacle. The flimsy clasp came undone as I dumped it in, tipping her belongings out, and it may have worked out for the best because it prompted me to turn off her phone when I saw it there.

Satisfied I had everything, I clipped Xanthe's bag back up, but that clasp really was on its last legs. She may as well have been carrying it all around in a teacup. I headed out.

Back in the office the next morning, I was operating purely on adrenalin, waiting for the stationery cupboard to open and the corpse to tumble out. But after an hour, no one had needed stationery. Everything was so normal, it felt strange that no one was rushing to get themselves a notepad, and to see what else they might find in the cupboard. But no one gave it a second glance.

I started to get impatient. Much as I was enjoying the morn-ing without Xanthe, and without any possibility of Xanthe, I wanted to move the narrative on. I thought about going to get something myself, but my desk was always well-stocked with everything I might need. If I were the one to find the body, it could draw unnecessary attention, when there was currently no reason to suspect me. I was both excited and frustrated.

I struggled to drag my gaze away from the cupboard, giddy with anticipation. Then Jayne brought the post over – a good-sized pile that day – and other matters demanded my attention. I lifted the letter opener from its place and applied it to the first envelope.

'Letter for Dave,' I said, putting the letter down on the desk and reaching for the staple remover as Gareth attacked his first envelope. 'Letter opener, Gareth?'

He looked surprised. To be fair, I am normally very stingy about sharing my letter opener. I usually leave him to hack his way through the Basildon Bond with an implement that is not much more than a butter knife. 'Don't mind if I do,' he said, taking it from me and setting-to enthusiastically on a well-stuffed A4.

'I'm desperate for the ladies,' I said. 'Alright if I leave you to it for a minute?'

'Of course,' he said, waving the blade theatrically in the air. 'I can hold the fort.' And he saw off a few imaginary attackers.

Leaving him to get his DNA all over the weapon, I went first to the toilets, where the smell of bleach was almost undetectable. Then I took the scenic route back to my desk, taking in views of gridlocked Newport Road on one side of the building, the prison on the other, the magistrate's court and the streets off into Adamsdown just visible from the far corner.

Back in sight of the desks, a vision assailed me. Sean, Dave and Mike were standing beside Gareth and none other than Sean himself was making some kind of point, tapping the end of the letter opener on the pile of letters, and getting his fingerprints all over it as he did so! Helping me out!

'Morning!' I almost squeaked with the excitement as I took my seat.

'Morning, Julie,' Sean said, putting the opener back on the desk. 'You haven't seen Xanthe on your travels?'

'Not this morning,' I said.

'She's not turned up for work or phoned in sick, and she's not answering when I call her.'

'Oh,' I said. 'Is that bad?'

'Well, it's not like her. And she left a sad face made out of paperclips on her desk, which is worrying.'

'No point worrying over things we can't change,' I said, and Gareth and Sean both gave me a sideways look. 'Meanwhile, we have quite a pile of post to get through.' I offered Gareth the opener and he took it from me, returning to his work as Sean took his phone out of his pocket and went to try to rouse the murder victim once again.

'It's rather worrying about Xanthe, isn't it?' Gareth said when it was just the two of us.

'Is it?' I said. 'I think she's just gone off somewhere.'

'While you were at the loo, Sean was saying Xanthe went to the gym yesterday after work, but when she got there, she realised she'd left her kit here. She was going to come back for it, but she disappeared.'

I nodded, so that explained the sports bag I saw. 'Must've changed her mind,' I said.

'So where would she have gone instead?' Gareth asked. 'She didn't go home, she didn't go to meet anyone. She just vanished.'

'I'm sure she'll turn up,' I said, with absolute certainty.

'Did she make it back here?' he asked. 'Did you see her? What time were you working until? You were still hard at it when I left, and Xanthe had already gone by then. It's only a few minutes to the gym, so it can't have been long between her leaving here and turning around again to come back.'

I didn't like the direction this was going in. I was going to ask him what his point was, but that would have been inviting further speculation, so I just said, 'I didn't see her.'

Gareth was quiet for a few minutes, then, 'If she'd had an accident, you'd think we'd know about it by now. She was in the city centre: someone would have found her.'

I'd always considered Gareth an ally, but I was having doubts now.

'Not if she fell in the river,' I said.

'She wasn't anywhere near the river.'

'She could've headed over that way.'

'But *why*? It doesn't make sense.'

'Maybe she had a breakdown and came over all suicidal.'

'Because she left her gym kit in the office?'

'No, because she's been feeling like that for weeks, or months, or years and that was just what pushed her over the edge.'

Gareth looked at me, his eyes narrowed, and I could tell he wasn't convinced.

'I think Sean should call the police,' he said. 'I'm going to tell him. Are you sure you didn't see her? What time did you say you were working until?'

'I didn't,' I said. 'I didn't see her. I wasn't here all that late. Look, the post is really piling up.'

But instead of helping me with the post, Gareth went off to share his concerns with Sean. For the first time in living memory, he didn't have a smile on his face. Nor did I.

Sean, I believe, did call the police, just for appearances sake. Luckily, he mentioned that her dad had been ill not so long ago and when the police heard that, they were of the same view as me, that she'd just decided the gym was too much trouble that night and had gone off to do something different. So, Sean spent much of the rest of the day making himself look innocent by trying to call Xanthe, while Gareth and I worked on fudging the evidence.

'Ooops, sorry!' I said as I nicked him with the point of my blade, drawing a drop of blood from his arm.

'Watch what you're doing, will you!' he replied, already snappy from our earlier conversation.

Yet still, no one needed any stationery. I wondered if we might eventually be led to her by the smell of decay. I've never smelt it myself, but I've heard the stench is unmistakable and unforgettable.

After the post was dealt with, the spreadsheets got themselves into a right tangle, which took my full attention and I forgot all about Xanthe until the next day when, mid-morning, a blood-curdling scream rent the air, proclaiming the big reveal.

Without even giving us time for a proper look, 999 was dialled and we were evacuated from the building. We waited outside, folk from other offices passing us by, imagining it was just a fire drill. They wouldn't know until they watched the evening news that it was something far more exciting.

It wasn't long though before the police arrived and started wrapping the outside of the building in crime scene tape. Police vans parked up in the driveway and senior managers couldn't get their cars out of the executive car park.

Gareth managed to drag himself away from his friends in our neighbouring department and came to stand with me.

'What time did you say you left the office?' he asked me again.

'Not long after you. What time did you leave the office?'

'About five.'

'There you go then,' I said.

'Who else was there?' he asked.

'I can't remember. Not Xanthe.'

'Did you see her? Because now we know she made it back to the office.'

'No, I didn't see her.'

Gareth looked perplexed. 'It just doesn't make sense,' he said. 'If you didn't see her, where was she between leaving the gym and—' He waved his hands in the air as a finish to his sentence.

To my relief, Marcus came around telling us we could go home once the police had our details, asking if everyone was OK, and that we would be in the offices across the road the next day, while simultaneously telling us we could take a couple of days off if we needed to. I skedaddled, before Gareth could ask me any more questions, hoping he would be one of the colleagues who took this as an opportunity to malinger their way through a couple of Netflix days and that after that, he would have forgotten all about it.

CHAPTER THIRTY

2010

I woke the next morning in a happy mood, Gareth's questions no longer bothering me. After all, the last thing he had said was that he was confused as to how Xanthe could have ended up in the stationery cupboard if I hadn't seen her. He was some way away from suspecting me. I showered, breakfasted, nipped next door to give Mabel her stabbing and polkaed my way to the train.

I alighted, as usual, at Cardiff Queen Street station and almost skipped the short walk to the office. As I neared the entrance, I reached into my bag for my security pass, before remembering, we were working from another office for the foreseeable future! Laughing at my forgetfulness, I made my way over the road to the ornate Victorian building that stood opposite the 1970s concrete block that was our usual home.

Once there, I bopped my way into the office and dropped my bag onto the desk beside Gareth.

'Morning!'

He looked up at me. 'Steady,' he said and returned to his work.

Sitting down, I logged onto my computer. I opened a spreadsheet, tinkered with a formula and hummed a cheerful ditty. The only fly in the ointment was the absence of Sean, but I knew he had to play his part and keep a respectable distance for a while. Yet without Sean, we were missing our early drinks.

'Tea?' I asked Gareth.

He nodded. 'Please.' He reached into his pocket and pulled out his wallet. 'You have to pay for the drinks here.'

My jaw dropped. With the number of drinks we all guzzled in an average day, that was going to get very expensive. In fact, we could all find ourselves running at a loss.

'It's only 5p,' he said.

That was a relief. 'In that case, it's my treat.' I dove into my bag, pulled out my purse and waved goodbye to Gareth as I headed off to find the machines.

I had a good look around as I searched. The building had a lot of what they call 'original features': ornate cornices, sash windows and boarded-up fireplaces, but it was chilly and smelt damp. The grass is not always greener. I was already hoping we'd be back in our concrete eyesore before too long.

As I travelled, I passed a meeting room. Clearly not part of the original interior, it had a glass front, to which large sheets of paper had been stuck from inside the room. They covered the glass from the top, to about calf-height, so all you could see were people's legs going to and fro or sitting at their desks. I crouched down to get a better look. About ten people were milling around the room, most in suits, four in police uniform.

A woman in a suit glanced down and saw me.

'Can I help you?' she asked, opening the door.

'Which department is this?'

'The police department. We've set up a temporary office in here and we'll be taking statements from all of you soon.'

'All of us?'

'All of you.' She frowned at me. 'It's not meant to be fun.'

I went on with my search for drinks, eventually locating the machine at the far end of the building and returned to my desk.

'Found it at last,' I said, putting the drinks down carefully.

As Gareth turned to take his drink from me, desperately thirsty by now, his elbow knocked my bag off the desk, and to my horror, I realised I'd left it wide open. All my possessions spilt out onto the floor.

All my possessions, and one of Xanthe's.

Gareth reached down and picked up a tube of lipstick. He turned it over in his hands. 'Is this yours?' he asked.

I nodded.

'I've never seen you wearing lipstick.' He looked at the label on the bottom. 'Deadly Biteshade? I wouldn't have thought that would suit your complexion.'

I thought he was going to say something else, but he continued to examine the lipstick, turning it over and over in his hands, bringing it close to his eye and squinting. I held my hand out for it and he ignored me.

He took the lid off and held the stick up to the light.

'It looks very much like Xanthe's colour,' he said. Then, 'You did see her.'

Oh, how a mood can change in a moment. Gareth rose, his face full of fury, refusing to make eye contact with me, and made his way towards the police room, lipstick in hand, as my spirits plummeted to the depths of the earth.

I tried to console myself with the thought that no one would be interested in what Gareth had to say about lipstick. But if just one other person said they thought that lipstick was Xanthe's, or agreed Deadly Biteshade was not my colour, questions would be asked.

They'd take it as evidence, they'd do experiments on it and they'd find Xanthe's DNA all over that gaudy little stick. They were never going to believe it was mine.

I resolved to throw the blame back at Gareth – it was his word against mine that it had fallen out of my bag. Who's to say that, having murdered Xanthe, he didn't tuck it away in his own pocket, just waiting to plant it on some unsuspecting bystander? After all, his fingerprints would be all over it. It was tenuous, but it was all I had.

When Gareth returned to his desk, his silence was overwhelming.

The incident with the lipstick seemed to get me bumped up the queue and soon it was my turn to go to the incident room, where a young whippersnapper calling himself DC Dalton asked me questions, overseen by an older woman who was introduced as DS Whittaker.

'Are you nervous, Julie?' DC Dalton asked, as I swayed to and fro, unable to keep completely still. His demeanour was very intense, anyone would be nervous. 'It's nothing to worry about, we're talking to everyone. What time did you leave work last night?'

'A bit after five,' I said. My spirits rose at such a mundane opening. This seemed like something I could cope with.

'Did you know Xanthe well?'

'We're a very close-knit department.'

'Had you ever met her before she came to work here?'

'No.'

'Did you ever see her outside work?'

'I saw her at the Christmas do.'

'Who was she friends with?'

'All of us.'

'Anyone in particular?'

I shrugged my shoulders. 'Dave?'

'Had she had a falling out with anyone?'

'Everyone.'

'Everyone? You just said you were all friends.'

'Yeah, but nobody really liked her, it could've been anyone.' I became aware I was speaking very quickly. The two officers looked at each other. DS Whittaker made a note.

Then she leaned forwards, her expression world-weary, her face was lined, her roots desperately needed doing. She placed Xanthe's lipstick on the table. 'Do you know anything about this?' she asked. It was in a see-through bag, presumably to stop it being contaminated with even more fingerprints.

'That looks like the lipstick Gareth tried to plant on me this morning.'

'He says it's Xanthe's and it fell out of your bag.'

'I say it was in his pocket. Test it, his fingerprints are all over it.' I was calling their bluff, I was desperately hoping his fingerprints would have obliterated mine.

'Why would Gareth have Xanthe's lipstick in his pocket?'

'He's always hated Xanthe, he's always had his eye on that lipstick. It's not my colour at all, but Gareth's like a magpie, he can't keep away from bright things.'

'No one else has said he hated Xanthe. Couldn't he just buy his own lipstick?'

'Kills two birds with one stone the way he did it. So to speak. Or with one letter opener.' No! I tried to keep my face impassive, but my heart lurched at my mistake. They hadn't mentioned the letter opener. No one had. I'd been getting over-confident and slipped up.

'You think she was killed with a letter opener?' DS Whittaker asked.

'Someone said she was stabbed,' I replied. 'That's the only sharp thing we're allowed in the office.' I thought it was a good recovery, but DS Whittaker made another note.

They let me go, but with the words, 'don't leave the country, Julie!' I knew this wasn't going to be the last I heard from them.

My shaky legs carried me slowly back to my desk where I tried to strike up a conversation with Gareth, but he huffed and turned away from me. Later, when he went to get drinks, he only got one for himself. Towards the end of the morning he went into a meeting room with Marcus and bloody Ffion. At lunch-time he moved desks and I was alone, several desks away from my nearest neighbours. No one visited, no one brought drinks, no one stopped for a chat.

I looked around at all the heads turned away from me and blinked back a tear.

In the office the next day, I still seemed to be in Coventry. I don't believe I exchanged a single word with anyone all morning, not until a courier came looking for me with an envelope.

Inside was an invitation to nip down the road the next morning, to the magistrate's court, for a hearing in regard to a restraining order that was being made against me.

It was being made by Sean. He really was going over the top with his efforts to throw them off the scent. But there was too much to do here for me to be messing about with performances at court. I had no doubt it would be a storm in a teacup, I didn't intend to attend. I dropped the letter in the bin and continued with my work.

As I was about to go home, an email from HR pinged into my inbox.

CHAPTER THIRTY-ONE

2010

'Thank you for coming, Julie,' Ffion said the following after-noon, as if I'd had a choice in the matter. 'I won't keep you long.'

They had really gone all out on this one. To my left, in his role as union rep and supposedly here to fight my corner, was Dave. In front of me was Ffion, to her left was a young girl taking notes, and to her right we had, not team manager Marcus, but Marcus's manager. His name was Pete.

'Do you know why you're here, Julie?' Ffion asked.

She shoved a piece of paper in front of me. It had a Cardiff County Court motif at the top of it. I suspected she'd done it herself with some kind of home design software, until I remembered the invitation for the court hearing I'd so recently thrown in the bin.

'We've spoken to you before about your behaviour towards colleagues and at that time we offered you help, which you declined.'

She paused and looked at me, presumably waiting for some kind of response, but I didn't give her one. She continued.

'In light of recent events, I am sorry to say that Sean O'Flannery has had no choice but to take out a restraining order against you. This copy is yours to keep, you must abide by its terms. Take a minute to read it.'

I wasn't able to concentrate on the words. My vision blurred, as I saw my name and then Sean's name, joined at last on a piece of official documentation, but separated by the words that told me I was not allowed to come within 500 metres of him.

'What?' I said. I looked at the words again, but other than my name and his, they were meaningless. 'I don't understand.' Surely Sean hadn't actually gone through with this charade?

'It's a restraining order,' Ffion said, and she pointed to the words at the top, as if she were helping a small child to read. 'It means you can't go within five hundred metres of Sean O'Flannery.'

'That's ridiculous!' I said, convinced now it was a sham. 'How am I supposed to know if I'm within five hundred metres of him? Are we to be given tracking devices? Is it five hundred metres as the crow flies, or in terms of the length of pavement to cover? It's completely impractical, I think you've made this up.'

I snatched up the court order and examined it, looking for evidence it was real. It had a court stamp on it, but I had no doubt you could buy a stamp like that in Toys'R'Us. I cast my eye around the room in case they'd left it lying about.

Ffion shoved a map across the desk. Someone had gone a bit mad on it with a yellow highlighter.

'You must not set foot on any of these streets,' she said, pointing to the highlighted area.

'I dispute this,' I said, taking a deep breath, pulling my shoulders back and clasping my hands together to stop them shaking. 'There are no grounds for a restraining order.'

'When we've finished here you can head over to the court to check,' Pete said. 'Or it should be up on their website soon.'

'But there are no grounds for a restraining order!' I really was perplexed. 'I haven't done anything to him!' My voice was high with outrage and disbelief.

'A restraining order can be granted where there is a threat of violence,' the girl taking notes said, reading from a printout from a government website.

'There you go, then,' Pete said.

'What threat of violence?'

Dave muttered something about investigations and DNA and tests and imminent results, and they all nodded wisely.

'So, you see the problem?' Ffion said, but I didn't. 'We can't have you both in the same office.'

'It doesn't mean at work!'

'It does.'

'I'm sure it doesn't. How would businesses operate if staff members were having to keep miles away from each other at the drop of a hat?'

'To the best of my knowledge,' Ffion said, 'in a hundred years of trading, this is the first time this has happened here.' She looked at Pete and he nodded.

'Well, what do other businesses do?' I asked. There had to be a precedent.

'Exactly what we're doing now, I imagine,' Pete said. 'Julie Tudor, with immediate effect, you are suspended from work, pending an investigation into your behaviour. I can't comment on what the outcome of that investigation will be, but bearing in mind the restraining order lasts for twelve months, it's hard to see how we could have you back in the office in the foreseeable future.'

I felt myself beginning to shake.

'You're making me sound like a common criminal,' I said, and they all shrugged and looked away. I took a breath. 'I think there's been a misunderstanding. I've been a loyal servant of this company for nearly thirty years. I am the life breath of compliance new business, the blood that runs through its veins. The department won't function without me.'

They all looked away.

'What if you lose a spreadsheet formula and I'm not there? The whole floor will grind to a halt.'

'She does have a point there,' Dave piped up.

They said they'd deal with the spreadsheet issue when they came to it. They'd hire a spreadsheet specialist if they had to, they'd use a calculator, they'd buy an abacus. It seemed anything was better than keeping their fully fledged, fully trained spreadsheet expert.

'Do you have any personal possessions here?' Ffion asked.

'Only my letter opener, but that's . . .'

'I don't think they usually return the murder weapon to the murderer,' the girl taking notes said and a gasp went round the room. 'I mean . . . I think . . . I'm sure there's a protocol, but I doubt murder weapons are returned to general circulation.'

Well, bluster as she liked, the bit she said first had not gone unnoticed. I waited for Dave, as my union representative, to jump in and threaten her with court action, but he was staring hard at the carpet.

'I think the letter opener is company property,' is all he said in the end.

'Do you have a coat or anything you would like to collect?' Pete asked me. 'Before we escort you from the building.'

'Now?' I said. 'You want me to leave now?'

'The suspension is with immediate effect,' Ffion reminded me.

'But Sean's not even at work today.'

'He could come in at any moment.'

I looked hopefully at the door. If they were expecting him any minute, he could explain to them that there had been a huge misunderstanding.

'I meant in theory,' Ffion said. 'He's on compassionate leave. If he chose to visit the office at any time, he would be welcome to.' We stared at each other. 'So, we can't have you in here.'

'Has anybody collected Julie's belongings for her yet?' Pete asked, looking around the room.

They all shook their heads. My hopes rose. Maybe if I went back down there to collect my possessions, I could just slide into my seat and carry on with my work. Then all this would be forgotten. It would all be so normal, this would just be a blip in the space-time continuum.

'I'll just nip down and get everything, then,' I said, but Pete said security would bring it to me at the front door. 'But how will they know which desk it is?' I asked, and he assured me someone would know.

'I'll escort you off the premises, then,' Ffion said, smiling with relief.

'Well, you'll at least let me see the week out?' I asked. I had loose ends to tie up, people to say goodbye to, the department would surely want to do a whip-round. They shook their heads. 'I've been here more than twenty-five years,' I reminded them. 'That qualifies me for a carriage clock. Or a watch, or something.'

Again, they shook their heads, but I'd seen it on the company intranet, I was entitled to a gift for my length of service.

'You're suspended, pending a review. You're not retiring,' Pete said.

'I'll stay to the end of the day, then. Hand things over properly.'

'Julie, are we going to have to call security?' Pete asked.

My eyes fell on a paper weight. Their eyes followed mine and they all shuffled their chairs backwards. They needn't have worried, it was only a small, ornamental thing, not much more than a marble; I couldn't have done them any damage with that. I cast my eyes around for an alternative, but the best I could see was a staple gun. Nasty, but not debilitating.

I held my head up, I kept my eyes dry and the wobble from my voice as I spoke. 'You're making a huge mistake. I'll see you in court if I have to and British justice will do its thing.'

Pete nodded. 'Hopefully.'

I saw Ffion glance at the girl. It must have been an unspoken code because the next thing I knew, she ran out of the door, two security guards rushed in and I was being carried, horizontal, out of the office, clinging to the door jamb, begging for one more chance to state my case as the guards hauled me away.

As my fingers slipped from the door frame, I heard Pete asking Ffion, 'Do you think you'll be safe walking home?'

I didn't hear her reply as I flailed for something to hold on to along the wall. Down came the pictures of the CEO, the Head of HR, and a glowing sunrise with an inspirational quotation beneath it. I looked down the corridor as curious heads poked out of offices.

'Lift?' one guard asked the other. I didn't hear a reply, but they must have decided against it because the next thing I knew, we were on the stairs and I was able to grab at the banister, slowing our descent. The plastic on the top railing squeaked as my hands were pulled along it.

'Owwwww!' I shouted as my fingers started to burn. The guards stopped for a moment, and I began to wriggle.

'If we put you down, are you going to walk out sensibly?' one of them asked.

'Never!' I shouted, the heat of the moment putting words into my mouth. And they continued their trudge down the stairs, with me still hanging between them.

The main door gave them pause for thought, as it is a rotating one that only allows for people in a standing position. For a moment I thought I'd won and all I had to do was to remain horizontal, but then the receptionist opened the delivery doors for them, and I was dumped out amongst the empty boxes.

'Wait there and we'll bring your stuff,' the guard said, and a moment later the doors reopened, and my bag and jacket were thrown my way. Before they closed again, I glimpsed Gareth talking to the receptionist as he cleaned his hands with some kind of wipe, a grimace on his face.

I sat where they left me, the words 'restraining order, restraining order, restraining order' ringing in my head. For a moment I almost forgot I was sacked.

CHAPTER THIRTY-TWO

2010

For the rest of that day and most of the night I painted vivid, angry pictures while I waited for them to realise their mistake and call me back. I painted an abstract vision in navy and black, I painted the whole of HR in the pits of hell, I painted myself with a Ffion-shaped shadow looming over me.

I mused over Sean and the restraining order. *A year.* Presumably he didn't mean for us to stick to that? Maybe things had got out of control at the court hearing. Perhaps I should have gone after all.

The next morning, I woke at the same time I had done for decades, but with nowhere to go I lay in bed watching the hours pass by and thinking of my normal daily routine. I thought of the train pulling in and the train pulling out, the short walk to the office, the ride in the lift. Now Gareth would be tipping the contents of his pockets out onto the desk and regaling everyone with his exploits of the night before. Now it would be time for coffee. Now the post would be arriving with some pithy comment from Jayne from the post room about the postman, or the weather, or *EastEnders*.

Now the spreadsheets would need updating. I wondered if they'd crashed yet and who would put them right and a tear formed in my eye.

When I rose from my bed, I turned first to the Facebook and spent some time looking for Sean's page, but he seemed to have vanished. I wondered why. Did he think the police were onto him too?

I wondered if he'd call into work and if my desk would be the first place he'd look. Although in the alternative office we were using, the seating arrangements were different and he wouldn't necessarily know where my desk was. Maybe he'd look to where Gareth was sitting, assuming my desk was alongside, not knowing how Gareth had abandoned me.

Next, I turned to my television. I watched the morning news where there was a report about a gruesome murder in an office in Cardiff. Police inquiries were continuing and they were confident of making an arrest soon. Did they have someone in mind? Was it me? Was Xanthe's lipstick really such a clincher? Or the letter opener? When they dusted it for fingerprints they'd find mine, Gareth's and Sean's.

At least two of us – Sean and I – had a motive, but no one else knew about it. Then I remembered the song and dance they'd made about a certain update in regard to our relationship status on the Facebook: that would probably be rehashed for the police to muse over and twist to their own purposes. I found myself hovering at the window, watching for a marked car to turn the corner into my street.

I watched all the true crime I could find. I learnt about something called catfishing, which, strangely, is nothing to do with catfish, and over the following days I thought long and hard about the possibilities a false identity could open up.

I learnt they can find out if someone is in the area by looking at which mast their mobile phone is connecting to.

I learnt everything I could about DNA testing. I discovered that they had a database and somewhere in there must be the hair I had left at the Pearsons' house. Felicity had survived my attack and eventually made her way out of intensive care, but only as far as a custom-made wheelchair, designed to keep her upright as she sat: she was so badly brain damaged she couldn't hold her own perfectly coiffed head up, let alone identify or testify against me. As long I kept a low profile, I considered myself safe. But now it seemed it would only be a matter of time before that affair reared its head again.

I watched prison dramas and wondered in how many different ways I would be assaulted in prison.

At night I would dream of letter openers, bodies in cupboards, hairs on pillows, chains of evidence and police officers putting two and two together. Sometimes I dreamt of prison and woke with relief to see an unbarred window. I closed my eyes again and saw DS Whittaker smiling at me: 'Tell me about Susannah, tell me about the Pearsons.' Her smile stretched wider, her mouth opened and she leant forward to swallow me whole. I'd wake screaming and sometimes I found my hands were shaking.

I tried to think of happier things, but it's hard when you have nothing to do all day but ponder your fate. I wandered around the house with a tension that wouldn't go away.

On the third full day after being sacked, I thought to bolster my spirits with a catch-up with Gareth. He was bound to be over his sulk about the lipstick by now and I'd be able to get an insight into how things were in the office: is Sean back yet? Any word on reinstating me? So, I sent him a text. 'Shopping? Drinks? Let's get together!'

He didn't reply straight away, but it was early evening and knowing what a busy life Gareth had, I knew he was probably in the middle of something. When he didn't reply at all that evening, I reasoned that he was most likely out having a few drinks.

I felt uneasy when I still hadn't heard from him by the next morning and by midday, knowing how often he checked his phone, I knew he hadn't missed it. I checked to make sure I hadn't sent it to the wrong person. The list in my phone was:

Dad, dentist, doctors, Frank, Gareth, Marcus (work), Mum. It didn't take long to check.

I sent another one, just to make sure, 'How's the office without me?' Nothing.

I sat in the house, alone. I noticed for the first time how loudly the kitchen clock ticked, I could hear it counting the hours down in every room in the house.

I was about to make my way upstairs one afternoon when there was a knock at the door. The police, I thought. I froze. I wanted to run up the stairs and hide, but there is a glass panel in my front door and whoever was outside could probably see the movement. Then they'd be coming through with a battering ram.

The caller knocked again and I jigged nervously on the stairs. I was going to have to make a decision.

'Are you in, Julie?' a voice called. It was Frank! I went to open it and there he was, harmless, friendly Frank. 'Are you alright?' he asked. I was almost crying with relief and I think it showed.

'Yes,' I said. I found myself a little breathless. 'Yes.'

'I just wondered if you'd like to go painting again?' he asked.

No, I thought. I wanted to stay in the house and drink and hope that the police would forget about Xanthe and leave me alone. But I could hardly say that.

'I'm rather busy at the moment,' I said instead. He looked as if he was about to argue, so I threw in a couple more reasons. 'I'm a bit tired as well and I'm waiting for an important phone call. On my landline.'

'Well, I didn't mean this minute,' he said. 'At a time of your choosing. Maybe in a day or two or even next week.'

I didn't tell him that making plans for next week was a trifle ambitious.

'Didn't we have a lovely time last time?' he said.

I found myself nodding. We had had a lovely time.

'Is that a yes?' he said.

'Ummm . . .'

'Will you be free tomorrow?'

I didn't know, so I said, 'Probably.'

'I'll pick you up about this time tomorrow then, shall I? Any problems, or if you want to go earlier, just give me a bell.' And smiling, he headed back to the Jacksons'. I watched him go, half looking forward to the outing, half terrified by the reasons why it might be cancelled at short notice.

But it wasn't cancelled, and we started our outing with a visit to Costa, but this time we purchased takeaway drinks and sat on the grass outside the castle.

If truth be told, although I seemed calm on the outside, I was still rather jittery under the surface. Yet, as we started to paint, a calmer mood edged in. I glanced over at Frank and he looked across and smiled. The sting of being ignored by Gareth still hurt, but Frank's attention was taking the sharpness off: the police may be on my track, but in that moment they seemed a million miles away. I breathed deeply and felt my shoulders relax for the first time in days.

Suddenly, all I wanted was to sit on the bank outside Caerphilly Castle and paint without a care for the rest of my days. To be like all the other people around, free to sit in the open air and to do so again the following week and for the weeks and months and years afterwards. No memories of corpses, or promises of prison, to haunt them. I looked up at the blue sky and listened to the birdsong. I breathed in the clean, fresh air and held it in my lungs for a moment. I wished I could hold it there forever.

'Maybe we could go in sometime,' Frank said, nodding at the castle gate – the time had already passed for last entry for today.

'Maybe,' I replied. It had never occurred to me to actually go inside.

'What are your plans for the weekend?'

Getting arrested and banged up for life. 'I think I'll spend some time in the garden, maybe give the house a good clean.'

'It's hard when you're just there on your own, isn't it,' he said.

'What do you mean?' I felt rather criticised.

'I mean I find I have to face up to the thoughts in my head. Even when they are uncomfortable, or they might lead me to do things I shouldn't do.'

I was both intrigued and terrified. I wanted to ask him what was going on in his head that was so terrible, but if he told me, I might have to reciprocate.

Frank looked down at his lap. He took a deep breath. 'I suppose you should know, if we're going to keep meeting like this. My issue – the reason I've been away – wasn't just a busy schedule, or the pressures of life. It was because I made a few mistakes in years gone by. You see, back in the day, I liked a little flutter on the horses. No harm in it, you might think, just a bit of fun at the weekend.'

Well, I thought, we all like to let our hair down after the working week.

'But I took it too far,' Frank said. 'I was obsessed, and when I got paid on Friday, it was always all gone by Monday. I sold everything I owned of any value and I borrowed money I couldn't pay back. Eventually, I ran out of money and I ran out of ways of getting it legally.' He paused and dropped his gaze to the floor. 'I stole, Julie,' he said, it was barely audible. He raised his voice and repeated it. 'I even broke into people's houses. And . . .' He dropped his head again, while I waited for the grand finale. 'I spent a bit of time in prison.'

I exhaled. I had harboured a concern that if Frank knew my full life story, he would think I was not his kind of person. I had believed him to be straightforward, carefree and without problems. I'd taken him to be someone who had breezed through his life. I'd even worried that, if he knew about my great depths of passion, he may think I was not someone he wanted to be associated with. But this put rather a different light on it. I had never broken into someone's house to *steal*.

'So that's why I've been away. But I've learnt my lesson. You have nothing to fear from me.' He looked over nervously.

'Well,' I said. 'That's quite a skeleton you have in your closet. Or out of your closet now, I suppose.'

'I'd understand if you wanted to call it a day,' he said.

It didn't put me off him. In fact, I felt we had more in common than I'd thought. For a moment I toyed with the idea of giving him an insight into my world, but I still had my freedom to lose, even if I was only a hair's breath away from losing it, so I kept quiet on that front.

Back at home, I checked my phone, still hoping that Gareth might have got back to me, that his silence was a mistake, that of course he'd meant to reply, he'd just been caught up in all the drama. There was nothing from him. I started to understand that there would always be nothing from him now.

My mind kept recalling happier times: chatting as we went about our work, our shopping trip together, the Summer Ball, and I realised there would be no more. The days stretched ahead of me, long and empty. No Sean, no Gareth.

I watched the second hand on the clock ticking round, counting down a minute, then another. Counting down to what, I asked myself. Prison? Certainly, to nothing good.

I wondered if I could get another job. I nipped out to buy a local paper – the front page screaming BLOODBATH IN THE OFFICE. At home I read the article: the police had several lines of inquiry. Then I searched for the jobs pages, but there were none. Apparently, it was all done online these days. It was hard to know where to start, so in the end I googled 'how to find a job' and a number of recruitment agencies appeared on my screen.

I began putting together a CV, but in truth, my heart wasn't in it. There was no point in me looking for a job. The police were coming back and sooner or later I was going to be otherwise engaged. And even if I wasn't, the only place I wanted to work was where I had been working for my entire career.

Restless, I paced through the house and watched the street from an upstairs window. A few people returned home from work, a few people headed out. With nothing else to do, I went downstairs, turned the TV on and watched the national news. It ended and the local show began.

Then suddenly, there was Sean! Right in front of me, on my TV, being interviewed on *Wales Today*. He was asking the person who had committed the murder to turn themselves in and face the music – clearly a message intended for me, but cryptic.

'Do the police have any idea who did it?' the journalist asked.

'They've got someone in their sights,' Sean told them. 'But they can't name names yet.'

Was that a warning for me? Or a reassurance? The interview ran on.

'How do you feel about the person who did this?'

'I never want to see that person. Other than in the dock.'

Well, those were mixed messages if ever I heard them. After that, Sean came over all weepy and they faded the interview out. When they came back, he was looking red-eyed, you could hear the interviewer saying, 'Are you alright?' and Sean nodded bravely and whispered, 'Yes. It's important I do this.'

They moved on to talking about what Xanthe was like. She was so forgettable, I can't remember a word he said about her.

The local press were really having a field day. They seemed to be hanging around outside the temporary office and asking everyone who came out of there whether they had known Xanthe and who they thought might have done such a thing.

'Well, there was someone, but she's not here anymore,' said the receptionist.

'A right weirdo, lurking at the back of the office . . . looked like the Grim Reaper . . . she kept a bottle of vodka in her desk drawer, she mixed it into the coffees . . . no, it was absinthe . . . no, it was strychnine . . . no, it was the cakes that had the strychnine . . .' said my counterpart from the department across the aisle, her friend who came to meet her for lunch, the bloke who occasionally came down from IT, a manager who visited from time to time, a woman who had moved to the floor above and a youth who seemed to be on an extended work experience placement.

Then there would be a clip with the police asking people not to speculate because it could prejudice a court case.

With that in mind I began to record the local news. I watched every interview several times, keeping an ear out for a comment that I thought went too far and could get me an acquittal. But listening to those comments over and over again began to get to me.

After two more days, the police finally knocked on the door. I opened it casually, thinking it was Frank again, and got the fright of my life. Instinctively, I tried slamming the door shut, but DC Dalton already had his foot in it. I kept trying, flinging myself against it, after all it was one foot against my entire bodyweight – but it was no good. The uniformed officer behind him pushed it open, as easily as if he were fighting a hamster.

'Julie Ann Tudor,' DC Dalton said, 'I'm arresting you on suspicion of the murder of Xanthe Irving.' And he went on to do the whole 'you do not have to say anything' palaver.

They marched me out of the house and into a police car, with Bert and Mabel watching from their front window. In the car I began to go into shock and we had to stop for a few minutes until my breathing returned to normal and my dizziness passed. I had never been more scared in my life. For the entire journey I prayed that a disaster would befall us to stop us reaching our destination. I would rather have had an aeroplane land on us or earthquake swallow us up than arrive at the police station.

However, once there, the immediate situation was not quite as bad as I'd anticipated. I was not physically thrown into a cell. I was not hauled into a dingy room, with a bare bulb hanging above me, to be interrogated. I was not threatened with splinters under my nails, or having my teeth extracted. I wasn't even water boarded.

Instead, the sergeant at the desk politely asked for my name and details. He asked me if I wanted legal advice, which seemed like a very good idea. He asked me if I needed the toilet, or anything to eat or drink, which I did not, and he asked me if I wanted to let anyone know that I was there. I have no idea why he thought I might want to do that. Did he think I would want to post it on the Facebook?

'No,' I said.

After that, they put me in a cell, while we waited for my solicitor to arrive. By the time he did, I was feeling much more like my usual self.

'Can you take us through the events of that evening, please, Julie?' DC Dalton asked me, once we were settled into an interview room, staring me down with unblinking eyes, DS Whittaker sitting to the side of him with her careworn expression.

'Which one?' I asked, artfully making myself look innocent of all knowledge of the time of Xanthe's death.

'Tuesday 30th,' DC Dalton said. 'Which did you think?'

I cast my eyes to the ceiling, trying to remember which direction you're meant to look in if you're telling the truth and which one means you're lying. To be on the safe side, I looked both ways.

'What time do you call evening?' I asked. 'Five o'clock? Six? Seven?'

'What time did you finish work? Who else was there? When did you leave the office? By which door? Which way did you walk? Did anything unusual happen between turning off your computer and exiting the building? Like killing a colleague with a letter opener?'

'Leading question,' my solicitor said.

'Hmmm,' I said, 'Tuesday, Tuesday, Tuesday.' I cast my eyes back to the ceiling, an innocent bystander, trying to recollect the humdrum events of an ordinary day.

'It was less than a week ago, Julie, it can't be that hard,' DC Dalton snapped. 'I'll give you an example. On Tuesday evening I finished work about six, I took my boy to rugby and we bought chips on the way back. Then he played on his laptop and I had a beer and watched a documentary about shipbuilding.'

What a boring evening.

'That's the kind of thing we're looking for,' DC Dalton continued. 'Off you go. I may ask for more detail when you've finished.'

I took a deep breath. 'On Tuesday evening I finished work sometime between five and half past five. There was a gremlin in one of the spreadsheets and I had to stay to fix it; no one else really understands the formulas.'

DC Dalton nodded me on.

'Spreadsheets fixed, I made my way out of the office, to the lifts, down seven floors and out via the usual route.'

I paused, looking at them to see how my story was going down, but their faces were blank. I continued. 'I walked to Queen Street station and from there I caught the 5:55 train home to Caerphilly.'

DC Dalton looked bored, but he nodded me on. Feeling more confident, I began to pick up speed.

'Once home I began preparation of a Lancashire hotpot. It's quite an involved process. Not only do I have to peel and chop the vegetables, to sear the lamb, brown the onions until golden, parboil the potatoes, sprinkle flour and allow to cook for . . .'

I stopped, appalled. I'd made a mistake – you don't parboil the potatoes for a Lancashire hotpot, you slice them thinly, place them on top of the casserole and allow to cook for an hour and a half, until crisp! I stared at DC Dalton in horror, waiting to see if he'd noticed.

'What's the matter, Julie?'

I recovered myself and pretended to wipe a tear from my eye. 'A hotpot always brings to mind my beloved cat, Fluffy, God rest her soul. She loved a hotpot.'

DC Dalton nodded. 'And what time was this?'

'A hotpot is thirty to forty-five minutes preparation time and an hour and a half to cook,' I said, trying to remember which train I said I'd caught and work it out from there.

'A lot of faff for a weekday,' DC Dalton said. 'What time do you eat?'

'I enjoy cooking,' I said, nodding and smiling and hoping to avoid telling him I'm usually too drunk to remember when – or if – I've eaten.

'What do you think happened to Xanthe?' he asked.

'I understand she was murdered and shoved into the stationery cupboard,' I said.

'But by whom?' he asked. 'Who do you think held a grudge against Xanthe?'

'A passing burglar?'

He shook his head. 'With all that security to get in and out?'

'The security's not all that great, to be honest. A couple of years ago one of my colleagues did a sponsored "how many times can I get into the building without my pass before I am caught?" for Children in Need and the answer was fourteen.'

'I believe they've made some changes since then, though?'

'They sacked the colleague, so I suppose that was a change.'

'Tell me about Sean O'Flannery,' Whittaker said.

'He's a case handler in the department in which I work. Worked. He's about twenty-five years old—' or less, I realised I didn't know exactly how old he was. Well, age is just a number! 'He's around five-foot-ten, medium build, short hair, brown . . .'

'Tell me about your relationship with him.'

So, they admitted I had a relationship with him? They were more astute than Ffion. I looked at my solicitor. He shrugged.

'Didn't you post a rather misleading comment on Facebook about him?' Whittaker asked.

'That's personal,' I said.

'You posted it for anyone who wanted to, to see.'

They probed a bit further and it occurred to me that when I'd said 'that's personal,' I should've said 'no comment.' For the second half of the interview, I pursued that line and it all went by much more quickly.

'How did you get on with Xanthe?' No comment. 'Who else was there when you left the office?' No comment. 'How many other people use your letter opener?' No comment. 'Why did you encourage Gareth to use your letter opener on the day after the murder?'

'Leading question,' my solicitor said.

In the end my solicitor said it was going to be hard to get a conviction based on the fact my fingerprints were on a letter opener I had used every single day for years; the discovery of a lipstick, currently of unknown origin, and a Facebook post. Did they have anything else? They let me go 'pending further investigations'.

'If I were you, I wouldn't sleep too well, Julie,' DS Whittaker said to me. 'We'll find Xanthe's killer. It won't be long.'

Well, I didn't imagine I'd sleep too well in prison either, so it was a bit of a moot point.

The phone rang when I got home. It was my mother who said she knew that it was early, but had I made any plans for Christmas and if not, would I like to go to theirs?

'I think I might be otherwise detained at Christmas,' I said, wishing for the first time in about 30 years that, actually, I could go to theirs. A family Christmas, with all its irritations, suddenly seemed very appealing. I wondered what would be going on at the Jacksons' and if Frank and I could perhaps have been a part of that.

Later that night, I looked at myself in the mirror and remembered the colleague who said I looked like the Grim Reaper. I couldn't entirely agree with that, I was not skeletal, in fact I had a bit more flesh than I needed to have. I didn't own a scythe either, but I did have a hoe. I fetched it from the shed and had a good look at myself in the mirror. No, I couldn't say I agreed that I looked like the Grim Reaper.

But nor did I look like Xanthe, or Susannah. I never did. I once was young, I once was thinner, but in truth I was never friendly, or personable, or carefree.

I saw myself now, from the outside. A woman bulging at the waist, slightly sagging in the face. A woman with an outdated hairstyle. A mousey woman who sat at the back of the office and was only noticed when the cases didn't come through properly.

And I saw some of the young girls you see out and about. Some of them rude, or uncouth or stupid, but many of them bright and lively and pretty and fun. I thought of Susannah, vapid, but giggly; and I thought of Xanthe, dreary, but laid back.

I saw what Gareth was seeing when he said maybe I should accept Sean wasn't interested.

The police were going to get their woman and I was going to be taken from this house, put into a cell, interviewed, tried and put into another cell. I was not going to be allowed to return home. I was not going to be allowed out to work, or to shop, or to walk around town. I was going to be locked in with someone I did not choose and likely would not choose. Someone who may be bigger than me, stronger than me, possibly more violent than me, or with a propensity for violence for violence's sake. There would be no respite, no hope of a reprieve, just the never-ending torment.

And for what?

I took the restraining order and the map that accompanied it out of the recycling. I studied the streets around Danescourt. Now I had a much better idea than I had previously of where Sean lived, but for what purpose?

I looked at his name, Sean Daniel O'Flannery – I hadn't known that was his middle name – and I looked at mine as well, Julie Ann Tudor, RESTRAINING ORDER written in bold print across the top.

I felt the sting of his rejection and I realised I'd been harbouring a hopeless hope.

CHAPTER THIRTY-THREE

2010

So, Sean had meant it when he took out the restraining order. The truth of the matter settled within me. At first I wondered when his feelings had changed: I couldn't believe the passion that had sparked when we first met was only on my side. It couldn't be true that our chats, our drinks, our night together were nothing but a footnote to his day. But as I thought it over, I saw his comments in a new light. He called my new wardrobe 'the dressing-up box', he had gone to Casanova with Xanthe when he had said he'd be with me, he had thought of Wilma Flintstone when we were together. He did not love me as I loved him.

Yet, a supernova burns brightest when it is in its death throes. I understood now that Sean wanted to sever our connection, but I couldn't just let go. My new understanding of the situation did not change the way I felt about him. In fact, my desire intensified. I had to have him. I had to have him here and to possess him. However brief our union might be, I had to be with him.

'If I can't have you, no one can.' Suddenly I understood that phrase better than I had ever understood a phrase before. No more Xanthes, no more Susannahs, no more anyone, except me. I knew I could not keep him, but for however short a time, I would have him.

I thought back to the programme I had seen about catfishing. I had, in fact, found it so interesting, I had watched it three times.

When I watched it, I saw the opportunity to know what it would be like to be someone else. To be someone with no history, someone no one had any preconceptions about, to be viewed as they all viewed each other and to be spoken to by other people as if I were someone else. I wanted Sean to see me as I saw him.

I borrowed a picture I found online, a picture of one of those bright, lively, pretty girls, Cherry from somewhere in California, I believe, and created a new Facebook profile: Tasha from Cardiff. I spent some time scrolling through the recent charts and cinema releases and added some music and film favourites: 'Bad Romance', 'Empire State of Mind', 'Bulletproof'; *Inception*, *Harry Potter*, *The Hangover*.

From my new page I searched for Sean – and there he was. He hadn't disappeared from the Facebook at all, he had just found a way to hide from me. His profile picture was a request for information about Xanthe's murder, but it was indisputably him, the same list of films and all his old posts. There were umpteen messages of condolence on his page, but he'd kept uncharacteristically quiet, although I could see from a post he was tagged in that he had been in a bar called Revolution a few days before.

I left him for later and began searching the Facebook for names I knew. Then I scrolled down their friend lists, asking to connect with those who had the highest number of friends – those whose lists I could go on unnoticed. They started accepting my requests almost straight away. By the end of the day, I had more than a hundred friends. I spent some time looking through people's pages, seeing what they wrote and how they spoke to each other on there.

Then I added a post:

'Hey guys, this is my new page. Had to close the other one down because of you-know-who . . .' To make it more credible, I asked how to set up privacy settings and someone was quick to provide that information, adding that they hoped I'd seen the last of that madman. 'Fingers crossed,' I wrote and got 37 likes.

I ended the session by mentioning that it had been a great night out with the girls last night and came offline.

After that I spent a bit of time limbering-up my back. It had never been the same since the episode with Mrs Pearson and the cast iron umbrella stand all those years ago. Lugging Xanthe around the office had triggered a relapse and I was going to need it to be strong soon.

CHAPTER THIRTY-FOUR

2010

I renewed my Facebook-befriending efforts the next day and by the end of it I'd topped the 200 mark. After that, catfishing as Tasha, I sent Sean a friend request. He was quick to accept and I left it there. For now.

'Did your work let you go?' Bert asked me as I arrived for Mabel's jab.

I looked at him, wondering where he'd heard that, before I realised they must have noticed I was around during the day.

'No.' I couldn't admit to it. 'I'm taking a sabbatical.' I turned to their chaotic room. 'You know, it really would help if you got into a routine and had a place to keep the insulin.' A place for everything and everything in its place was the antithesis of life at Bert and Mabel's. 'Where did you last see it?'

Bert rubbed his stubble. 'That'd be yesterday, when you were here last.'

'Where, not when.'

It had been on the coffee table the day before, the table that currently looked as if they'd tried to pile half the contents of the house on it. I began picking through it: a pile of cutlery, a couple of ornaments, a skirt, for some reason, but no insulin.

Bert followed me as I did a brief recce of the kitchen and dining room. No sign of it.

'Alright if I look upstairs?'

Bert nodded, a look of concern on his face now.

With Bert behind me I started in the bathroom, where toiletries and first-aid supplies bulged out of cupboards, but not a drop of insulin was in sight.

'The bedroom?'

Bert nodded. 'I'm just going to take a leak. You go on.'

With trepidation, I moved onto the master bedroom. And there, bingo! In the first drawer I opened, right on top of a pile of underwear, I found a treasure trove of insulin, at least ten vials, along with the pen and a spare. I couldn't help but pocket a few doses. And the spare pen as well; they probably didn't even know they had an extra one.

I went downstairs with the remaining insulin, and it was smiles all round as I administered the jab. I put the rest away in a kitchen cupboard, explaining clearly to them where I'd put it and why: 'It really is vital that you remember. Mabel, *your life* depends on this.' I had no doubt they would be missing again the next morning.

Weighed down with illicit medication, I bid them a good morning and made my way home with a sense of accomplishment.

I put the insulin and the pen in the drawer of my bedside cabinet, ready for action as soon as I needed it. Then I spent the rest of the day reading the Facebook posts of my new 'friends' and ignoring the news. As evening fell, I went to my room, donned the dress I wore for the summer ball and stepped into a pair of stilettoes. I piled my hair on top of my head and covered my face with make-up; I wanted to get into character. Then I turned to the Facebook and, in the guise of Tasha from Cardiff, sent Sean a message.

'Howdy, stranger,' I wrote, all casual and in the style of a Southern belle, as I had seen on one of the Facebook pages I had looked at. 'Did I see you in Revolution the other day?'

He hadn't been online when I sent my message and it took him a while to reply, but eventually he came back with, 'Might have seen me, I didn't see you. Where were you?'

Good question. 'Standing up by the bar,' I said, 'some of the time. And some of the time on the seats nearest the door.'

'Who were you with?' he asked.

'Girls,' I said, wanting to lure him in further, then realised that sounded more like me than Tasha. 'My bitches,' I corrected, thinking back to some of the language I'd seen used.

'You hanging with your bitches? Lol!' he wrote.

'Hanging like I always do on a Friday,' I said.

'Friday? I don't think I was there on Friday,' he said. I must've got the day wrong! Lesson number one – don't be too specific.

'I thought it was Friday, could've been another day; I've been a real social whirlwind recently!'

'A social whirlwind?' he wrote and I realised I'd made another mistake. Was that something Tasha would say? Probably not.

'Out every night last week,' I said, hoping that would set us back on the right track.

'A veritable tornado,' he replied. 'Gotta shoot.'

'Nooo!' I howled as the green dot vanished and he slipped from my grasp. Had he sensed something was wrong? Had it been the whirlwind comment? Or the bitches?

The early evening news told me that the police believed they were closing in on Xanthe's killer and would be holding a press conference at the end of the week. The immediacy of the situation somehow made me more haste, less speed as I logged myself onto the Facebook, clicking here, there and everywhere, my fingers refused to obey my brain, whispering 'come on, come on, come on,' as I finally homed in on Sean's page.

But still no Sean. I watched the late news, which contained the same comment from the same police officer.

And then, the green dot. I waited for him to notice me – or Tasha – and initiate a conversation, but nothing. So, I played my hand. After all, he had 500 and something friends, he might have simply forgotten about Tasha.

'You out next week?' I messaged him, deliberately dropping the 'are' from the beginning of the sentence as I had seen the younger users do.

He waited a few minutes, then replied. 'Nah, not out much at the moment. Got something on that's keeping me in. Just desperately needed a blowout when you saw me last week.'

'Work?' I asked.

'Not exactly.'

I wondered how to follow that.

'Where do you work?' I asked.

'You know the investment company in town?'

'In the city centre?' I took the chance: 'Wasn't there a bit of trouble there recently? No one you knew, I hope.'

'That's the thing. It was. It was my girlfriend. So, I won't be out much for a while. I was out last week because I thought it would help, but actually, it made it harder. I smashed the lounge up when I got in. Drinking is the only thing that helps and I can do that at home. It looks like I'm coping but I'm not, I was drunk when we messaged before. Drunk now.'

'It's the only way to be sometimes,' I wrote, and refrained from adding, 'I'm the expert.'

'I can't sit around here thinking about it sober, my head will explode. I saw her body, I can't get it out of my mind. Every time I close my eyes . . .'

And the green dot vanished. Funny how people will tell their deepest feelings to a random photo from the internet.

I went back to scouring for pictures of drunk young people. When I found one of a large group, faces pretty much unrecognisable, I posted it on my Facebook page. Then I looked for some mutual friends of Sean and mine. I named a few of them, and Sean, with the comment that I couldn't remember for certain who was there that night. Then I wrote, 'When times are tough, we drown our sorrows.'

I couldn't sleep. I paced the floor. I watched Facebook. My post had a few likes and the odd comment about how sorrow floats.

At about 2am, when most people were asleep, a little green dot reappeared by Sean's name.

'I took your advice,' he wrote. 'It's drowning.'

'I'll join you,' I wrote back and for the sake of method acting, I grabbed a glass of wine.

'You not got work tomorrow?'

'I'm between jobs.'

'They've given me time off work because of what happened to my girlfriend It's too much time to fill, but I can't think about anything else, so I can't do anything else. Where did you work?' he asked. 'Trying to figure out where I know you from.'

'We were at uni,' I said. 'Not on the same course. We met in the union.'

'Never used to go to the union,' he replied. 'Our house was miles away. I lived in Birchgrove.'

My heart started to race. I had only ever heard of Birchgrove on train announcements.

With shaking fingers, I typed, 'You must've gone into town sometimes. Put your glad rags on and headed for the city lights!'

'Glad rags,' he typed back. 'You sound like someone I used to work with. A right old bag. A glad bag!'

Who? I wanted to ask, but I didn't want to hear the answer. Instead, I gathered my wits and gave his terrible joke a 'lol!'

Unfortunately, Sean elaborated. 'She was a right weirdo, sitting there giving people death stares, always dressed in black.

Think there will be news about her soon, but I can't say any more at the moment. She's not there now.'

Well, well, well. I wanted to be spoken to as other people were spoken to, but I did not want to be spoken to about myself as other people spoke of me. Certainly not.

I had to step away from the laptop while I regained my equilibrium. I returned a few minutes later and wrote, 'Imagine!'

'Anyway,' he said. 'I think I remember you now. Didn't you have longer hair at uni?'

I took a deep breath, it seemed we were back on track. 'I did back then. Did you prefer it long?'

'I liked it then. Like it better now. You still living local?'

'I live in Caerphilly these days. Just bought a house off some-one who moved to London.'

'Really? That old glad bag I was talking about lives in Caerphilly, I once . . .' I waited for him to go on, but all he added was ''nuff said.' I recoiled, but soon rallied round again:

'Painful memory?'

'Not exactly.'

There was a pause and I began to panic, trying and failing to think of something to follow that up with and terrified he'd go. But then he replied with:

'Were you the one at uni who was obsessed with the *Scream* films?'

'They are very good films.' I replied. I'd heard of them, I'd never seen one.

'That used to make me laugh, how often you watched them. How many times can you jump at someone standing behind a door?'

'I like other films as well,' I typed, scrolling down his list.

'Such as?'

Top of the list was *In Bruges* but it seemed a bit obvious to work my way down in order, so I skipped a couple.

'*500 Days of Summer,*' I wrote.

'That's a real girls' film!' he said. I nearly typed 'isn't that on your list?' but stopped myself in time.

Instead, I wrote, 'I'm a real girl.'

'All the fixtures and fittings?'

My stomach did a flip.

'All of them,' I said.

'Show me the taps,' he wrote.

That was a bit direct! Suddenly I felt a little shy, but he was typing again:

'Don't send it on Facebook! You never know what's going to happen! Text a pic to this number.' And he typed in his mobile number, followed by 'Your taps'.

My stomach somersaulting, I went to my bedroom, took my top off and stood in front of the mirror, stretching tall to iron out any of the giveaway wrinkles of age. I held my phone at what seemed a good distance and snapped.

I'd held it a bit too close. If you didn't already know you wouldn't have even guessed it was part of a human body. Holding it further away, I snapped again. The second attempt was better, but not prize-winning stuff. I was about to go for third time lucky when I heard the ping of another message arriving 'I'm waiting . . .' Sean said.

I loaded the second picture up and sent it off.

A moment later my phone beeped and when I opened the message a picture of his manhood appeared on the screen – aroused – with the caption, 'My piping. You again.' He obviously hadn't made a note of my number when I sent it to him following our night of passion, otherwise, he may have reacted rather differently on receiving my message.

I took a third picture of my cleavage and sent it away.

'Nice,' he said, 'but I was hoping for something a bit more revealing.' And he sent me a picture of his dick from a different angle.

I went into the bathroom, took off my top and snapped close-ups of my chest until I had a winner.

I sent it over, Sean sent his compliments and asked for more. I told him it was his turn and he obliged with the same organ from yet another angle.

I realised this could be a very long evening.

Then, 'You want to make this a booty call?' he asked.

'A what?' I was about to type back, but I stopped myself. It sounded like something Tasha would know. I googled it and realised he was propositioning me! 'Yes.' I typed back.

'No strings, I'm not wanting to get into anything. I could just do with a bit of company.'

'No strings,' I lied and I sent him directions.

'Really no strings?' he repeated. 'It's just with Xanthe and everything.'

There are always strings, I thought, looking at where the insulin was kept, but I typed back, 'Really, no strings.'

Then there was a long pause, until, 'I'm not sure,' he said. 'It doesn't seem right.'

'There are no rights or wrongs in bereavement.' That had been on a poster on the staffroom wall on one of my nursing placements, all those years ago. 'Might take your mind off things for a while.'

'I'll be there in half an hour.'

Well, that was quick, I'd been worried I'd still be dangling the bait when the police arrived.

I cleared the lounge and hall of anything he might recognise – including that picture of us losing ourselves in passion.

I made sure everything of a personal nature was in the wardrobe. There was very little left out anyway, but I hid away pictures and coasters and a couple of ornaments that he might remember. There was still a risk Sean would recognise the house and make a quick about-turn, but really, what did I have to lose? This was one last roll of the dice for my dreams of us being together.

Then it was down to the detail. I spent some time arranging a pile of clothes under the duvet to create a rise about the size and shape of an average female body. I pulled the duvet right up over the pillow and left a dark t-shirt just peeking out.

I closed the curtains and turned the lamp on. In the dim light it would look like the top of a head to someone who was expecting to see the top of a head. I took a condom out of a packet in the drawer – the packet I'd bought before Sean and Susannah's wedding – and gave it pride of place on the beside cabinet, beneath the glow of the lamp.

I stood back and surveyed the scene. The prone shape perhaps wasn't quite the sight Sean expected to meet his eyes, but it would do the job. Bearing in mind the prelude to this encounter, I couldn't imagine he was going to be too fussy about the initial position of his quarry.

Nervous with anticipation, I jumped out of my skin when my phone beeped.

'Nearly there. You ready?'

With the bedroom door open, I sat myself behind it and prepared the insulin pen. How many times can you jump at someone standing behind a door?

I sent a message: 'The front door's unlocked, come straight in.' He replied with a 'gr8'.

It was only a few more minutes when the phone rang and I froze when I realised it was him. I picked up before it had time to go to the answer phone. I hadn't expected this – would he recognise my voice? I thought probably not; he would hear what he was expecting to hear. But just in case, I manufactured a deep purr for myself. I may have sounded a bit strange, but as long as I didn't sound like me, it would work.

'Hello?' I said into the phone, trying not to laugh at the strangeness of the sound.

'Hello, sexy,' he said. 'I think I'm a bit lost. I'm outside a house with a black garage door and a little well in the garden. The door looks black in this light anyway.'

'Keep walking away from the roundabout and turn left,' I told him.

'I think I've been round here before, that well looks familiar.'

'You said you knew someone in Caerphilly,' I reminded him, treading what could be dangerous ground.

'Yeah, but I only went there once and I was hammered,' he said. 'It could've been Timbuktu for all I knew.'

'To be honest,' I said, keeping my tone neutral after that kick in the teeth, 'a lot of these streets look the same and wells are rather popular. Are you nearly here?'

'Yep. House number two, three, four . . . I'm coming!'

He ended the call. A moment later I heard the front door as he shut it behind him.

'Hello?' he called out. I didn't dare reply, but two minutes later he hadn't moved, so I sent a message. My heart was pounding as I wrote:

'That you? Come upstairs. Second door on the left.'

Seconds later I heard him climbing up the stairs.

He moved slowly down the landing and to my surprise, I started to feel a bit annoyed – what was so hard to understand about 'upstairs, second door'? Hurry up and let's get this over with!

Eventually I heard the floorboards shift as he stood in the doorway. He paused. *Move!*

'Tasha?' he whispered. Of course there was no answer. He took a step forward. 'Tasha?' he said again. I saw his head move to look at the bedside table and I think that maybe the sight of the condom on display emboldened him. He took off his jacket, dropped it on the floor and moved to the bed. I restrained myself from picking the jacket up.

'You haven't fallen asleep, have you?' he said, leaning towards the heap of clothes.

Certainly haven't, I thought and I lunged towards him, with the pen held high. He heard me and started to turn. His face registered surprise, then horror and he put his hands forward to defend himself. But it was of no matter, I only needed the needle of the pen to go through a thin layer of clothes. Beneath his jacket he was only wearing a t-shirt.

I brought it down in a stabbing motion. The pen went in, I plunged the top down.

Sean roared and reared backwards, like a wounded beast. Which I suppose he was. He swayed and staggered around the room. He regained his balance and headed for the door. I pounced on him, leaping up and wrapping my legs around him to stop him escaping.

It slowed him down but didn't entirely stop him. With a small roar of my own, I let go, then leapt again, landing my full weight on his back and dragging him downwards. But he continued his shuffle towards the bedroom door.

I hung like a dead weight. My arms were already starting to tire, but I could feel Sean weakening as the insulin took effect on his drunken body; I wouldn't have to hold on much longer.

Then he was out of the door. I felt a surge of energy from him as the stairs came into view. I dropped down and hung onto one leg. He tried to shake me off, but I clung tight and his balance didn't seem to be all it could be. He hopped forward, flailing his arms for balance and finally righted himself for a moment between the banister and the wall.

He stood on one leg, catching his breath. Neither of us spoke.

After a moment he dropped to the floor. Tentatively, I released his leg. He didn't move. I rose to a crouch. He remained inert. I stood and he still didn't move, but I wasn't taking any more chances. I knelt on his back as I stopped to think. The bathroom door was ajar, and I ran through a quick inventory in my mind. I stood and went to fetch the heaviest thing I had in there.

I'd been right not to trust him. When I returned, seconds later, with the bathroom scales in my hands, he was starting to rise. Without delay, I clunked him as hard as I could on the head with the scales. They didn't have the weight or the power of the umbrella stand I had clobbered Felicity Pearson with all those years ago, but it was enough to knock him back down. I fetched a magazine to read, then I sat on his back and waited for the insulin to take full effect.

It took longer than I'd expected, but when he was finally unconscious, I gave him a second dose for good measure and tried to think back to my nursing course – were you meant to sit coma patients up, or to lie them down? One was good and one was bad. If I chose the wrong one he could be up and at me again before I was ready for him.

I ran to google it, but Google was no help.

Then I recalled that on the wards, coma patients spent their days lying flat. I braced my back and pulled him upright.

'Let's get that blood away from your brain,' I said.

He slid downwards to his left. I pulled him back up and he slid to his right. I tried a couple more times, but he would not stay upright, so I dragged two chairs from the dining room upstairs and positioned one either side of him. They held him up, tilting gently to the left.

I stepped away, rubbing my back. I couldn't keep hauling bodies around, this had to be the last one. Yet, a sense of accomplishment swelled through me. Here he was, at last, in my home,

just me and him and that was how it would stay, although probably not for long.

At the Jacksons', I had a supply of insulin with which to keep
him docile, but I would need to keep topping him up. How long
that could continue for until Sean had one dose too many was
unguessable. Insulin could be an unpredictable thing. Our union
would be, like the dying supernova, brief, but brilliant.

CHAPTER THIRTY-FIVE

2010

I still had work to do before I could relax and enjoy our time together. I hadn't thought the aftermath of my plan out well.

I realised in the following hours that I hadn't considered how I was going to move Sean around the house or feed him. I hadn't even thought properly about what I was going to do with him on that first night, so intent was I on just getting him there.

I left him where he was while I put the clothes from the bed away, hung his jacket in the coat closet and had a general tidy.

I had planned to move him onto the bed, but the hour was late, and my energy was flagging. So, after checking he was still as I had left him, I brushed my teeth, put my pyjamas on and went to bed. But with all the drama, I couldn't sleep. I lay awake, thinking over what had happened and making plans for the morning. From time to time, I got up and went to check Sean was still unconscious. Shortly before dawn, exhaustion overcame me and I dozed, waking soon after to the sound of birdsong proclaiming morning.

I rose stiffly from my bed, the muscles in my back giving me no chance to forget what had happened the night before and went to assess the level of damage done so far. Sean's eyes were closed, but he was still alive. When I gave him a pinch, he didn't react. I gave him a kick as well, just a gentle one, to check he wasn't bluffing. There was no reaction, so I tied his hands to the chairs and his ankles to the banister for safety's sake, had a shower, dressed and headed over to the Jacksons'.

'Sounded like herd of elephants was running through your house last night,' Bert commented as he let me in.

'There was just a small one passing through,' I said and he laughed at my joke. 'Where's the insulin today?'

'All in the kitchen, in the cupboard on the left of the sink. Bottom shelf,' Bert said, heading for the lounge and leaving me to find it. Amazingly, it was exactly where he said it was. I pocketed a few for my own use and took the morning dose through to Mabel.

'You'll need to go to the clinic on Monday,' I said, 'you're running a bit low.'

'Are we?' Bert sounded surprised. 'I thought we had a good stash.'

'Go and see for yourself.'

Back in the house, I hurried upstairs. Sean was more or less where I'd left him, just slumping a little more to the left. His eyes were open now, but his body didn't flinch when I checked his reflexes with another gentle kick.

'How are you getting on?' I asked.

'Grrrug,' he said.

'Oh, well. Shall we see about a bit of breakfast?' I pulled at his arm and realised moving him from one part of the house to another was going to be quite a challenge. 'Can you shuffle along at all?'

But his head rolled sideways and all he said was, 'Urrrrm.'

I went to the airing cupboard and took out all my spare sheets. 'No point crying over spilt milk, is there, Sean?' I began tying them together. 'When life gives you lemons. Let's get you down-stairs. This will be fun.'

The plan was to use the sheets to create a pulley system with which I would be able to hoist him easily up and down the stairs, but I'd hardly started before there was a knock on the door. I froze. Then I relaxed, if I ignored it, they would go away.

They didn't go away. 'They' turned out to be Frank. 'Julie!' he called. 'Are you in there?'

'Yeah, she's in there,' I heard Bert saying. 'I saw her going in after she'd been here.'

With that encouragement, Frank knocked again. 'Julie!'

I thought about shouting that I couldn't come to the door, but I couldn't think of a reason why not.

'Keep quiet,' I whispered to Seán and headed for the stairs. I turned back, looking for something to gag him with.

'Julie!' Frank called from outside.

Hoping the phrase 'put a sock in it' was good, practical advice, I stuffed one in Seán's mouth, a clean one. 'Don't choke, don't suffocate,' I warned him, then, leaning out of the window, I shouted 'Coming!' and went to answer the door.

Frank was staring upwards when I swung it open.

'Oh, there you are,' he said, sounding surprised when he saw me. Had he been expecting me to shimmy down the drainpipe? 'Everything alright?'

I felt my heart going into panic mode. Had he seen something? 'Yes,' I said. 'Why?'

'It's just Mum and Dad said the police were round the other day. I wondered if something had happened?'

He'd previously been very honest with me, so I decided on a middle course between truth and obfuscation. 'I had to go to the police station. A few loose ends they wanted to tie up. They're talking to everyone.'

He nodded. 'Loose ends about what?'

My impending doom had been so preoccupying me, I'd forgotten the Jacksons didn't know the murder the local news station was so obsessed with had taken place in my office. I gave him a summary. His eyes widened.

'So, you knew her? The victim?'

I nodded and wondered if I should wipe away a tear. Instead, I said, 'Not well. I know her partner, though. I know him very well. He didn't love her, he was going to end it. There was someone else involved.'

'They think he did it to be with this other woman?' Frank asked.

'Something like that.'

'Strange way of going about it, when you think he could probably have done it in the privacy of his own home and had a better chance of hiding it.' He looked over my shoulder, into the house, and my heart started to race again. Had he seen something? I was desperate to turn around and see what he could see, but I couldn't risk it.

'Hmmm,' I said.

'It's mad, the things people do, would it really have been so bad for him to just end it with her?' Frank said. 'She's dead, and sooner or later he's going to be spending years in prison. I hope this other woman was worth it. Say, are you up for going painting again sometime? Or just out somewhere? It doesn't have to be painting.'

I nodded and shrugged at the same time, hoping to convey both enthusiasm and reserve.

'Are you sure you're alright?' Frank asked and I nodded. 'A bit shaken up about things?' And I nodded again, with some relief.

A siren sounded in the distance and my legs started to shake.

'You look like you've got a lot on your mind,' Frank said. 'I'll leave you in peace.'

'Speak to you soon,' I replied and watched as he did a little salute and headed back towards the Jacksons'. As soon as he was gone, I turned and looked up the stairs to see what he could see. There was no sign of anything awry. To be certain, I stepped outside, stood where he had been standing and looked. Nothing.

I went inside, fetched the little step I use to reach into high cupboards and put it where he had stood, to get exactly the same view, although Frank isn't that much taller than me. Still nothing.

Starting to relax, I picked the step up to go back into the house. As I did so, I glanced to my right and saw Bert staring at me.

'Lovely morning,' he said and went inside.

I ran upstairs and took the sock out of Sean's mouth. He hadn't choked and he hadn't suffocated.

'That was a close one!' I said, laughing slightly manically at how easily Frank could have knocked a few minutes later – with Sean hanging halfway down the stairs.

I regained my composure and returned to the pulley, but I don't have the mind of an engineer and when I tipped him over the edge, the sheets unravelled almost immediately and he bounced most of the way to the ground.

I ran down after him. 'Sorry! Wasn't meant to go like that.' He stared up at me, he perhaps couldn't speak very well, but he could convey fury with his eyes. 'I'm sure we'll laugh about it later,' I said. Promising him tea and cake, I hauled him into the dining room. There, I left him propped up in the corner while I went to make the tea.

I abandoned the idea of cake, it had been an impractical suggestion. Indeed, as I took our teacups into the dining room I was having doubts about even liquid.

'Let's see,' I said, lifting the cup to his lips.

I tilted it and Sean's eyes rolled wildly. 'Naaaagh!' he said.

'Is it still a bit hot?' I took it back into the kitchen, tipped a bit away and topped it up with cold water.

I tried again. 'Naaaagh!' he said again.

'It isn't poisoned.' I tipped it again, but the rim was quite wide and most of it spilt over his chin and down onto his t-shirt.

I persevered and half an hour later, with our respective drinks drunk, we sat, both of us on the floor, looking out at the garden. Every muscle in my body felt as if I'd done a marathon workout and I was enjoying the tired, but happy, feeling it brought. The shrubbery outside bowed and lifted again in the breeze. Sean's breathing, which had been laboured, was now becoming more normal, I was going to have to give him another jabbing soon. But for now, I felt at peace.

'Do you like my garden?' I asked him. 'The bluebells are just coming through.' He didn't reply. I gave him a small kick in the ankle and asked him again.

'Ooof,' he said.

'What's that? If you don't mind me saying, you're not quite the conversationalist you used to be. You remember our little chats? Putting the world to rights. Where did it all go wrong, Sean? Why did you let it come to this?'

'Rrrrogh!' He had quite a range of grunts and groans. It was going to be fun working out what they all meant. I glanced towards him and to my horror, Sean seemed to be moving of his own volition, making an attempt to move forwards. I ran upstairs for the insulin and gave him another dose. His eyes closed.

It was mid-afternoon before he stirred once again.

'Would you like to watch TV now?' I asked him.

With my back protesting loudly, I managed to haul him into the lounge and point him towards the TV. Then I selected *The Proposal*. I watched him to see his expression as the story unravelled. There were certainly similarities with our story: a strong go-getting woman, with a less enthusiastic younger man, who comes slowly to accept his fate. His expression remained blank.

'You could show a bit of gratitude,' I said, settling myself down next to him, 'I've done a lot for you today: the pulley – although I admit it wasn't a roaring success; the tea; this film.'

'Foooff,' he said.

As the film reached its romantic denouement, it occurred to me that this was the moment I'd been waiting for, Sean and I together, alone in an amorous situation. I looked at him, head lolling, in need of a change of clothes.

'More tea, Sean?'

'Naaagh!' he said. I think that one meant 'no'.

As night fell, I looked at my useless pulley and acknowledged to myself the hopelessness of trying to get him back upstairs. Tiredness made me dispirited for a moment. This situation was not as I had imagined it, and I could not change it.

Yet, things always looked better in the morning. I gave Sean a bedtime shot of insulin and headed upstairs.

At daybreak I was heartened to see Sean regarding me with a less hostile stare than he had done earlier.

'More tea, Sean?' I asked, although I was going to have to feed him something sooner or later.

'Naagh.'

'Well, I'll make you some anyway.'

And so, we fell into something of a routine: tea, conversation and films all day, with regular stabbings, which seemed to be taking longer and longer to wear off.

We had some fine weather and to perk us both up, I opened the French doors wide and set up my easel outside. I hauled Sean into the dining room, so he could look out as well. He could see the trees, the shrubbery, the skies with the birds to-ing and fro-ing. He could probably hear Bert Jackson in his garden and the traffic from the main road in the distance.

From my seat in the garden, I could hear Sean gurgling away and now and then I had to nip in to wipe up the dribble.

I couldn't help thinking back to my dreams of Sean and I, of our cosy nights in, our glamorous evenings out and our nights of passion. And I looked at Sean propped up against the wall, incontinent and drooling and I contemplated the gap between imagination and reality.

There was a knock on the front door; Sean and I were not expecting anyone so we ignored it. They knocked again, this time they sounded pretty insistent, but still we ignored it. A girl's home is her castle, so I sat tight.

There was another knock on the door and Bert Jackson poked his head over the fence. 'Morning,' he nodded. 'Police car outside.'

I didn't go down without a fight. I was there with a pen full of insulin, primed and ready to use, when they broke the door down. But the police were quicker with their taser and before I knew it, I was lying on the ground shouting, 'That really hurt!'

One of them picked up the pen and looked at Sean, in his fragile state, before asking, 'Do you need a shot of this, mate?' and jabbing it in, as I laughed through my pain.

CHAPTER THIRTY-SIX

Ten years later

Between the bell for lockup and the five-minute warning for lights out, I spend a bit of time on my Open University course. Then I like to review my letters.

I've never been so popular! I get all sorts: letters from fans, letters from journalists, from psychiatrists and criminology students, all wanting to know more about me. I get letters from charity workers, wanting to help me atone.

I keep every single one. I reply to a fair few as well – those that dare to put their address at the top.

Most importantly, I get letters from Frank.

Frank, you can imagine, was somewhat taken aback to learn that still waters ran quite as deep as they did with me and that our relationship was going to take a different form to that which he had fondly imagined. He was amongst the spectators when the paramedics stretchered Sean out of my house and off to his hospital bed. There he remained for several years, like Sleeping Beauty, incapacitated by the prick of a needle, before their stories diverged and Sean succumbed to unspecified complications. But Frank soon rallied and was the first – after my solicitor – to visit me on remand.

And he continued to do so. Now that I am ensconced in HMP Bronzefield, Frank comes when he can, usually once a month. He brings me the art materials I am allowed and keeps me up to date on what Bert and Mabel are up to, and the comings and goings in my street. My house is currently rented out to a young couple, whom he describes as 'very nice, but none too fond of gardening,' which is always a pleasure for me to hear.

At first it was difficult to find tenants, given the publicity, but eventually the property management service managed to let it out, at a discount, to a couple of devil worshippers. Once they'd been there for a while, the taint seemed to have washed off and it was easy to rent out afterwards.

After ten years, I'm quite a senior figure amongst the other inmates. My trial was a cause célèbre and I've maintained my status through the years. Indeed, myths and legends have grown up around me: it is widely believed in here that rather than stabbing an average-sized man with an insulin pen, I strangled a rugby player with my bare hands, along with the tale that I led the police on a merry dance for years on end. Consequently, many of those on shorter sentences come to me for advice on how to take revenge upon those who need to be revenged upon when they get out. I never disappoint. In return, I am rewarded by never being attacked or having my meagre possessions stolen.

In my spare time, I am doing an Open University course in environmental science. By the time I leave here I will be fully qualified, but I shan't be working in that field. I shall be retired by then; I was sentenced to life, with twenty years to serve before I can apply for parole.

When I am out of here, Frank is keen for us to visit some art exhibitions and talks about us taking up golf. He would like me to move in with him, rather than go back to my own abode, and we will watch TV together on Saturdays and sleep in late on a Sunday. We will try restaurants and become regulars in the park. It keeps me going, to lie on my bunk at night and think of the times ahead.

Sometimes I wonder what it might be like if things had been different, if I'd met Frank before I met Sean. If Sean and Xanthe were still tripping the light fantastic all over Cardiff. If Susannah, even, were still alive. Although I maintain her allergies were going to get her sooner or later.

Lately, I have been experiencing the first moans and groans of age and I suspect time is not on my side. In darker moments I consider that my plans with Frank may be just dreams to give hope to a hopeless situation. Incarceration is not good for your health; I look older than my six decades. In truth, my chances of leaving here are low.

The days are rhythmic in prison, punctuated by a bell to rise, a bell for morning work, for lunch, the afternoon, association and so on. I have a job in the launderette. It's boring and I find myself marking the time by counting how many sheets I have folded and how many are left to do. How many days have gone by, how many to go. My life broken down into moments I have wished away, the passing of an hour an achievement.

We swap gossip about each other to relieve the tedium. Some of it is based in truth, but in the absence of any real news, it can be entirely made up. The minutiae of the day to day is magnified in prison, and slights and insults, real or perceived, often end in a fight: which we all enjoy.

The most exciting thing to have happened here for a long time is that there's a new male governor and he's the spitting image of Dr Pearson, wonky eyes and all.

He likes to be 'visible' and to make himself 'accessible' – his words, not mine – so he takes walks around the prison during association time. He can't always remember everyone's name and crime, after all, most of the nobodies here are in for sentences of less than ten years, some for only weeks or months. But everyone knows me, the Sinister Spinster.

My cellmate is younger than me, and blonde and skinny and she simpers and giggles and hangs on his every word.

'Won't have to worry about me much longer,' she says, fluttering her eyelids. 'I'm up for parole in a few weeks.'

'The very best of luck to you,' he says.

'Be a pity to leave you behind,' she says. For a moment he pauses and looks as if he's about to say something more and I am wracked with images of them outside the prison gates – not that I can remember what the prison gates look like – hand in hand, running to freedom.

But I know by the way he always leaves me until last on his rounds that I am the inmate for him, the one who will still be here long after these petty thieves and council tax dodgers have been released. And in some cases, readmitted and released again.

I still love a project, so I am fashioning a knife of sorts from my paintbrush. I whittle away at it, making the handle sharp. I have a different kind of freedom in mind for my cellmate, and for him as well if he doesn't stop his indiscriminate flirting.

One of the governor's favourite jokes is that prison would be fine if not for the prisoners and when he passes me, he stops and says,

'It would all be dandy here if not for those pesky prisoners, eh, Julie?' As if I am not one of those prisoners myself.

I think of my paintbrush and I say, 'I can help you with the "pesk" control.'

Acknowledgements

To start with, I'm *sorry* about the pets. I'm a cat owner myself. First I had Fable who I thought was the loveliest thing in the world and I treated him like royalty. Now I have Kismet, aka Chaos. She is a vandal and a hooligan, but still, her life will be as long as I can make it.

I was trying to do something nice with Julie's pets, she was alone in her house and I thought it would be good for her to have some furry company. When I started out, I imagined the guinea pigs had lived long lives and she was too devastated to bury them afterwards. But Julie just evolved. I had no idea about Fluffy or Tweety until it was too late and she was set on that course.

Strangely, I found it easier to write these things than I do to read them in other books, maybe because it wasn't based on anything I know to have happened.

Lastly, on the subject of Julie: her views on the Yorkshire accent are entirely her own.

And on to the humans. I have to thank my agent, Ariella Feiner, who picked Julie Tudor up, had huge enthusiasm for her and opened the doors. Also at United Agents, Amber Garvey and Alex Stephens who are always helpful and patient.

Thank you to Phoebe Morgan at Hodder for choosing this novel and giving it such care and attention, and to rest of the team: Kate Norman, Zahraa Al-Hussaini, Claudette Morris,

Helena Fouracre, Ella Young and Ellie Wheeldon. And to Alyssa Ollivier-Tabukashvili.

In the US, thank you to Shana Drehs at Sourcebooks.

My writing groups, Tuesday Night Writes and Cardiff Writers' Circle, without them I wouldn't have kept going. In particular, Tuesday Night Writes, thank you for the title!

Also, Nick Paul, Sherif Gemie and Sara Hayes for the early beta reads, and the Cheshire Novel Prize (Sara Cox) for the feedback that got it over the line, as well as the impetus to start sending it out to agents. And, of course, friends and family, for their enthusiasm for this.

Reading Group Questions

1. What do you make of Julie Tudor? Is she a good person?
2. Julie uses her worry dolls as effigies of those she hates, but also as a kind of stress reliever. Do you have anything like the worry dolls that you use to relieve stress?
3. Are Julie's neighbours overly nosy, or are they simply caring neighbours? How much contact do you like to have with your neighbours?
4. Most of Julie's story plays out during the dawn of social media and the Facebook era. What was it like to be learning social media at that time? How does social media in the 2000s differ from social media today?
5. How does Julie keep getting away with her crimes? Is she just that clever, or is she being helped in some way by her father, by luck or by something else?
6. Compare Julie's perspective on the world versus actual reality. How does she perceive the women in her 'lovers'' lives? What do you think they are actually like?
7. How do Julie's pets reflect her view on life, and how does that feed into why she keeps killing them?
8. What do you think of Gareth and Julie's relationship? How does Julie interact with someone she considers a friend, versus someone she's pursuing (or plotting against)?
9. Do you think Julie has learned her behaviour from somewhere, or was she born this way? What evidence does the book give either way?

10. Consider Julie and Frank's relationship. How are they similar to each other, and how are they different? Why do you think Julie is able to connect with Frank when she couldn't connect with anyone else she was trying to pursue?
11. Do you believe justice was sufficiently served in the end?

Author Questionnaire

1. How difficult was it to write all the different timelines? Was there a timeline that was more challenging than another?

To my surprise, the hardest time to write was the years around 2009/10. I expected that to be easy because it seems recent in my memory, but I was forgetting that, with the internet and social media, everything changes quickly and constantly, so I got into a bit of a tangle from time to time trying to remember what we did and didn't have, and what we could and couldn't do.

The years I chose were when Facebook was the reigning social media channel. It wouldn't have been very practical to have Julie spreading herself over several social media channels, and I can't really see her mastering TikTok, Instagram, X and so on, so she is in a time when Facebook was well used by all generations.

Going back to the '70s and '80s, the main difference was taking Julie back to before she was the serial killer she developed into. As I wrote it, it started to feel like a natural progression to go back and look at what had shaped her, and how she began her killing career. At the same time, I was in the swing of writing her the way she was in her later years, so it took a bit of thought to consider that she hadn't always been that way and to think about how she may have been in her childhood. I didn't want to go too mad with making her parents really unpleasant – I don't think they were necessarily horrible to her, not deliberately, they just liked Angela better.

Everyone did, and one way or another, it showed in Julie's development.

2. What kind of research went into this novel?

I think the main research was around the 1980s years, looking back to all the little details, like where the Pearsons might have bought their vase and how much they might have paid for it. When I started writing it, it wasn't my intention to go as far back in time as the '80s, and certainly not into her childhood in the '70s, largely because I didn't envision it as a novel that would need more than the recent past. I thought at first it would all be in the modern day, and I would be able to do it all from memory. But once I got started on the '80s, I really enjoyed it – 18p for a bar of chocolate, and that was considered a bit steep! I actually moved it all back a year because I thought Bucks Fizz winning the Eurovision Song Contest was too good to leave out. (This is a very big deal in the UK!).

The office she works in was based largely on offices I have worked in, in terms of both the layout and decor, as well as the day-to-day activities. Specifically, this is one I worked in in Cardiff, although I've taken a couple of small liberties with the view. The people I have put in it are fictional, of course.

Julie was always meant to be almost cartoon-like and not a realistic portrayal of any personality type. I've been asked a few times if she's autistic, and it's a good question that I had to give some thought to, but in the end, I think she's not. I think she was just so badly damaged by her early years, she can't relate to anyone in a normal way. I suppose it's part nature, part nurture, but I think Julie suffered from always being in Angela's shadow.

3. Was it difficult to get into the mind of someone like Julie?

It was frighteningly easy to get into the mind of Julie Tudor! I had the idea after I'd finished reading *Rebecca*, and I thought that *Rebecca* reminded me of *Jane Eyre* in that, in both novels, the protagonist got her man when he was a lesser, or damaged, version of himself: Maxim de Winter in *Rebecca* was revealed to be a murderer and Mr Rochester in *Jane Eyre* was disfigured.

Then I thought that, here, in the twenty-first century, a story like that would never happen because now a girl wouldn't wait for her man to be damaged, she'd get out there and damage him herself. So, I started off with a general idea of a beginning, middle and end, and once I started, Julie's voice took over and led the way. When we were editing, from time to time I'd be asked to make something funnier, or more Julie-ish and I'd think, 'Oooh, I don't think I can,' but then Julie would step in and come up with something.

It was fun to write her. It was a licence to say, think and do pretty much anything.

4. Do you have a favourite character?

Gareth is my favourite character. He takes people as he finds them and assumes everyone is a friend, until they prove otherwise.

5. What do you want readers to take away from this story?

In its way, it's quite a sad story. Although Julie's misfortune is ultimately her own doing and she could have behaved differently and changed the outcome, she was quite often treated badly in her early years, and it obviously left its mark.

But I don't expect people to feel sad, after all, she wasn't completely destroyed at the end. She kept some things, such as her art, and she had a status in her new world. I think prison would suit her nicely – she has a structure to her days, a place in a community where people can't get away from her if her company isn't to their liking, and a certain amount of respect in there. So, in that way, it's a happy ending. The importance she thought she had in her job was always something she valued highly, and now she has it for real.

It was fun to write, and I hope people will feel that the time they've spent with Julie was enjoyable. There isn't a moral to the story – unless anyone needs to be reminded you shouldn't kill your colleagues, no matter how tempting that may be.